P. G. Wodehouse
Four Plays

This volume offers the pick of Wodehouse's considerable output of theatre writing – he wrote or co-wrote eighteen straight plays, not to mention thirty-three musical comedies. His theatre career spanned forty-five years, from 1911 to 1956, and his collaborators and the stars who appeared in his work included Jerome Kern, George and Ira Gerschwin, Cole Porter, Ivor Novello, George Grossmith, Douglas Fairbanks, Beatrice Lillie and Gertrude Lawrence.

The four plays in this book include two social comedies from the twenties, both adapted from the Hungarian: *The Play's The Thing* and *Good Morning, Bill* (which he later novelised as *Doctor Sally*). Both have been successfully revived in recent years. The other two are *Leave It To Psmith* (1930), dramatised from his own novel, and *Come On, Jeeves*, from the fifties, later novelised as *Ring For Jeeves*. Both bring famous members of the Wodehouse menagerie on to the stage.

The Introduction is by David A. Jasen, author of *The Theatre of P. G. Wodehouse* and the biography, *P. G. Wodehouse: A Portrait of a Master*. He is also the editor of Continuum's Wodehouse Collection and has compiled *The Theatre Lyrics of P. G.* Jerome Kern.

GW00669849

The front cover illustration is 'At One' by H. M. Bateman and is reproduced by arrangement with London Management. The photo of P. G. Wodehouse on the back cover is from the BBC Hulton Picture Library.

Other volumes in this series

John Arden
PLAYS: ONE

Brendan Behan
THE COMPLETE PLAYS

Edward Bond
PLAYS: ONE   PLAYS: TWO

Noël Coward
PLAYS: ONE   PLAYS: TWO
PLAYS: THREE   PLAYS: FOUR
PLAYS: FIVE

Ibsen
PLAYS: ONE   PLAYS: TWO
PLAYS: THREE   PLAYS: FOUR

Molière
FIVE PLAYS

Clifford Odets
SIX PLAYS

Joe Orton
THE COMPLETE PLAYS

Harold Pinter
PLAYS: ONE   PLAYS: TWO
PLAYS: THREE   PLAYS: FOUR

Terence Rattigan
PLAYS: ONE

Strindberg
PLAYS: ONE   PLAYS: TWO

J. M. Synge
THE COMPLETE PLAYS

Oscar Wilde
THREE PLAYS

P. G. WODEHOUSE
Four Plays

The Play's The Thing
Good Morning, Bill
Leave It To Psmith
Come On, Jeeves

With an introduction and chronology by
David A. Jasen

METHUEN · LONDON

This collection first published in 1983 in simultaneous hardback and paperback editions by Methuen London Ltd, 11 New Fetter Lane, London EC4P 4EE

The Play's The Thing previously published in an acting edition only by Samuel French, Inc., n.d.
Good Morning, Bill first published by Methuen Ltd., 1928.
Leave It To Psmith previously published in an acting edition only by Samuel French Ltd., 1932
Come On, Jeeves previously published in an acting edition only by Evans Brothers Ltd., n.d.

Printed in Great Britain by
Richard Clay (The Chaucer Press) Ltd,
Bungay, Suffolk

ISBN 0 413 53020 5 (Hardback)
0 413 53030 2 (Paperback)

CAUTION

These plays are fully protected by copyright throughout the world. All enquiries concerning performing rights should be directed to the respective agents as follows:
The Play's The Thing and *Good Morning, Bill*: International Copyright Bureau Ltd.,
Suite 8 D & E, 26 Charing Cross Road, London WC2
Leave It To Psmith: Samuel French Ltd.
Come On, Jeeves: A. P. Watt Ltd., 26/28 Bedford Row, London WC1R 4HL.

CONTENTS

Pelham Grenville Wodehouse:

A Chronology

15 October 1881	Born at 1 Vale Place, Epsom Road, Guildford, Surrey, third son of Henry Ernest Wodehouse, a Hong Kong magistrate and Eleanor Deane Wodehouse. He is called 'Plum' by family and close friends.
2 May 1894	Enters Dulwich College, specialising in Classics.
1899	Member of the First XI and First XV teams. Co-editor of *The Alleynian*, the school magazine.
February 1900	First article, 'Some Aspects of Game Captaincy,' published (*Public School Magazine*). Begins free-lance writing career.
July 1900	Leaves Dulwich. Enough slacking, must go to work.
September 1900	Joins the Hong Kong and Shanghai Bank as a clerk in their London office – his first job.
16 August 1901	Writes his first 'By The Way' column in *The Globe*, which he eventually edits.
9 September 1902	Leaves the bank and joins *The Globe* staff full-time.
17 September 1902	'An Unfinished Collection' begins historic 65-year association with *Punch*.
18 September 1902	*The Pothunters* published, his first of 97 books.
16 April 1904	First trip to the United States. Meets boxer Kid McCoy, establishes contacts with newspapermen and sees many Broadway shows.
10 December 1904	'Put Me In My Little Cell,' Plum's first lyric in Owen Hall's musical, *Sergeant Brue* (Strand Theatre, London). It is also published and recorded. This musical is the first of 33 in which he participated.

July 1905	'The Wire-Pullers' begins a 35-year relationship with *The Strand Magazine*.
March 1906	Becomes staff lyricist for Seymour Hicks, meets and collaborates with Jerome Kern in *The Beauty of Bath* (Aldwych Theatre, London).
May 1909	Second trip to the United States, this time selling two short stories to *Cosmopolitan* and *Collier's Weekly* after which he resigns from *The Globe*.
24 August 1911	Opening night of *A Gentleman of Leisure*, Plum's first of 18 plays, which is a dramatization of his novel by the same name (The Playhouse, New York).
28 August 1913	*The Little Nugget* is Plum's 17th book but the first published by Methuen (London).
3 August 1914	Meets Ethel Rowley the day after he comes to New York City. Accepts position of Drama Critic for magazine, *Vanity Fair* (New York).
30 September 1914	Marries Ethel Rowley in the Little Church Around the Corner (Madison Avenue & 29th Street, New Yok City). They move to Bellport, Long Island.
January 1915	Signs with literary agent Paul Reynolds for a 30-year hitch, whose first sale of the serial 'Something New' to the *Saturday Evening Post* starts a record 50-year affiliation.
25 January 1915	Meets life-long collaborator and friend, playwright Guy Bolton, at opening night party of the Bolton-Kern musical, *Ninety In The Shade* (Knickerbocker Theatre, New York).
18 September 1915	Jeeves makes his debut in 'Extricating Young Gussie' (*Saturday Evening Post*).
25 September 1916	*Miss Springtime* opens (New Amsterdam Theatre, New York). First show worked on by 'the Trio of musical fame, Bolton and Wodehouse and Kern.'

11 January 1917 · *Have a Heart* (Liberty Theatre, New York) is first original show written entirely by the Trio, who were to have six shows on Broadway this year.

20 February 1917 · *Oh, Boy!* is the first of the Trio's Princess musicals. Also biggest success with 475 performances at the Princess Theatre, New York and many more with touring companies over the next ten years. Opens in London two years later as *Oh, Joy!*

May 1918 · *Piccadilly Jim*, a best-selling novel, issued by Herbert Jenkins (London), his first book with the firm who publish him regularly for the next 56 years.

30 November 1923 · *Leave It To Psmith* published by Herbert Jenkins (London) after having appeared in the *Saturday Evening Post* (United States) as a serial, but with a changed ending for book publication. The second Blandings Castle novel and the biggest seller in England.

3 November 1926 · *The Play's The Thing* (Henry Miller's Theatre, New York) opens and establishes itself as a major comedy – a theatre classic. This production enjoyed a run of 326 performances.

28 November 1927 · *Good Morning, Bill* produced at the Duke of York's Theatre (London). Fine press reception.

28 March 1928 · *Good Morning, Bill* issued by Methuen in a hard cover edition. Splendid seller.

8 May 1930 · Arrives in Hollywood under a one-year contract to MGM studios.

27 September 1930 · *Leave It To Psmith* (Shaftesbury Theatre, London) first produced.

16 March 1934 · *Thank You, Jeeves* published, the first of eleven novels featuring Jeeves and Bertie Wooster.

10 October 1936	Hollywood and MGM again for six months.
May 1937	*A Damsel in Distress*, an RKO film from Plum's novel, is the only film with a significant contribution from Plum. Stars Fred Astaire, Joan Fontaine, Burns and Allen.
21 June 1939	Honorary D. Litt. degree from Oxford University.
1940–1945	Interned by Germans. Spends duration of war in Poland, Germany and France.
26 April 1947	Wodehouses settle permanently in the United States. Live in New York City and Remsenburg, Long Island.
Summer 1954	*Come On, Jeeves* produced in English provinces.
16 December 1955	Becomes a citizen of the United States. Lives year-round in Remsenburg.
27 January 1960	Elected to *Punch* Table.
November 1974	First published biography, *P. G. Wodehouse: A Portrait of a Master* by David A. Jasen.
1 January 1975	Knight Commander of the Order of the British Empire (K.B.E.).
14 February 1975	Plum dies at 93 of heart attack in Southampton Hospital (Long Island, New York).

INTRODUCTION

P. (for Pelham, his family and friends called him Plum) G. (for Grenville) Wodehouse (pronounced Wood House), the most famous and successful humorist of the twentieth century, had an important career in the theatre. Indeed, with Guy Bolton and Jerome Kern, he created what became the American Musical Comedy.

Plum Wodehouse started his amazing writing career in February 1900, and kept it up until he died. Not only did he write plentifully, but he did so in every possible literary form: novels (more than 70), short stories (more than 300), plays (18), musical comedy librètti (33), song lyrics (more than 200 published), memoirs (3), humorous articles, essays and poems.

With the creation of such series characters as Bertie Wooster and Jeeves, Lord Emsworth, Mr Mulliner, The Oldest Member, Uncle Fred, Ukridge, and the hangout for all his young gentlemen, The Drones Club, Plum became one of the most popular humorists in the English-reading world. The world of Wodehouse's novels and stories was one of his own creation, peopled not with beings from real life but from his imagination. His popularity was gained not by caricaturing the real world or by holding up a mirror, but by taking universal traits and easily recognizable habits and making us see ourselves through his make-believe people in perfectly constructed, yet enormously complicated make-believe situations.

His was the humour (very rare indeed) of geniality, of kindheartedness. Many earlier critics made the mistake of calling him a satirist, but there was hardly anything about which he was truly satirical.

Atmosphere is one thing that separates the good comic writers from the bad. Plum was particularly adept at establishing an atmosphere and maintaining it throughout. Although he worried all his life about his plots – which were nearly all the same – it was his use of the English language, mixing formal locutions with slang to produce hilariously unexpected results, that gave his readers such extreme delight: 'He was in evening dress and hysterics'; 'Chimp Twist was looking like a monkey that had bitten into a bad nut, and Soapy Malloy like an American senator who has received an anonymous telegram saying "All is discovered. Fly at once."'

Before the triumvirate of Bolton-Wodehouse-Kern took charge, American musicals were either musical burlesques of then current non-musical theatrical productions or else imported (usually Viennese) operettas which were neither humorous nor colourful. As a result, the American musical very much resembled a group of vaudeville specialists hired to do their renowned routines dressed up in outlandish costumes.

Elisabeth Marbury, a charming and resourceful literary agent, had an idea to produce musicals on a small scale: have only one or two sets, eleven musicians, a small cast and a strong book. She convinced F. Ray Comstock, lessee of The Princess Theatre, New York, a 299 seat house, to produce such a show. Naturally, they couldn't afford top names, but she knew the Trio and thought they could provide the proper material, especially since they had been airing their views on what constitutes a proper musical to whomever would listen. And, what constituted a proper musical comedy was a very strong book, funny dialogue, lyrics which either carry the plot along or else further characterization, and each chorus girl her own person.

The Princess musicals caught on and established the team of Bolton-Wodehouse-Kern as the leading creators of musical comedies. In 1917, Plum had five shows on Broadway at the same time. Guy Bolton (1884–1979) wrote the book, Wodehouse helped him with the dialogue and wrote the lyrics, and Jerome Kern (1885–1945) composed the sparkling music.

Wodehouse's theatrical career was such that in the course of his thirty-three musicals and eighteen straight plays, he worked with every major theatrical composer of his time and was associated with all of the major producers.

His co-workers and other future-lyricists have praised his efforts through the years: 'Before Larry Hart,' wrote composer Richard

Rodgers, 'only P. G. Wodehouse had made any assault on the intelligence of the song-listening public.' And, songwriter Howard Dietz wrote, 'Over the years I have held Wodehouse as the model of light verse in the song form.' Several Wodehouse novels have a theatrical setting and several others have been turned into plays.

As he was getting his feet wet by taking his novels and short stories and adapting them to the stage, he became the drama critic for what was the artiest magazine in the United States, *Vanity Fair*. In fact, he was its first, in a rather distinguished line including Dorothy Parker, Robert Benchley and Robert Sherwood. 'I had always wanted to be a dramatic critic,' Plum once wrote. 'A taste for sitting back and watching other people work, so essential to the make-up of this sub-species of humanity, has always been one of the leading traits in my character. I have seldom missed a first night. No sooner has one periodical got rid of me than another has had the misfortune to engage me, with the result that I am now the foremost critic of the day, read assiduously by millions, fawned upon by managers, courted by stagehands. My lightest word can make or mar a new production. If I say a piece is bad, it dies. It may not die instantly. Generally, it takes forty weeks in New York and a couple of seasons on the road to do it, but it cannot escape its fate. Sooner or later it perishes.'

His theatre and his novels were firmly linked in Plum's world. Critics have traced various influences in his writings, such as the verses of W. S. Gilbert, Shakespeare, the Bible, Conan Doyle and the 'good grey poets'. But the greatest and most lasting influence came from the theatre. From the period 1917 to 1927, when he was doing so much for the theatre, it was giving him the expertise to use the mechanics of a musical comedy to the best advantage in the construction of his stories. Plum often described his novels and serials as musical comedies without the music. All of the Wodehouse plots can be broken down into their components of acts, chorus numbers, duets and solos. The dialogue is crisp and concise, the entrances and exits are carefully prepared and vividly executed.

In a letter to a novelist friend, he said, 'In writing a novel, I always imagine I am writing for a cast of actors. Some actors are natural minor actors and some are natural major ones. It is a matter of personality. Same in a book. Psmith, for instance, is a major character. If I am going to have Psmith in a story, he must be in the big situations. One big character is worth two small ones. Don't diffuse the interest. Generally, the trouble is that you can't switch Character B's stuff so that it fits Character A. The absolute cast-iron rule, I'm sure, in writing a story, is to introduce *all* your characters as early as possible – especially if they are going to play important parts later. I think the success of every novel depends largely on one or two high spots. The thing to do is to say to yourself, 'Which are my big scenes?' and then get every drop of juice out of them. I believe that when one has really got a bit of action going, it can extend as long as you like. Guy Bolton says the great thing in writing plays is never let your characters sit down – i.e. keep the characters buzzing about without a pause. He also thinks it's a mistake to give the audience too much to think about at any one time. In other words, in a play, one mustn't try to develop two threads simultaneously.'

The first of Plum's straight plays was an adaptation. In fact, with one exception, all of his plays were adaptations, either of his own material or by some foreign playwright. His collaborator on *A Gentleman of Leisure* (1911) was the American, John Stapleton, who furnished the technical expertise transforming the novel into an exciting drama. Douglas Fairbanks, Sr. was the star.

In his next play, *Brother Alfred*, Plum did the adaptation himself. It was taken from his and Herbert Westbrook's short story, 'Rallying Round Old George'. It was commissioned by Lawrence Grossmith, who starred in it at the Savoy Theatre in London in April, 1913.

It wasn't until the summer of 1926 when producer Gilbert Miller commissioned Plum to adapt *Spiel im Schloss* for American audiences from the Hungarian of Ferenc Molnar that he wrote his next play. As *The Play's The Thing*, it opened at Henry Miller's Theatre in New York and starred Holbrook Blinn and Catherine Dale Owen. It was a smash hit, running for 326 performances. On 4 December 1928, it was presented at St James's Theatre in

London with Gerald Du Maurier and Ursula Jeans in the leading roles. On 28 April 1948, it was again presented by Gilbert Miller at the Booth Theatre, New York with Louis Calhern and Faye Emerson in the leading parts. This revival, once again, was a hit, racking up 244 performances. It has subsequently attained the status of a standard comedy with performances given regularly in repertory companies on both sides of the Atlantic.

Good Morning, Bill was presented on 28 November 1927 at the Duke of York's Theatre in London with Lawrence Grossmith, Ernest Truex and Vera Lennox in the featured roles. This was another adaptation from the Hungarian of Ladislaus Fodor. From the successes of these two plays, Plum should have been made an honorary Hungarian! Plum's skill in adapting foreign plays is all the more remarkable in the light of his ignorance of any language other than English. His agent would provide Plum with a translation, usually only a plot synopsis, and he would then create and embellish accordingly.

Methuen, who had published Plum sporadically since 1913, decided to issue this play as a hardbound book on 28 March 1928. Both Plum and Methuen had such a fondness for this play, that when Plum made a novel out of it, Methuen published it on 7 April 1932 under the title, *Doctor Sally*. This publication led to a new production of it on 20 March 1934 at Daly's Theatre in London. It starred Lawrence Grossmith once again, with Peter Haddon and Winifred Shotter. It was serialized in *Collier's* in the United States under the title, 'The Medicine Girl,' and issued there in the collection of stories entitled *Crime Wave at Blandings*.

Leave It To Psmith (the 'P' is silent as in pshrimp) was the dramatization by Ian Hay and Plum himself of Plum's most successful novel in England. As Plum recalled the collaboration, 'Ian and I had a lot of interests in common. We were both keen on golf and public schools. I read all his stuff and liked it enormously. I liked collaborating with Ian because it's like collaborating with Guy. He liked doing all the stuff himself. I was just to contribute the book. We talked it all over and got our scenario and the characters and everything and then he wrote it.' It wasn't quite that easy for Plum, however, as he actually blocked out all of the scenes and acts, with Ian doing the rewriting. They had formed a syndicate in 1928 to produce adaptations. The first was from Plum's novel, *A Damsel in Distress*, the second was *Baa, Baa, Black Sheep*, which was based on a short story by Hay, and the third was *Leave It To Psmith*. The company was actually a professional repertory company with Basil Foster, Jane Baxter, Clive Currie, Reginald Gardner and Aubrey Mather in the three productions. Plum couldn't be at the opening on 27 September 1930 at the Shaftesbury Theatre in London, as he was in Hollywood working on scripts that would never see the light of day. Toward the end, Plum was writing the third act and mailing it to Ian, who also supervised the rehearsals. Despite the failing economy, the amusing comedy ran 156 performances.

Come On, Jeeves was the last three-act farce written by Plum and his major theatrical collaborator, Guy Bolton. The basic plot of Jeeves to help an impecunious young peer to become a Silver Ring bookie was Guy's. He and Plum worked it all out during the summer of 1952. They originally called it *Derby Day*. When it was discovered that there was a film of that title, the authors then came up with *Come On, Jeeves*. In a reverse procedure, instead of adapting a novel to a play, Plum took this play and turned it into the novel, *Ring For Jeeves*, which was published 22 April 1953, over a year before it was to reach production as a play. This was the one exception mentioned earlier. Here is an original idea (originally by Bolton) which then turned into Plum's sixth Jeeves novel. Intended for a West End opening, it toured the English provinces during the summer of 1954 but never came to London. It was published originally by Evans Brothers Ltd. in an Acting Edition in 1956 but apparently wasn't registered for copyright until 15 January 1960. In their nineties, Plum and Guy returned to this play to rework it as a musical comedy with the music by Robert Wright and George Forrest. This, too, under the title *Leave It To Jeeves* has yet to be produced. So, here we have the only play to star Plum's greatest character, Jeeves. His own introductory remarks need no further comment.

Plum Wodehouse is constantly being rediscovered. Although he, in typically modest fashion, made a joke of 'humanity remaining a message short' from his writings, humanity in the form of a continually expanding reading public is not to be fooled. New readers are quick to appreciate Plum's important message of learning to get along with one another in a kindhearted manner. That simple, but profound message, along with his freshness of style and vitality of his prose, may destine P. G. Wodehouse for immortal fame.

DAVID A. JASEN

The Play's The Thing

A comedy in three acts by Ferenc Molnar adapted by
P. G. Wodehouse

The Play's The Thing was first staged on 21 October 1926 at Irving M. Lesser's Great Neck Playhouse, Great Neck, Long Island, by the Charles Frohman Company, Gilbert Miller, Managing Director. The play was presented for the first time in New York City under the same auspices at Henry Miller's Theatre on 3 November 1926, with the following cast:

SANDOR TURAI, *a famous dramatist*	Holbrook Blinn
MANSKY, *his collaborator*	Hubert Druce
ALBERT ADAM, *a young composer*	Edward Crandall
ILONA SZABO, *a prima donna*	Catherine Dale Owen
ALMADY, *a leading actor*	Reginald Owen
JOHANN DWORNITSCHEK, *a footman*	Ralph Nairn
MELL, *the Count's secretary*	Claude Allister
LACKEYS	{ Stephan Kendal { John Gerard

SCENES

The action takes place in a room in a castle on the Italian Riviera, on a Saturday in summer.

ACT ONE: 2:00 A.M.

ACT TWO: 6:00 a.m.

ACT THREE: 7.30 p.m.

ACT ONE

―――――――――

As the curtain rises a distant orchestra is heard playing Leoncavallo's 'Mattinata.' The stage is almost dark. The only light comes through two large French windows at the back. Through them we see the moonlit Mediterranean far below, the vague outlines of the precipitous coast, twinkling lights along quays and esplanades, and here and there the faint glow from some lighted window. A lighthouse blinks intermittently in the far distance. Within the dark room three darker shadows loom against the moonlit windows; the lighted ends of three cigarettes prick the blackness. There is a long pause. It is almost embarrassingly long. Just before one wonders if anything is ever going to happen a man's voice breaks the silence.

THE MAN'S VOICE: When you stop talking, Sandor, for sixty consecutive seconds, there's something wrong. [*One of the shadowy forms is seen to rise and cross to the right wall. We hear the click of an electric switch and instantly the stage is flooded with the warm glow of several electric sconces and candelabra lamps. The light reveals a room beautifully furnished in Italian Renaissance. At the back one shallow step leads up to a raised portion which runs the whole width of the room. Behind it are the French windows, now closed, with a balcony beyond them. To the right a short flight of steps leads to a landing and a door to a bedroom suite. To the left one step leads up to a door to the hall and the remainder of the castle. Occupying the right wall of the lower portion of the room is a great fireplace with a corbelled chimney. A long table stands near it. At the left is a grand piano. Below the piano in the left wall is a door to another bedroom. All these doors are closed. Above the piano toward the centre is a small stand with a telephone on it. There are comfortable chairs here and there. The ceiling is beamed and carved. The whole room reflects wealth and beauty. The speaker, who has just lighted the room, is a large and portly man of middle age. His name is* MANSKY. *He is in a dinner jacket, as are his two companions,* SANDOR TURAI, *seated in the*

5

centre, and ALBERT ADAM, *near the piano.* TURAI *is also middle-aged, but younger-looking and less portly than* MANSKY. *A glance shows him to be a man of consequence and dynamic personality. He is wearing a monocle.* ALBERT ADAM *is a dreamy, handsome boy just over the threshold of manhood. The distant orchestra has stopped playing.* MANSKY *reseats himself to the right of* TURAI, *and speaks again.*] What's on your mind, Sandor?

TURAI: I was just thinking how extraordinarily difficult it is to begin a play. The eternal problem of how to introduce your principal characters.

ADAM: I suppose it must be hard.

TURAI: It is – devilish hard. Up goes the curtain, there is a hush all over the theatre, people come on the stage. Then what? It's an eternity – sometimes as much as a quarter of an hour before the audience finds out who's who and what they are all up to.

MANSKY: I never saw such a fellow. Can't you forget the theatre for a single minute?

TURAI: No. That's why I'm such a great dramatist.

MANSKY: You can't be happy for half an hour unless you're talking shop. Life isn't all theatre.

TURAI: Yes, it is – if you write plays. You know what Alphonse Daudet says in his 'Memoirs'? When he stood by his father's deathbed, all he could think of was what a wonderful scene it would make for the stage.

MANSKY: It's silly to let your job become an obsession.

TURAI: Well, that's the theatre for you. And of all the brain racking things in the world, beginning a play is the worst. Take this scene here, for instance. We three – Curtain goes up on three ordinary men in ordinary dinner jackets. How is anybody to know even that this room we're sitting in is a room in a castle? And how are they to know who we are? If this were a play we would have to start jabbering about a lot of thoroughly uninteresting things – to the accompaniment of slamming seats – until the audience gradually found out who we were.

MANSKY: Well? Why not?

TURAI: Think how much simpler it would be if we were to cut out all that stuff and just introduce ourselves? [*He rises and addresses*

6

the audience.] Ladies and gentlemen, good evening. We three arrived tonight to spend a couple of weeks at this castle. We've just left dinner where we did ourselves remarkably well with some excellent champagne. My name is Sandor Turai. I am a playwright. I have been a playwright for thirty years. I make a very good thing of it. I bow and step back leaving the stage to you.

[TURAI *steps back and* MANSKY *steps forward and addresses the audience.*]

MANSKY: Ladies and gentlemen, my name is Mansky. – I, too, am a playwright, and this gentleman's life-long collaborator. We are probably the best-known firm in the business.

TURAI: Come to Mansky and Turai for all comedies, farces and operettas. Satisfaction guaranteed.

MANSKY: I, too, make a very good thing out of it.

TURAI: Which brings us –

MANSKY: – to the remaining member of the trio.

[*They indicate* ADAM, *who rises and addresses the audience in similar fashion but with more diffidence and none of their assurance.*]

ADAM: The last and least. I, ladies and gentlemen, am Albert Adam. I am twenty-five years old and I compose music.

TURAI: Very good music, too.

ADAM: I have done the score for the latest operetta by these two kind gentlemen. My first effort. They discovered me. Without them I am a complete non-entity. I have no parents, no reputation, and no money.

TURAI: But – he's young.

MANSKY: And gifted.

ADAM: And in love with the prima donna.

TURAI: You don't have to tell them that. An audience takes it for granted that the young composer is in love with the prima donna. That's tradition, isn't it?

ADAM: Thank Heaven.

TURAI: At any rate, here we are. Free at last from the dusty world of make-believe; out of the reach of thin-skinned actors and thick-skinned managers. What's more, there is nothing to worry us. Our operetta is finished and off our minds. Moreover, it is summer. The weather is perfect, the night is gorgeous, the sea —

MANSKY: Yes? What's the matter with the sea?

TURAI: It's moist! And the world is the world. Now, there you are. Wouldn't that be the simplest way to begin a play?

MANSKY: Very crude. If that were all there was to it, any fool could write plays.

TURAI: A great many do. You should know that. But you can see how absurdly simple it is.

MANSKY: All right, all right. For heaven's sake, stop talking shop. I've had enough. Save it for tomorrow.

TURAI: At any rate, it's been a great day — and we must remember it — August the twentieth.

MANSKY: Friday.

TURAI: What of it?

MANSKY: I wish it wasn't.

TURAI: Don't be such an old woman.

MANSKY: No one should arrive anywhere on a Friday.

ADAM: What difference does it make — Friday, Saturday, Sunday — life's always wonderful.

TURAI: My unlucky day is Tuesday. Among other things [*Indicates* MANSKY], he was born on a Tuesday. During, I believe, the Second Crusade —

MANSKY: Well, look at it for yourself. Here's today's little bag of bad luck. Midday — blowout — followed by violent thunderstorm. Set us back an hour. Early afternoon — ran over dog. More delay. And when we arrive, who is out? Our princely host. Who else? Everybody. All gone off on a picnic. Friday! And the beautiful, the one and only, our adorable prima donna, where is she? Also off on a picnic. Is she expected home tonight? No. When is she expected? No one knows. Friday!

TURAI: Oh, she'll be back.

MANSKY: Well, that won't spoil Friday's record because it's Saturday now.

ADAM: And I've got to wait a whole night before I can see her. It's cruel.

MANSKY: Just Friday.

8

TURAI: Well, now listen to me. I'll give you my version of the day's proceedings. Midday – capital lunch including some really drinkable coffee. During the meal, a few drops of rain. Result: perfect roads, no dust. We did injure a dog – but our Friday good luck held. The dog made a miraculous recovery and when last seen was sitting up taking nourishment. We arrived here a few hours late. But what a bit of good luck that was. Nobody in the house to expect tired men to make conversation. What's more, we dine on as fine a curried chicken as ever I tasted.

MANSKY: I loathe curry.

TURAI: You would! Now, in conclusion, let me give you the crowning piece of good fortune of this magical Friday. The room next to this is – Ilona's.

ADAM: What!

TURAI: Yes! Through that door is the room of the beautiful prima donna, the one and only. And I managed to get this suite for us. What a piece of good luck that was.

MANSKY: For him.

TURAI: No, no. For all of us. When a composer is happy, he writes song hits. When a prima donna is happy, she occasionally sings on key. And the librettists gather royalties from the resulting triumphs.

MANSKY: Sordid brute. You've no poetry in your soul.

TURAI: But I have a balance in my bank account, and that's far more important. As for Ilona being away, think what a piece of good luck that is. Think of the pleasant surprise she'll get. The little darling comes home from her picnic. All unsuspecting, she goes into her little room, she sinks upon her little bed –

MANSKY: Why on earth must everything always be so little?

TURAI: I never gave it a thought. Why not?

MANSKY: Damned sentimentalism. I know the house well. She has a *huge* room and an *enormous* bed.

TURAI: The point is she doesn't know we're here. That we've brought her the unfinished operetta – and that I am going to sing her the waltz song from Act Two.

MANSKY: God help her! Do you know it's past three? Let's go to bed. You can do your singing tomorrow.

TURAI: I've no objection to postponing the little surprise party. Suppose we wake her in the morning with the waltz.

ADAM: Suppose she finds out we're here?

TURAI: Oh, I've attended to that. I've particularly impressed on the butler that no one must know we're here until tomorrow morning. He's a very important man, that butler – practically runs this house.

ADAM: Then I'm going to have a bath.

TURAI: I don't follow his logic, do you? What has the importance of the butler to do with your having a bath?

ADAM: I hate logic. When you're tired and sleepy and looking forward to something particularly nice – well, it's wonderful to lie in a tub of lukewarm water with your eyes closed.

TURAI: Young! [*Laughs.*] And an artist must pamper himself, eh? You're a lucky boy. You're going to escape the struggles that most young artists suffer before they reach the top. You've got a very clever man behind you – pushing you on.

MANSKY [*significantly*]: Yes. *Two* clever men.

TURAI: I beg your pardon? Oh! Of course, *two* clever men. So run along, my boy, and have your bath – and sleep and dream and love. And enjoy your youth in this not so beautiful world – what's left of it.

MANSKY: You ought to be ashamed of yourself. He should be learning by this time that life isn't all music and roses and happiness.

TURAI: Why be in such a hurry to teach him that?

MANSKY: I'm not in a hurry.

TURAI: Then why must he be in a hurry to learn it?

ADAM: Good night, Uncle Sandor.

TURAI: Good night, my boy. And don't forget who will presently be sleeping on the other side of that wall. Say! There's an idea for a scene. The lovers separated by the wall.

MANSKY: What lovers?

TURAI: Pyramus and Thisbe. 'And thou, oh wall, oh sweet, oh lovely wall! Oh wicked wall, through whom I see no bliss!'

MANSKY: Shop again! Always shop!

ADAM: And what about you two?

TURAI: Oh, we're all right. Our room is on the far side of yours.

ADAM: Are you two sharing a room?

TURAI: We have to. Real collaborators never separate for a moment. Or the most priceless ideas might be lost forever. Besides, I talk in my sleep. I'm told that's when I say some of my best things. Mansky is a light sleeper, and wakes up and jots down whatever I say.

ADAM: Well, gentlemen – one last word before I go. I am very fond of both of you. I am finding life very beautiful. And I am very happy. [*Exit upstairs.*]

TURAI: Which startling announcement seems to call for a glass of very old brandy.

MANSKY: Make it two.

TURAI: Right. It's good to see the boy so happy. Now that I've reached the shady side of fifty, I find myself full of parental affection and nobody to lavish it on. His mother was a gentle, beautiful woman. They're still dancing down there on the terrace of the hotel. With that dark blue sky in the background and the coloured lights on the water. Yes, the boy's right – life is beautiful.

MANSKY: Sandor.

TURAI: Yes?

MANSKY: I didn't like to tell you before.

TURAI: Tell me what?

MANSKY: Something rather unpleasant. A little piece of news. Rather unpleasant.

TURAI: You're an odd sort of fellow. Just when a man is feeling happy for five minutes, you have to come along and take the joy out of life.

MANSKY: It concerns you, too. It's rather unpleasant.

TURAI: Well, come on, old friend. Ruin my evening for me.

MANSKY: I was looking in the visitors' book downstairs, and I saw a certain name. Yes, it's rather unpleasant.

TURAI: Don't sit there making my flesh creep. What name did you see in the visitors' book?

MANSKY: Almady.

TURAI: The actor?

MANSKY: Yes.

TURAI: He's here?

MANSKY: He is.

TURAI: H'm. This *is*, as you say, rather unpleasant.

MANSKY: You realize what this means?

TURAI: It means that you're thoroughly happy.

MANSKY: Not at all. I may be a pessimist, but unfortunately, I'm a tender-hearted pessimist. When I am proved right, I do not enjoy the fact. The fact is that Mr Almady is here.

TURAI: But how? He hasn't been invited here for ten years.

MANSKY: I suppose he fished for an invitation. He probably had his reasons.

TURAI: Does our young friend know anything about that business?

MANSKY: No! If he knew the part Mr Almady has played in his fiancée's life, it would be a terrible shock to him.

TURAI: Well, how much of a part was it? When she was starting on the stage he gave her lessons in voice production. And then – well, it was just the usual business – the romantic leading actor and the little pupil. The sort of thing that lasts a couple of months at the outside. And, besides, it was all over and done with long ago.

MANSKY: Apparently it is *not* over and done with.

TURAI: Rot! Because by *pure* chance he happens to be in the same house?

MANSKY: It isn't pure chance. It's impure intention. Use your intelligence, man. Ilona was Almady's discovery – he took her out of the chorus and taught her all she knows.

TURAI: That's a thing of the past. Ilona's in love and she's engaged to be married. And you know how passionately an actress can be engaged to be married. I'm bound to say I'm not remarkably enthusiastic about this match, but if it makes the boy happy that's the main thing. My dear chap, you're crazy. She wouldn't be such a fool – with a worn-out elderly actor – a father with four children. She's got too much sense.

MANSKY: I never said a word about that. I merely said I had seen his name in the visitors' book. That means he is staying here. Is that pleasant? No. It is unpleasant. That was all I said. I now say something more. We ought to have wired Ilona that we were coming tonight.

TURAI: I admit it. You're right again. So be happy. Never surprise a woman. On several occasions in a longish life I have prepared a joyful surprise for a woman, and every time I was the one surprised. The telegraph was invented for no other purpose than that woman should not get surprises. [*There is a knock at the door.*] Come in. [*A* FOOTMAN *enters from the hall. He is an elderly man in blue livery.*] What do you want?

FOOTMAN: What do *you* want, sir? You rang, sir.

TURAI: Oh, yes, cognac.

FOOTMAN: Any particular brand, sir?

TURAI [*to* MANSKY]: Do me a favor, old man, and go up and make sure Albert stays out of here. I want to have a few words with this fellow.

MANSKY: Don't drink both the brandies. [MANSKY *goes out through door at right.*]

TURAI: What's your name?

FOOTMAN: Mine, sir?

TURAI: Yes, yours.

FOOTMAN: Johann Dwornitschek, sir.

TURAI: Johann?

FOOTMAN: Dwornitschek.

TURAI: Ah – Age?

DWORNITSCHEK: Fifty-two, sir.

TURAI: Born?

DWORNITSCHEK: Yes, sir.

TURAI: I should have said, where were you born?

DWORNITSCHEK: Podmokly. In Bohemia, sir.

TURAI: Nice place.

DWORNITSCHEK: No, sir.

TURAI: Ah – married?

DWORNITSCHEK: Yes, sir, thank you, sir.

TURAI: Wife living?

DWORNITSCHEK: Well, in a sense. – She ran away two years ago with a soldier, sir – thank you, sir.

TURAI: Don't thank me – thank the soldier. Now – Johann Dwornitschek. Here are more questions. That room next door there is Miss Ilona Szabo's?

DWORNITSCHEK: Yes, sir.

TURAI: Has she been out long?

DWORNITSCHEK: Yes, sir. They left at six o'clock this afternoon.

TURAI: They? Who's they?

DWORNITSCHEK: The entire houseparty, sir, including the master. They were going to San Pietro, I think, sir.

TURAI: Is that far?

DWORNITSCHEK: The yacht would take them there in about an hour and a half, sir.

TURAI: When do you expect them back?

DWORNITSCHEK: Well, sir – they took a considerable quantity of liquor with them.

TURAI: My question was, 'When do you expect them back?'

DWORNITSCHEK: That is the question I'm answering, sir. Hardly before tomorrow morning at the earliest.

TURAI: I see. Who's in the party?

DWORNITSCHEK: The core or centre of it, if I may use the expression, sir –

TURAI: Certainly you may use the expression. It's a beautiful expression.

DWORNITSCHEK: Thank you, sir. The core or centre of it is an American family, distant relatives of the master. Every time a holiday comes around, they insist on a picnic.

TURAI: What holiday is today?

DWORNITSCHEK: I don't know, sir. They have two every week here. They always go off at night in the big yacht. They're quite wild about the young lady. She sings for them on the yacht.

TURAI: Now, look here – do you know a Mr Almady?

DWORNITSCHEK: Oh, yes, indeed, sir. I know Mr Almady. I know Mr Almady very well. He has been here three days.

TURAI: Here in the castle?

DWORNITSCHEK: Yes, sir, on this floor.

TURAI: And – he's a member of the yachting party?

DWORNITSCHEK: Yes, sir. Along with the young lady.

TURAI: What do you mean, *along* with the young lady?

DWORNITSCHEK: Well, sir, he escorted her to the boat. They're working together – like – like – as it were – partners. Mr Almady gives recitations on the boat.

TURAI: My God! How did you find that out?

DWORNITSCHEK: They took me with them, sir, last Tuesday.

TURAI [*into each life some rain must fall*]: Tuesday?? Yes, it *would* be on a Tuesday.

DWORNITSCHEK: Yes, sir – Tuesday.

TURAI: Yes, I heard you. Thank you. That will be all.

DWORNITSCHEK: Excuse me, sir. Would it be taking a liberty if I inquired why –

TURAI: Why I began by asking you all those personal questions?

DWORNITSCHEK: Exactly, sir.

TURAI: Quite simple. It's a little matter of psychology. When you want a man to speak the truth, begin by making him tell you all about himself. It gives him a feeling of responsibility and makes him afraid to lie later on. That is from a little detective play by Mansky and Turai. You may take the tip as some slight return for your trouble.

DWORNITSCHEK: Thank you very much sir.

TURAI: Don't mention it.

DWORNITSCHEK: And which shall I bring you, sir?

TURAI: Which? What which?

DWORNITSCHEK: Which brand of cognac?

TURAI: Which brands have you?

DWORNITSCHEK: All the best brands, sir. Hennessy, Three Star Martel, Biscuit DuBouche – Excuse me, sir. I rather fancy that's the young lady coming back now. [*They listen. From the adjoining room at the left a soprano voice is heard singing casually but clearly a well-known aria from an operetta.*] Yes, sir. That's the young lady, all right.

TURAI: It is. It's she. Splendid! Then never mind the cognac. Champagne is clearly indicated. See that it's well iced and hurry it along.

DWORNITSCHEK: You wish it here, sir?

TURAI [*going into room at right*]: Of course. Of course.

DWORNITSCHEK: Very good, sir.

    [*Exit* DWORNITSCHEK.]

TURAI [*in the room at right*]: Hey! Stop that bath. You haven't time for baths now. She's back! Sh! Hurry up. Quick, both of you. [*The voices of* MANSKY *and* ADAM *are also heard.*] I tell you she *is*. She's in her room. Do be quick. I've ordered champagne. Here, I'll help you dress.

    [*The door at the right is closed from the inside. From inside the adjoining room on the left the singing continues until interrupted by* ALMADY'S *voice raised in protest.*]

ALMADY: What do you mean by this singing? I believe you're doing it just to annoy me.

ILONA: Well – it's pretty cool to come walking into my bedroom at this hour.

ALMADY: I came with you.

ILONA: Now, listen. Everything's over and ended. I'm engaged to be married and I intend to be a good little wife. You've no right to behave like this.

ALMADY: No right? I, who made you? I, with whom you have lived so many wonderful, unforgettable –

ILONA: Do go away, and leave me alone. Don't touch me. [*A pause.*] Stop. I won't let you kiss me. Can't you understand my fiancé will be arriving any day now?

ALMADY: I'll kill him.

ILONA: You'll do nothing of the kind. [ALMADY *sobs loudly.*] Oh, stop *crying!* The idea – a grown-up man, the father of four children.

ALMADY: But I love you so, Ilona. Don't you love me – still – just a little?

ILONA: You're nothing but a great big baby. All right, then you *may* kiss me. [*A pause while they kiss.*] What are you doing? Don't take off your coat.

ALMADY: I want to say goodbye.

ILONA: Well, you don't need to say it in your shirt-sleeves. [*Pause.*] *Now* run away and let me get some sleep. I'm worn out.

ALMADY: I'm only waiting till you're in bed. Is there anything to drink here?

ILONA: You'll find it in the ante-room. [*Pause. Shouting.*] Look in the sideboard. And stay where you are till I've got my nightie on. Don't come *in* and don't *look*.

[*There is a silence during which the door right is opened and* TURAI, ADAM *and* MANSKY *tiptoe in like three mischievous boys. They speak in whispers as they cross to the door to* ILONA'S *bedroom.*]

TURAI: Hush! She's gone to bed.

ADAM: Do you think she's asleep already?

TURAI: I doubt it. Come on. Get as close as you can get. [*They group themselves in a row as near the wall as the furniture will permit. Whispers.*] Ready? Now – Ilona, Ilona, Ilona – take the time from me. [*Raises his hand like a conductor; at the same moment* ALMADY'S *voice is heard.*]

ALMADY: I worship you – I adore you.

[*The* THREE *are riveted where they stand, transfixed with amazement.*]

ILONA: Are you starting all over again?

ALMADY: Yes, I am. All over again. I love you as the church steeple loves the cloud that settles above it and floats away with the first passing breeze. I can't go on living without you. Not a week, not a day, not an hour.

[*The* THREE MEN *turn simultaneously.*]

ILONA: [*contemptuously*]. Just words.

ALMADY: It's the truth. I'm crazy about you. And you – you've used me up and squeezed me like a lemon, and now you want to throw me away.

ILONA: I don't want to throw you away, silly. Oh, come on, then. Come here and let me kiss your beautiful classic brow.

ADAM: She said – did you hear what she said?

ALMADY: That's not a kiss – that's a tip – Nothing but a paltry tip.

[MANSKY *sinks into chair.*]

ILONA: Don't shout like that.

ALMADY: I will shout. I'm a squeezed lemon. That's what I am – [*Sobs*] – a lemon! The whole world shall know that I'm a lemon.

ILONA: Get off your knees. And, oh, please, do stop crying. You know how fond I am of you.

[TURAI *and* MANSKY *clap their hands to their heads.* ADAM *collapses on the piano stool.*]

ALMADY: Those nights of love – those flaming wonderful nights! Have you forgotten them so completely?

ADAM: Why – That's Almady!

MANSKY: You can't be sure.

ILONA: Stop! Control yourself.

ALMADY: You ask me to control myself – when I look at *that* – at that perfect shape. The rose flush of that skin.

ILONA: Hands off!

ALMADY: My God! How round it is! How smooth, how velvety – and how fragrant. [*A pause.*]

ILONA: Don't bite!

ALMADY: I must – I am so *hungry* –

TURAI [*to* ADAM *and patting him on the shoulder*]: I think you had better go, old man. Go and turn in in our room.

ADAM [*bitterly*]: And I thought she was a Madonna. Holding her in his arms – stroking – [*Rising in sudden fury and rushing to the door*] – God, I could kill him!

TURAI: Steady, old man, steady.

[ADAM *covers his ears with his hands.*]

ALMADY: Ah, well! I see I am nothing to you any more.

ILONA: Oh, for goodness' sake, I swear that no man has ever meant so much to me as you. From the top of your head to the soles of your feet you are a *man!* Who should know that better than I?

TURAI: Come, come, my boy – let's get out of this.

MANSKY [*goes to* ADAM]: Come on, old chap. You're going to sleep in our room. [TURAI *and* MANSKY *lead him to stairway.*]

ADAM: Sleep! [*He goes out at right.* TURAI *and* MANSKY *are on the landing.*]

ILONA: Oh! Don't look so pathetic. – Well, come here – kiss me.

MANSKY: I was right – We ought to have sent a telegram. [*He goes out.*]

ALMADY: I want you to remember that kiss forever.

ILONA: It was your old kiss. Sweet and burning – like hot punch. But do be a dear and go away now. It was mad of you to come

18

here. If my fiancé ever hears of this I'll kill myself. Oh, damn my idiotic sentimentality for getting me into this mess. You must leave here tomorrow on the first train. He'll be here any day now. [TURAI *shifts uneasily*.] Every day I've been expecting a telegram. [TURAI *groans*.] Get out, I tell you, get out!

ALMADY: If you insist, dear heart, so be it! Your word is law. I am going to bed now. Farewell, dear heart. But grant me one last kiss.

TURAI [*to himself*]: Damn all fools who don't know when they've had enough.

ILONA: Go *now* –

ALMADY: So be it. Good night, dear heart.

ILONA: Good night, you baby.

[*Silence. A door is heard closing.*]

TURAI [*to himself*]: At last! Good night, dear heart! [*After a moment he sits down in armchair. Pause.* MANSKY *re-enters.*]

MANSKY: This silence – what does it mean?

TURAI: This silence is a highly moral silence. The baritone hero has departed. And the fair heroine has deposited herself in bed.

MANSKY: After depositing *us* in the worst mess in my whole experience. Wasn't it awful?

TURAI: Awful? Well, how is he?

MANSKY: I got him to bed. Poor little Pyramus. A jolly wall that, isn't it? Church steeple! Lemon!! The damned fool.

TURAI: I can't look the boy in the face.

MANSKY: You managed to get this suite for us. Marvellous luck! Pyramus and Thisbe! 'Oh, sweet wall!' Well, I hope you're satisfied.

TURAI: Oh, go to the devil.

MANSKY: I don't want to be unkind, but whichever way you look at it, you're to blame for this catastrophe. Why the deuce was it necessary to put the boy next to his lady-love? Friendship is friendship, but there are limits.

TURAI: I was merely trying to be sympathetic and helpful. I meant well.

MANSKY: Never mean 'well'. It's fatal. See what's happened as a result? Bride gone – love gone – waltz gone – operetta gone. All a total loss. On the other hand, the dog didn't die and the coffee was good. Well, Friday has certainly made a nice, clean, efficient job of it this time!

TURAI: What about the boy?

MANSKY: What about our operetta? The lady kissed the lemon's classic brow. After this, can you see her playing the part?

TURAI: To hell with all that. What about the boy? Did he say anything?

MANSKY [*gloomily*]: *One* of his remarks was: 'I'll tear up the score and kill Ilona.' The round and fragrant one. And the problem that presents itself to me is this: if he tears up his music and kills the prima donna, what sort of a first night shall we have?

TURAI [*thinks a moment, then with emphasis*]: We'll have a first night, I promise you that.

MANSKY: What, after all this?

TURAI: Yes, after all *this*. Don't worry, we'll have a first night all right.

MANSKY: With that music?

TURAI: With that music and that composer and that prima donna. And I'll tell you some other things. We'll have a hit, a wedding, and a happy ending.

MANSKY: Well, of all the optimists! It's just a suggestion, but wouldn't it be a good idea if you were to mention just what you propose to *do*. This is where Sandor Turai, famous for his happy endings, had better try to surpass himself. Get busy, my playwriting genius, and let's see how good you are.

TURAI: One can do but one's best. [MANSKY *goes out at right. A clock in the hall is heard to strike four.* TURAI *takes a blank sheet of music from the piano. He paces up and down in deep thought, occasionally glancing toward* ILONA'S *room. He jots down a few words.* MANSKY *re-enters.*] Well, how is he?

MANSKY: Lying in bed, staring at the ceiling. That's bad. He didn't even answer my question.

TURAI: What did you ask him?

MANSKY: I said: [*Plaintively*] 'Feeling better now?'

TURAI: What did you expect him to answer to a damn fool question like that?

20

MANSKY: Well, have *you* solved the problem?

TURAI: If I have I'm not going to tell you. You've ruined enough good ideas of mine already with your collaboration. This time I mean to work alone. Without a partner. All I ask of you is a little information. There are a few *facts* I require.

MANSKY [*huffily*]: That's all I'm good for, is it?

TURAI: That's all. Where are Almady's wife and family now?

MANSKY: At Lake Balaton, I believe.

TURAI: Lake Balaton. Address?

MANSKY: Verona Cottage.

TURAI [*putting it down*]: Verona Cottage. What's Ilona's mother's name?

MANSKY: Adele – Alma – something.

TURAI: Well, it begins with an 'A.'

MANSKY: Yes, I know that.

TURAI: Thank God! Mrs A. Szabo. What's her address?

TURAI: 70 Elizabeth Avenue, Fured.

TURAI: Would she be there now?

MANSKY [*petulantly*]: Oh God! How should I know? But, listen – [*Points to* ILONA'S *room*] My own humble suggestion would be to wake her up now and have a little chat.

TURAI: What about?

MANSKY [*starting across*]: I'll rout her out.

TURAI: For God's sake, don't do that! The only thing a woman can do is deny everything. And what could she deny? Could she explain her half-hearted resistance? Of course, she might point out that it was nice of her to tell the man not to bite.

MANSKY: Women have lots of other tricks. Falling on their knees – fainting – bursting into tears – laughing hysterically – or just going *rigid* all over.

TURAI: That might work all right for you – or me. But that boy is twenty-five, so think again.

MANSKY: Then there's no solution to the problem.

TURAI: There's a solution to everything. One has only to find it.

MANSKY: By Jove! Rather a good line, that.

TURAI: Oh, I don't think – . Well, it's not bad. Jot it down. [MANSKY *does so on his cuff.*] The thing to do now is to be tactful and understanding with the boy. You go and sit by his bed until he falls asleep.

MANSKY: He won't sleep tonight.

TURAI: Give him something to make him sleep. He's got a big day ahead of him tomorrow. One false move and he'll find himself the centre of a record scandal. That would break his heart. On his peace of mind, you know, depends –

MANSKY: Our success. Capacity business. A year's run.

TURAI: Beastly words.

MANSKY: And only yesterday – how beautiful they sounded.

TURAI: Look here. I'll take on this job. Leave everything to me. You know, it's a curious thing, but whenever you stop trying to help me, I can solve anything.

MANSKY [bows stiffly and turns towards stairs]: Thank you, my dear fellow.

TURAI: Not at all.

MANSKY: Good night.

TURAI: Good night. See you tomorrow. Till then, don't leave him for an instant. That's official. I've enjoyed our little talk so much. Good night.

MANSKY: Good night. [Goes out at right. TURAI goes to table, sits and jots down some more notes. There is a knock at door left to hall.]

TURAI: Come in. [DWORNITSCHEK enters with cooler and champagne, four glasses on a tray.]

DWORNITSCHEK: The champagne, sir – just as you ordered.

TURAI [motioning it away]: 'Mm, yes. But that was a long time ago. A very long time ago. Since then the world has changed quite a good deal. However, the motto of the Turai is: 'Never refuse champagne'; so put it down. [DWORNITSCHEK places tray on the table and the cooler on the floor.]

DWORNITSCHEK: Will four glasses be sufficient, sir?

TURAI: Three more than sufficient.

[DWORNITSCHEK leaves one glass on the tray before TURAI, and places the other three on the table. There is a pause, TURAI stares at him.]

DWORNITSCHEK: Something in the expression of your eye, sir, tells me that you are trying to remember my name.

TURAI: Quite right. What is it?

DWORNITSCHEK: Dwornitschek, sir.

TURAI: Still Dwornitschek? Well, well! All right, Dwornitschek, you can go to bed.

DWORNITSCHEK: Is there anything special that you fancy for breakfast, sir?

TURAI: No. Just ham, eggs, cold chicken, smoked salmon, cold beef, bacon, butter, milk, honey, jam, rolls and tea.

DWORNITSCHEK: With lemon?

TURAI: No! With rum!

DWORNITSCHEK: Very good, sir.

TURAI: What are you waiting for?

DWORNITSCHEK: I was wondering if there were any more questions you desired to ask me, sir?

TURAI: No, thank you.

DWORNITSCHEK: Thank *you*, sir.

TURAI: No, no, thank you.

DWORNITSCHEK: I love being asked questions, sir. It shows that gentlemen take an interest.

TURAI: You mean in Dwornitschek, the servant, eh?

DWORNITSCHEK: Yes, sir. You are sure you have nothing more to ask, sir? It would be a treat for me.

TURAI: There's nothing more, thank you. My stock of knowledge for today is complete. I wish it weren't.

DWORNITSCHEK: Then I will bid you goodnight, sir.

TURAI: Goodnight – One moment! There is something I'd like. I'd like some writing paper, some telegraph forms, some ink and a pen.

DWORNITSCHEK: The writing materials are in the library, sir. But I can bring them to you here.

TURAI: No, thank you. I'll do my writing in the library. That's a good idea – no chance of being disturbed.

DWORNITSCHEK: I'll go and turn on the lights, sir.

TURAI: One moment. [*Points to champagne.*] Might that come with us?

DWORNITSCHEK: Very good, sir.

TURAI: After you.

DWORNITSCHEK: Oh no, sir!

TURAI: I insist, my dear Dwornitschek – after you.

DWORNITSCHEK: At what hour do you desire breakfast, sir?

TURAI: What hour is it now?

DWORNITSCHEK: Quarter past four, sir.

TURAI: Then let us say at seven – or, no – make it six.

DWORNITSCHEK: Very good, sir. At six precisely.

TURAI: Look here, Dwornitschek, – when do you sleep?

DWORNITSCHEK: In the winter, sir!

CURTAIN

ACT TWO

As the curtain rises a clock in the hall is heard to strike six. Golden sunlight pours in the windows. The Mediterranean is as blue as tradition has painted it. SANDOR TURAI, *now jauntily attired in white flannels, is seated in the armchair at the centre, with the loose leaves of a manuscript before him. As the clock stops striking, the door at left to the hall is opened by* DWORNITSCHEK, *who comes down to* TURAI *bringing a newspaper on a salver.* DWORNITSCHEK *is followed by two* LACKEYS *in livery, each carrying an enormous silver tray piled high with* TURAI'S *breakfast. During the dialogue that follows, the* LACKEYS *place the breakfast upon the long table at right. This done, one of them stands at attention while the other goes up to the window, opens it, steps out on the balcony and lowers an awning which shuts off some of the now too brilliant sunlight.*

DWORNITSCHEK: Good morning, sir.

TURAI: Good morning. What's this?

DWORNITSCHEK: Morning paper, sir.

TURAI: You've read it, of course?

DWORNITSCHEK: Oh yes, sir.

TURAI: Anything about me in it?

DWORNITSCHEK: No, sir.

TURAI: Then take it away. [DWORNITSCHEK *gives salver with the newspaper to one of the* LACKEYS *and motions both off.*]

DWORNITSCHEK: Let me see, sir, I *think* it was ham, eggs, cold chicken, smoked salmon, cold beef, bacon, butter, milk, honey, jam and rolls that you ordered, was it not?

TURAI: Quite right.

DWORNITSCHEK: And tea with cut lemon.

TURAI: I loathe lemons.

DWORNITSCHEK: Yes, sir. Many people do. I once had an aunt —

TURAI: Suppose we don't talk about your aunt just for the moment.

DWORNITSCHEK: Very good, sir.

TURAI: Later on, perhaps.

DWORNITSCHEK: At any time that suits *you*, sir.

TURAI: You must make allowances for the artistic temperament, when I have been sitting up all night writing.

DWORNITSCHEK: I quite understand, sir.

[TURAI *has risen and crossed to the table, upon which he has put the manuscript. He now goes round to the right side where his place is set and examines the breakfast with evident satisfaction. He lifts the covers from several silver dishes, looks at their contents with pleasure, and smiles at* DWORNITSCHEK *with approval.*]

TURAI: You're really a wonderful fellow. How on earth did you manage not to forget anything?

DWORNITSCHEK: It was a labour of love, sir. My heart is in that breakfast.

TURAI: Your heart, too? [*After he has taken a sip of tea*] Ah! That puts new life into a man.

DWORNITSCHEK: You must have had very little sleep, sir.

TURAI: Not much.

DWORNITSCHEK: I hadn't any.

TURAI: Yes, I remember you told me you were essentially a hibernating animal.

DWORNITSCHEK: Nobody else is stirring as yet. This is the time when I sometimes manage to lie down myself for a few moments.

TURAI: Then you will get some sleep, after all?

DWORNITSCHEK: Just forty winks, sir. That's the advantage of being by the sea. Gentlemen stay in bed till noon. Very different from the mountains.

TURAI: They get up early in the mountains, eh?

DWORNITSCHEK: At about five or four-thirty. They like to go climbing. But there's always a bright side, sir; they go to bed at nine.

TURAI: You know, you're broadening my mind tremendously. Every time I see you, I learn something new.

DWORNITSCHEK: If it's not a liberty, sir, I should like to say something.

TURAI: I'll bet it's something good. Go on.

DWORNITSCHEK: You ought to take more care of your health, sir. You don't get enough sleep.

TURAI: I don't?

DWORNITSCHEK: And you smoke too much, sir. I found at least fifty cigarette butts in the ash-tray in the library.

TURAI: Wrong. Thirty-seven.

DWORNITSCHEK: Too many, sir.

TURAI: What's your daily allowance?

DWORNITSCHEK: Fifteen, sir.

TURAI: You'll live to be a hundred.

DWORNITSCHEK: Thank you – is that a medical opinion, sir?

TURAI: No, just a hope. This weary world needs men like you.

DWORNITSCHEK: No, no, sir. Like *you*.

TURAI: Well, shall we say like both of us?

DWORNITSCHEK: Would it be a liberty, sir, if I expressed the opinion that you have a heart of gold?

TURAI: Not at all. Thank you very much.

DWORNITSCHEK: Thank *you*, sir.

TURAI: No, no. Thank *you*.

DWORNITSCHEK: It's the way you take an interest that touches a man, sir. I wish there was something I could do for *you*.

TURAI: At the moment, I think the best thing you can do for me is to leave me alone. And if anyone asks for me, tell them I'm sleeping and must not be disturbed. Understand?

DWORNITSCHEK: Oh, yes, indeed, sir. [DWORNITSCHEK: *starts to go.* TURAI *stops him.* TURAI *pantomimes 'Wait a minute. I must remember your name.' He registers despair.* DWORNITSCHEK *smiles indulgently and whispers*] Dwornitschek.

TURAI: Thank you.

DWORNITSCHEK: Thank *you*, sir.

[*He goes out.* TAURAI *rises, listens at the staircase, then goes to the telephone and takes up the receiver.*]

TURAI: Hello. Will you give me Miss Ilona Szabo's room? [*He waits. Telephone bell rings loudly in the room at left. After a pause it rings again.*]

ILONA [*sleepily*]: Yes???

TURAI: Hello.

ILONA: Hello!!!

TURAI [*softly*]: Hello.

ILONA: Who's that?

TURAI: The unfeeling brute who has aroused you from your slumber is known to the police as Sandor Turai.

ILONA [*changing in a flash, delighted*]: Sandor! Dear old Sandor!

TURAI: Well, and how's the prima donna?

ILONA: Where are you speaking from?

TURAI: Next door.

ILONA: What!

TURAI: I thought you'd be surprised. I'm in the next room.

ILONA: How on earth? –

TURAI: My dear little Ilona, let's postpone the explanations. I want to see you at once – immediately.

ILONA: You're frightening me. What is it?

TURAI [*deliberately puts down receiver and speaks towards the wall*]: Don't be alarmed. Open the door, put something on, and come in. Or rather, put something on, open the door and come in.

ILONA: Do what? I can't hear you. There must be something wrong with this telephone.

TURAI [*now at the door*]: I say: put something on, open the door, and come in. Can you hear me better now?

ILONA: Yes. I can hear beautifully now.

TURAI: Good.

ILONA: I'll be right in. [*Enters.*] Sandor – what is it? I feel something terrible has happened. What's the matter?

TURAI: Sit down, my dear. You and I have got to do some quick talking.

ILONA: But what's happened? For heaven's sake, *tell me!*

TURAI: Sit down.

ILONA: Why?

TURAI: Because if you don't sit down now, you'll sit down later on when you hear what I've got to say – and you'll sit down hard. Better do it gracefully while you can. [*He pushes her gently into the armchair.*]

ILONA: I don't understand.

TURAI: You will. My dear little Ilona, in spite of the fact that you are engaged to my young friend Adam, you are still carrying on an affair with Mr Almady.

ILONA [*with indignation*]: It's an outrageous lie.

TURAI: Good! I thought you were going to say it was none of my business.

ILONA: I couldn't say that, because you're Albert's guardian, guide, philosopher and friend and God knows what else. And you're a friend of *mine* and write plays for me. So I simply say that it's a lie.

TURAI: I'm glad you do, because it's an observation which I can answer. I've been in this room since last night and the walls in this new wing are as thin as paper.

ILONA [*looks at the walls. As the truth dawns upon her she is horrified*]: Good God!

TURAI: 'Lemon.' [ILONA *hides her face.*] 'Lemon – Church steeple.' Well, dear Ilona. Suppose we talk this over? Something's got to be done – and done quickly.

ILONA: If you heard, you heard what I said, too.

TURAI: Every word.

ILONA: Then you know that I told him to get out – and he's *getting* out today. At twelve o'clock. So if you don't say anything – and of course you won't –

TURAI: Not quite so fast, please. If the thing were as simple as that, you would never have known from me that I had overheard you. I regret to say matters are much more unpleasant.

ILONA [*sinking back in chair*]: My God! You don't mean – ?

TURAI: I see you've guessed.

ILONA: Did – did – I can't say it.

TURAI: I will say it for you. Yes, the boy did hear it too.

ILONA: God! – He's *here* then?

TURAI: He is here.

ILONA: Where?

TURAI: Sh! He's up in Mansky's room – asleep. And last night he was in this room – awake.

ILONA: I'll take veronal, all there is in my bottle.

TURAI: That's not enough.

ILONA: Ten ounces?

TURAI: I was not referring to the veronal. I mean suicide is no solution.

ILONA: There isn't any solution that I could survive. There are only two things I can possibly do – kill myself or deny the whole story.

TURAI: Deny the whole story? Do you suppose if it were just a question of telling lies, I would have troubled you? I'd have told them myself long ago.

ILONA: Then we come back to the veronal.

TURAI: Exactly. We come back to the veronal – and find it safely tucked away in its bottle.

ILONA: Well, what *do* you suggest?

TURAI: I have my plan. And all I ask of you is not to hinder it.

ILONA [*almost crying*]: You know I worship Albert. If anybody knows that, you do. I've been a different woman since I met him. He looks on me as a saint. [TURAI *gives her a quick ironic glance.*] And he's right. I *have* turned into a saint since I began to love him. It was the only thing I wanted to do in life – to keep straight for his sake. I was so happy. [*She sinks into armchair crying.*] I love him so.

TURAI: And yet you can't be true to him.

ILONA [*indignantly*]: You've no right to say that. It was nothing but my damned sentimentality. You know very well that affair with that beast Almady didn't last a couple of months. First he gave me breathing lessons and taught me how to throw my voice –

TURAI [*with a significant glance*]: Yes, he taught you that, all right.

ILONA: I'm just a victim of my kind heart. I thought I was rid of him, but he got himself invited here. And he's always bursting into tears. A woman hates to see a man cry. He stuck to me like a leech. But why on earth would I want to start in with him again? I give you my word, Sandor, that last night was simply – like the last dying vibrations of a high note.

TURAI: You'd have done better to stop vibrating a little earlier. Still, there it is. What we've got to do now is get you out of the mess.

ILONA [*runs across to* TURAI *and throw herself on her knees, clasping him beseechingly*]: Sandor! Sandor darling! Do you really think you *can?*

TURAI: Yes, I can. But don't think I'm doing it for your sake, my dear; not for the sake of your beautiful eyes. You deserve to be drawn and quartered. I'm doing it for that poor decent boy who still retains a few ideals in this unpleasant world. Yes, my dear Ilona, I think I must ask you to be a little ashamed of yourself.

ILONA [*bitterly*]: Don't worry. [*Rises*] I am. What can I do?

TURAI [*goes to telephone*]: I am just going to tell you. And you won't enjoy it. Still, good medicine's rarely pleasant. [*Picks up receiver.*] Hello. [*To* ILONA:] What's the number of Almady's room?

ILONA [*apprehensively*]: What do you want with him?

TURAI [*into the telephone*]: Give me Mr Almady's room, please. [*Pause.*] Never mind about all that, my good man. I don't care what instructions he left – call him. And go on ringing till he answers. It's a matter of life and death.

ILONA: What are you doing?

TURAI [*into telephone*]: Mr Almady? Yes, yes, I know you gave instructions – Will you please be quiet for a moment? – This is Sandor Turai speaking. Here in the new wing – Last night, by car – Good morning – you were awake already! Capital! Would you mind coming here at once? Room number four – Yes, I mean now, right away – Yes, matter of life and death was what I said, but I made a slight error. I should have said a matter of death – yes, yes, this very minute – right. [*He hangs up the receiver.* ILONA *starts to go.*] Where are you off to?

ILONA: Is Almady coming here?

TURAI: You will kindly stay just where you were.

ILONA [*looking toward* ALBERT'S *bedroom*]: He looked on me as a saint. He thought I was everything that was fine and pure. He called me his Madonna.

TURAI: You should have thought of that a long time ago.

ILONA: Tell me – what did Albert say?

TURAI: I wouldn't ask that if I were you.

ILONA: God! What was the plan you said you had? – Can't you speak?

TURAI: Patience.

ILONA: It's too cruel – Just because I hate hurting people's feelings – [*She breaks off as a knock sounds.*]

TURAI: Come in.

[ALMADY, *who enters, is also in a state of nervous apprehension. He is attired in elaborate, not to say loud, house pyjamas. A tall and but recently handsome man, now well into middle age.* ALMADY *is first, last and always the actor. He dramatizes every moment of his existence. He does not walk, he struts; he does not talk, he declaims.*]

ALMADY: Good morning. [*Sees* ILONA, *surprised.*] Hullo, *You* here?

TURAI: Yes, she's here.

ALMADY: But what's the matter? Has something happened?

ILONA: Oh, do sit down.

TURAI: He'll sit down quite soon enough. I'm not afraid of his not sitting down.

ALMADY: You'll forgive me if I seem nervous –

TURAI: Glass of brandy?

ALMADY: Thank you. Never in the morning.

TURAI: Mr Almady, you are a married man and the father of a family. And you are forcing your attentions on another man's fiancée.

ALMADY [*indignantly*]: It's an outrageous lie.

TURAI: Good. I thought you were going to say it was none of my business. You would have been quite right. But a lie – no, I'm afraid that won't do.

ALMADY [*aggressively*]: Mr Turai, I would have you know –

TURAI: Shut up!

ALMADY [*outraged*]: 'Shut up!'

TURAI [*significantly*]: 'Lemon!' [ALMADY *sits down abruptly.*] I told you he'd sit down. [ALMADY *looks at the left wall.*] Yes, quite right. It's as thin as paper.

ALMADY [*rises*]: Now come, Mr Turai, between two gentlemen –

TURAI: I beg your pardon?

ALMADY: As one gentleman to another, I ask your discretion –

TURAI: Sit down.

ALMADY [*sitting down anxiously*]: Why? Is there something else coming?

TURAI: Yes, there is something else coming. Are you sitting down?

ALMADY: Yes.

TURAI: Then listen. I wasn't the only one who heard everything. Her fiancé was in this room with me at the time, and his hearing is excellent.

ALMADY [*strangling*]: Brandy!

TURAI [*pouring it out*]: In the morning? [*Gives* ALMADY *the brandy.*]

ALMADY: I always take it in the morning. [*He gulps it down.*]

ILONA: Well, what are you going to do now, you miserable idiot, you? You see what you've done. You've driven me to suicide. Oh, God! I shall die. I shall die!

ALMADY [*rising melodramatically*]: I'll die with you!

ILONA: I don't want you! I'm going to die alone.

ALMADY [*pompously*]: I am ready to give him satisfaction.

TURAI: That's the last straw. I'll tell you what you are going to do. You are going to do just as I order.

ALMADY [*starting up*]: Order?

TURAI: Sit down. [ALMADY *sits down.*]

ILONA: *Yes – order.* [*To* TURAI *– rapidly:*] Tell us, please. Never mind how much he rants.

ALMADY: Rants! You dare to criticize my diction?

TURAI: Oh! Damn your diction! Just thank your stars that I'm going to get you out of this. A married man! Father of a family. With four children at home – four little lemons! One word from you, and this telegram, all ready and written, goes off to your wife.

[ALMADY *looks again at the wall and groans.*]

ILONA: Look at him. Don't look at the wall. Last night was the time to have done that.

TURAI: In that room next door – last night – something occurred.

ILONA: Yes, yes, *please.* We know what occurred.

TURAI: That is just what you don't know. You are now going to hear. What occurred was the rehearsal of a play. Do you grasp my meaning?

ILONA: In the middle of the night?

TURAI: In the middle of the night.

ALMADY: How do you mean – the rehearsal of a play?

TURAI: Your very loud remarks, so loud that they actually penetrated the wall, were dialogue from a play. Now, do you understand?

ILONA: I do. [*To* ALMADY:] Don't you – idiot? It's the most marvellous, wonderful idea, you old darling – [*She is just about to embrace* TURAI, *when she stops in consternation.*]

TURAI: What's the matter?

ILONA: It's no good. He'd never believe it.

TURAI: Why wouldn't he believe it?

ILONA [*glances witheringly at* ALMADY]: Where on earth would you find a play in it with lines like those?

TURAI: Where? Here. [*Picks a script up from the table.*]

ILONA: What do you mean?

TURAI: Here you are. Here's the play. This is it.

ILONA: Who wrote it?

TURAI: I did. This morning – between four and six.

ILONA: What!!??

TURAI: After all, one is either a playwright or one isn't. Half of it I heard through the wall; the other half I wrote to fit. I feel this morning rather like an acrobat who for once has had the chance to use his skill to save a life. I don't suppose a play has ever been written with such altruistic motives. Well, there you are. There's the play. Read it, learn it – and play it.

ILONA: Play it!

TURAI: Naturally! How else can you make him believe that what you were saying last night was just dialogue? There will be a dress rehearsal this evening – then the performance.

ALMADY: Tonight? But where?

TURAI: At the concert, of course. After dinner in the ballroom. [*To* ILONA:] You're already down for something, aren't you?

ILONA: A couple of songs. [*Looks at* ALMADY *contemptuously.*] He's to recite some poems.

TURAI: Oh, my God. Then there'll be a slight change in the programme. He's going to have to act.

ILONA: But how on earth can I learn all this by tonight?

TURAI: Well, really! You knew it well enough last night! [ALMADY *sighs deeply.*] Why do you sigh?

ALMADY: Mr Turai, that was a sigh of relief. You *know* my wife.

TURAI: Didn't I tell you it was a matter of death?

ILONA: Oh, but listen – what earthly reason could we have had for rehearsing at three o'clock in the morning?

TURAI: That's what I asked myself, and I answered myself – quite simply. You had to play the thing tonight. You'd lost a lot of time at the picnic. Every moment was precious. And you were so conscientious that you insisted on rehearsing when you got home last night even though it was three o'clock in the morning.

ILONA: Well, we'd better get started. I'm a very slow study.

TURAI: One minute. Don't get excited. Who's supposed to be running this concert?

ILONA: The Count's secretary, Mr Mell.

TURAI: We must notify him of this change in the programme. [*Goes to telephone.*] Hello – Give me Mr Mell's room, please.

ILONA: But he'll be asleep.

TURAI: Oh, no, my dear. Not after this telephone bell has rung once or twice. [*He hands* ILONA *the receiver.*] There you are – ladies first.

ILONA [*taking telephone*]: But what am I to say?

TURAI: Keep calm. I'll prompt you.

ILONA: Hello! Is that Mr Mell? Yes, it is early, isn't it? [*She looks at* TURAI *for directions.*]

TURAI: Good morning.

ILONA [*into telephone*]: Good morning.

TURAI: How did you sleep?

ILONA [*her hand over the receiver*]: I *can't* say that. The poor man is furious.

TURAI: Use your own judgement.

ILONA [*into the telephone in her most seductive manner*]: Dear Mr Mell! [*Coos.*] I'm so dreadfully sorry to wake you up at this hour, but I wanted to tell you that there will be a little change in the programme tonight. I'm sure the Count will be pleased. I'm sure you will be pleased. I'm sure the audience will be pleased.

TURAI: Unanimous.

ILONA [*into the telephone*]: Instead of working alone, I'm going to appear with Mr Almady. Yes, Mr Almady. In an extremely witty, charming, brilliant little duologue. [TURAI *bows.* ILONA *listens at the telephone for a moment then she turns to* TURAI *and asks, as if she were still speaking to* MELL] What kind of a play is it?

TURAI: French.

ILONA [*into the telephone*]: French. [*As before.*] Who wrote it?

TURAI: Geraldy.

ILONA: Geraldy, I believe – [*Pause.*] Oh, isn't that nice!

TURAI [*apprehensive*]: What's nice?

ILONA [*hand over receiver*]: He says he knows every line that Geraldy ever wrote.

TURAI: Then it's by Sardou.

ILONA [*into the telephone*]: No I'm sorry. I've just been looking at the script again. It's not by Geraldy; it's by Sardou.

TURAI: The Great Sardou.

ILONA [*into the telephone*]: The Great Sardou! – Indeed?

TURAI: How is he up on Sardou?

ILONA [*covering receiver*]: He says the only thing of Sardou's he knows is 'Hedda Gabler'.

TURAI: That's the man for us!

ILONA: That's the man for us!

TURAI: No, no, no!

ILONA: Goodbye, and thank you so much, Mr Mell. You've been so sweet. – Oh, of course – as if we'd dream of having anybody but you as a prompter – The title?

TURAI: 'A Tooth For a Tooth.'

ILONA: 'A Truth For a –

TURAI: No, no. Tooth, tooth!

ILONA: 'A Tooth For a Tooth' – Yes, isn't it? Quite snappy. Well, goodbye. [*Hangs up.*] Why a French piece?

TURAI: So that nobody will know who wrote it. That's the beauty of French literature. There's so much of it. Besides, one has one's conscience, you know. I've stolen so much from the French in my time that it's only fair I should give them something for a change. Oh, Almady! So that no one will recognize my handwriting, it will be necessary for you to copy out the script.

ALMADY: All of it?

TURAI: From beginning to end.

ALMADY: You think of everything.

TURAI: Two copies!

ILONA [*who has been looking through the script*]: Oh, but this isn't right!

TURAI: What isn't right?

ILONA: This line. You have me say, 'Your kiss is revolting to me.' What I really said was –

TURAI: 'That was your old kiss. Sweet and burning like hot punch.' I know. My memory is excellent. But fortunately we got the boy out of the room before you got that far.

ALMADY: And may I be permitted to inquire *why* my kiss should be described as revolting?

TURAI: The line occurs in the second part of the play, where I was relying on my native inspiration.

ALMADY: You call my kiss revolting? I wish to know why.

TURAI: That is how I *see* it. I am the author of this play, and that is my opinion of your kiss.

ILONA: I do think you might have made some noise to warn us. Why couldn't you have coughed or something?

TURAI: Suppose I had, what should I have been able to do *now*? You overlook the fact that your very first words, my dear Ilona, left no room for misunderstanding. If I had stopped you then nothing could have averted the tragedy.

ALMADY: What a brain!

TURAI: You flatter me!

ILONA: No, he doesn't. He's right for once. Did this idea come to you the moment you heard us?

TURAI: No, I got it from you.

ILONA: From us?

TURAI: Yes, stupid of me, I admit. You see, I always assume the best of my fellowmen. And just for a minute I did think that you really were acting. Later on, I realized my mistake.

ILONA: You thought we were acting. Why?

TURAI: Because it all sounded so artificial. No ring of conviction. I refer particularly to the more erotic passages.

ILONA: I don't wonder. Considering I don't care one little bit for the man.

ALMADY: What's that?

ILONA: You heard.

ALMADY: You don't love me?

ILONA: No!

ALMADY: So you were lying!

ILONA: Yes.

ALMADY: Just to get rid of me?

ILONA: Yes. I hate the sight of you.

ALMADY [*sobs bitterly*]: Serpent!

ILONA: I'd like to murder you!

TURAI: Doesn't it tear your heart to hear a strong man weep?

ALMADY: What made you realize that we were not acting?

TURAI: The disgusting sloppy way you spoke to her. No author living would dare put such slush into the mouth of an actor who is supposed to be making love.

ALMADY: Slush?

TURAI: Utter slush!

ALMADY: Allow me to inform you –

TURAI: Shut up!

ALMADY: Oh, very well.

TURAI: My friends may be here any minute now. Please go and study your parts. [*To* ILONA, *who has been turning over the leaves of the script:*] That's a bit you'll have to learn particularly well.

ILONA: Which?

TURAI: These lines here. This loathsome series of speeches – the ones we overheard last night. [*Points*] From there to there.

ILONA: Odd – I hardly remember –

TURAI: I do. Nor is your fiancé likely to have forgotten.

ILONA [*reading*]: 'I worship you. I adore you. I love you as the church steeple loves the cloud that settles on its summit:' [ALMADY *turns away, embarrassed.*] Just words!

ALMADY [*takes script*]: 'You have used me up and squeezed me like a lemon.'

ILONA: Yes, now I remember –

ALMADY: It's all down. word for word. [TURAI *takes script*.]

TURAI: Yes, the passage is underlined in red ink. Three pages – here – from page sixteen. It goes on, 'Come here and let me kiss that beautiful classic brow' – and then – this is the worst bit, here – this mad outburst of sensuality – [*Reads rapidly:*] 'When I look at *that* – at the perfect shape. The rose flush of that skin – Just to stroke it! – '

ILONA: Yes, but I said –

TURAI: I know, I know. [*Reads:*] 'Hands off!' you said. But he evidently didn't obey you because he goes on, 'My God! How round it is! How smooth! How velvety!' And then he must have gotten very close, indeed, because his next remark is 'And how fragrant!' That's right, isn't it?

ALMADY: Quite right. It was fragrant.

ILONA: Yes, but I did try to –

TURAI: No, my dear, you did not. There was a complete silence until you were heard to exclaim, 'You mustn't bite!' [ILONA *rises;* ALMADY *turns away*.] Yes, I should think you would be ashamed of yourselves. All right, then; copy it, learn it, and play it. And if you ever studied parts in your lives, study these. I'll give you run-through here at seven-thirty – and Ilona – remember, we haven't seen each other for three months.

ILONA: All right, three months. [*Exit*.]

ALMADY: A colossal brain!

TURAI [*bows*]: *Thank you.*

[ALMADY *follows* ILONA *off.* TURAI *sits at table and resumes his interrupted breakfast. Throughout the following scene he goes on eating quietly, deliberately, and with apparent good appetite.* MANSKY *enters dressed in white flannels. He is more doleful and dejected than ever.*]

MANSKY: Have you been up long?

TURAI: I couldn't sleep. [*Goes on eating*.] How is the infant?

MANSKY: Woke up a moment ago. I left him dressing.

TURAI: You had breakfast yet?

MANSKY: Not a mouthful. Couldn't touch it. *You* seem to have no difficulty in putting it away.

TURAI [*with mock sadness*]: One must keep up one's strength.

MANSKY: I'm amazed, and, if I may say so, a little shocked. Sitting there gorging as if nothing had happened. Can't you realize we're absolutely ruined? I'm positively ill thinking about it.

TURAI [*mysteriously*]: Shall I let you into a secret, Mansky?

MANSKY [*with excited anticipation*]: Yes. Tell me.

TURAI [*with great deliberation*]: I am a man who weighs his words. I do not speak lightly. And I say to you solemnly, my friend – [*Dramatic pause.*] – that this is the best bit of ham I've ever tasted.

MANSKY [*furious*]: Bah! [*Crosses to a mirror.*]

TURAI [*continuing as before*]: Juicy – nutty – positively good. [*Solicitously.*] Did the boy sleep at all?

MANSKY: He dropped off about daylight out of sheer exhaustion. [*Looks in the glass.*] I'm pale.

TURAI: Say anything?

MANSKY: Not a word. Just stared at the ceiling. You know, that's bad.

TURAI: Ceilings aren't so bad. Walls are much worse.

MANSKY: What I can't understand is why a magnificent place like this should have walls like tissue-paper.

TURAI: Ah! These are deep waters.

MANSKY: Do stop eating!

TURAI: But I haven't finished.

MANSKY: Gobble – gobble – gobble! [*Looks in the glass.*] My God, I am pale!

TURAI: Suits you. Intellectual pallor.

MANSKY: What about that solution you were hinting at last night?

TURAI: There were several possibilities. I considered them all thoroughly in the night watches – while you lay snoring in your bed. Oh, yes, I heard you while I was changing my clothes. [*Points to the table.*] Telegrams, letters, all ready. Finally I hit on the best and simplest plan.

MANSKY: Which is?

TURAI: I'm going to do everything possible to make him break with her.

MANSKY: What for?

TURAI: Because that's the surest way of bringing them together. If he casts her off forever, in two weeks he'll be rushing after her and falling at her feet. The lady, after a little coaxing, will allow herself to melt. He will coax a little more. She will melt a little more. Finally she will melt altogether – and the curtain will fall on the lovers' slow embrace.

MANSKY [*with cumulative contempt*]: You thought of that in the night, did you?

TURAI: I did.

MANSKY: All by yourself?

TURAI: All by myself?

MANSKY: Well!!! I've noticed all this past year that you've been slipping. I realize now that you've completely lost your grip. Our last show died the death simply because you would write psychology into it. And now you've become simply drivelling. It's a great shock to me. Do you know what's happening? Little by little you're beginning to think – and that spells ruin for both of us. Haven't you grasped yet what a frightful knockdown blow last night's affair was to that boy?

TURAI: Sh! Here he is! [*Enter* ADAM. *He is also in white flannels. Very solemn and miserable. Pause. He passes them without a word and goes to balcony.*] Hullo! Not even a good morning?

ADAM: Oh, good morning.

[TURAI *rises;* MANSKY *looks longingly at breakfast things.*]

MANSKY [*to* ADAM *with his best bedside manner*]: Had breakfast?

ADAM: No. [MANSKY *goes to table and sits down; starts to eat.*]

TURAI: Sleep?

ADAM: No.

TURAI: Nor did I. [ADAM *looks at the wall.*] No. Nothing from there. Not another sound. He left and she went to sleep. *I* didn't on your account. [*To* MANSKY:] Hullo! Appetite picking up?

MANSKY [*starting guiltily and pushing his plate away.*]: No. I can't swallow. Too nervous. I'm a wreck.

TURAI: Try the ham.

ADAM: I – my dear Uncle Sandor – . I don't want to be a burden to you two any longer – now that my life has been blown to bits.

TURAI: Come, come, come!

ADAM: I mean it. I know what I'm talking about. There's a great crack in my heart, and –

TURAI: Come now, be a man. We had enough of that sort of talk last night. Tell me just what is it you want to do?

ADAM: Before anything else, I want to get away from this place.

TURAI: Quite reasonable. And then?

ADAM: Then I'll tear up the music I wrote for her – tear it into little bits and burn it.

TURAI: Right. And after that?

ADAM: Don't be so casual. You know I have nobody in the world but you – you two. If you hadn't been here, I'd have ended things long ago.

TURAI [*to* MANSKY, *who has once more started on the breakfast*]: That's right. Peck a bit.

MANSKY [*jumping up*]: No. It's no good. Absolutely can't swallow. I'm a very sick man.

ADAM: You see? I'm to blame for that.

TURAI: Now listen to me, my boy. Sit down. [ADAM *sits.*] What has happened, has happened. It's over, done with, a thing of the past. And I'm going to say something to you now which no young person will ever believe. You're twenty-five and you're gifted. The world's at your feet. And that world, let me remind you, contains a great many million women.

ADAM: What good are they to me? I only wanted this one. Can't we get away now – at once? I won't see her!

TURAI: Oh, yes you will! Everybody knows she's your fiancée. And you won't run away now. Mind you, I absolutely forbid any sort of reconciliation with her; but you will behave toward her quite naturally and nicely. I know it's going to hurt – it's a bitter pill to swallow. But, remember, today you're a man.

ADAM: Yes, you're right.

TURAI: Up with the head and out with the chin and damn everybody! That's the stuff. The day after tomorrow, when we leave, you shall write her a letter, and let yourself go as much as you like. And, no matter how it may hurt, you have finished with that woman forever.

ADAM [*with an effort*]: Very well. And if it should hurt *too* much, don't be afraid that I'll go back to her. I'll always have pluck enough to put a bullet through my head.

MANSKY: There! See where you have got us to with your psychology.

TURAI [to ADAM]: You ought to be ashamed of yourself.

ADAM [smilingly]: It's all right. It was silly of me to talk nonsense like that. I won't let you down. You shall be satisfied with me.

MANSKY: Good. Then you won't – er – tear anything up?

ADAM: No.

TURAI: You'll behave toward Ilona as if nothing had happened.

ADAM: Yes. Honour bright.

TURAI: I am satisfied.

MANSKY [sitting down to breakfast, a completely changed man]: It's an enormous relief to me to see you getting hold of yourself again so capitally. [Eats rapidly.] Bless my soul, yes, an enormous relief. I really feel a little better.

TURAI: I'm proud of you. [To MANSKY:] Haven't you finished breakfast yet?

MANSKY [delighted]: I can swallow.

TURAI: So I notice.

MANSKY: Come and join me, my boy. You'll find your appetite steals back, little by little. [To TURAI:] He's suffering. He can't get over it.

TURAI: We must try to make him.

MANSKY: Come on, my boy – just a mouthful. Try a little of this excellent ham.

ADAM: I don't want any ham.

MANSKY: Well, a slice of chicken, then – and some nice hot tea with a drop of brandy.

ADAM: Oh, all right. [Sits down.]

MANSKY [to TURAI]: Well, what's on your mind?

ADAM: After trying to cheer me up, are you going to be depressed yourself?

MANSKY: Do you know what I think's the matter with him? He's got another –

TURAI: You win. Another problem.

MANSKY: Theatre!

TURAI: As usual.

MANSKY: Good Lord!

TURAI: Last night I was thinking how hard it is to begin a play. Now I'm thinking how hard it is to finish a second act.

MANSKY: Oh, come and finish your breakfast.

TURAI: No, no. This is interesting. Take this situation of ours – just as we did last night. We've had a curious experience. We arrived here perfectly happy, and immediately got a terrible shock – a ghastly disillusionment. Oh, we've managed to survive it, and we've got ourselves in hand again. But, suppose all this had happened not in real life but on a stage. Suppose this were not a real room, but a painted set. Suppose we three were characters in a play who had just passed through the experiences that we have just passed through.

MANSKY: Well?

TURAI: Well, how would you end the act?

MANSKY: My dear fellow! It's ended already.

TURAI: Well, in a way, yes. But, at the last moment, just before the curtain actually falls, you need a new note of suspense. The act must end, and yet it mustn't quite end – if you know what I mean. Well, my distinguished collaborator, you've often told me how good you are. Try your hand at ending the second act of this dismal adventure of ours.

MANSKY: Simplicity itself. Now then. I'm all for the quiet curtain. One of those charming delicate things the French do so well. You know – sophisticated – lightly sentimental – the smile behind the tear. The three friends sit down to breakfast. Audiences always like to see actors eating. The storm has passed. The skies are still a little dark, but there is sunlight in the heart – and all that sort of thing. Let this sink in for a bit – everything very cozy and pleasant. [*Notices wine-glass on table.*] We each have a glass of wine. For a moment – silence – their thoughts are busy with what has passed. [*Pause.*] Capital. And then – [*He raises his glass.*] – you want a couple of smart lines, spoken with something of a flourish. [*Thinks.*] Oh, well – . My young friend, today you have become a man –

44

TURAI [*pointing to where he was sitting at the time*]: I said that.

MANSKY: For — always remember —

TURAI: Yes, that shows 'em it's coming.

MANSKY [*not heeding him*]: Always remember that in affairs of the heart it is not the first victory that makes us men, but the first defeat. [*Lifts his glass.*] To Woman's Treachery, which has made our child a man! [*Raises his hand toward the Curtain.*] Curtain. [*Curtain starts to come down. They put their glasses down on the table simultaneously, untasted.*] How's that?

TURAI: Rotten! [*Stops Curtain with a motion. Curtain slowly goes up again.*] Tame. Feeble. Nothing in the nature of a high spot. I'm not saying it isn't pretty and graceful. Charming even, but it lacks suspense. [*Pause. To* ADAM:] How would *you* do it?

ADAM: I? Feeling as I do now?

TURAI: Give us your idea.

ADAM [*with tremendous intensity*]: Very well, I'll give you my idea. We start from where Mansky gave that toast.

MANSKY: To Woman's — ?

ADAM [*rises*]: Treachery. That's it. I'd say — 'No. I won't drink any toast.' [*Throws glass against the wall, smashing it to bits.*]

MANSKY [*approvingly*]: Effective.

ADAM [*rapidly losing control of himself and becoming hysterical*]: That woman was not just an incident in my life. She was my first great passion. I promised to act as if nothing had happened. I meant to keep that promise. But when I remember that I gave her my life and that she whispers words of love to another man — and — and kisses another man, that's such unbearable, burning torture, that the only right solution — [*Grabs a small game carving knife from the table.*]

TURAI [*leaping forward*]: Hey! Stop that!

ADAM [*struggling with him*]: No! No!

MANSKY [*rushing forward*]: My God! You weren't really —

ADAM [*struggling*]: Let me go. I want to die. [TURAI *has got the knife away from him. He looks at it intently.* ADAM *stands, pale and defiant.*]

TURAI: What the devil do you think you're doing?

ADAM [*bitterly*]: Just — finishing the act. [*He sits down.* MANSKY

45

follows him and sits down. Smiles wanly.] Curtain! [*Curtain starts to come down.*]

TURAI [*stopping Curtain with a motion*]: Very bad. [*Curtain goes up again.*] My dear young fellow. You simply can't wipe out the young love interest at the end of the second act with a bread knife. That's crude. And there are the critics. [*Cringes.*]The critics dislike bloodshed. If there is to be any slaughter, they prefer to attend to it themselves. No, no, my boy. What we need is suspense. Suspense – and a quick curtain.

MANSKY: And now, I suppose, you could show us how it really ought to be done?

TURAI [*goes to telephone*]: Hello. Will you give me Miss Ilona Szabo's room, please. [*Bell sounds in* ILONA'S *room.*]

MANSKY: What on earth – ?

ILONA: Hello.

TURAI: Hello. Ilona?

ILONA: Yes. Who is that speaking?

TURAI: Don't you recognize my voice? This is Sandor Turai.

ILONA: Oh, how wonderful! Are you here, then? Where are you speaking from?

TURAI: Yes. I'm right here in the castle. Next door to you. Number four.

ILONA: What a perfectly delightful surprise.

TURAI: We came by car last night. All three of us.

ILONA: You don't mean Albert, too?

TURAI: Yes – and Mansky, if you think that worth mentioning. We're all three here in this room, and we've brought you the finished script of the operetta.

ILONA: Marvelous! That's something like a surprise!

TURAI: We were hesitating about waking you so early, but I particularly wanted to see you about something. Can you come in here for a minute? [*Replaces receiver and goes to door. Enter* ILONA *with assumed joy and excitement.*]

ILONA: Well, this is wonderful of you all. [*She kisses* TURAI *lightly and crosses quickly to* ADAM *who kisses her hands.*] What a surprise. Albert, darling! This *is* a surprise. Sandor! To think that it's –

TURAI: Three whole months –

ILONA: Three whole months since I've seen you. How brown you're looking. And younger than ever. Let me look at you. Wonderful! [*She crosses to* MANSKY *and kisses him on each cheek.*] And Mansky – how are you, Mansky dear? I think this is too sweet of you all. You don't know how I've been longing to see you. When did you get here?

TURAI [*very gravely*]: Just a minute, Ilona. [*He looks through door into her room.*] Why, Mr Almady! Of all people! Won't you come in? [*Enter* ALMADY.]

ALMADY [*nervously*]: Good morning.

TURAI: Fancy finding *you* here after all these years.

ALMADY [*pompously*]: Passing through. Just passing through. I only wanted to say how-d'you-do to the Count, but they wouldn't let me go. The – er – the shooting-party you know, and the concert. They insisted on my staying.

ILONA: I was so surprised to see him.

TURAI: Pardon me for disturbing you and possibly casting a slight gloom on what must have been a joyful reunion, but I have something rather important to say.

ILONA: What do you mean? Nothing – nothing unpleasant, I hope?

TURAI: Yes – extremely unpleasant. [*He motions them to sit down.*] Well, then. We arrived here last night – [*Long pause.*] And just now we were sitting having breakfast – we three – . Weren't we?

ADAM [*puzzled*]: Yes.

MANSKY: Well?

TURAI: Keep quite calm, please. We were sitting here, having breakfast – all three of us. [*He lowers his voice and speaks very earnestly.*] I must entreat you all to hear what I am about to say quite calmly – Don't lose your heads –

ILONA: For God's sake –

ALMADY [*uneasily*]: What is it?

TURAI [*holds up his hand*]: Please! [*Dead silence.*] What I am about to say – and I shall not detain you long now – must almost inevitably have a shattering effect on the lives – both the private and the professional lives – of all of us five people. I have asked myself – is it wise to speak? And I have answered myself – wise or not, it is unavoidable. Ilona – I have a question to ask you –

47

[*Breaks off. Dead silence. Then very simply to* MANSKY:] How's that for suspense?

MANSKY: Yes. Well? What now?

TURAI: Nothing. That's all. [*Smiles.*] Curtain! [*Curtain comes down while he offers* ILONA *his arm. The rest of the group breathe again and relax their tension.*] We've just been having an argument about the proper way to end a second act.

CURTAIN

ACT THREE

As the Curtain rises it reveals the room lighted up by the electric sconces and candelabra. A large and elaborately painted screen in silver and green has been placed in front of the window. It is painted to suggest an orchard. The screen shuts out the view of the Mediterranean, but to the left and right of it we glimpse the lighted esplanade, and many more twinkling lights than in the first act, for it is early evening. There are two garden chairs in front of the screen in the raised portion of the room; otherwise the scene is unchanged. MR MELL, *the Count's secretary, and the master of ceremonies, enters. He is a fussy, pale young man with a high pitched voice. He wears glasses and is in evening clothes. He is carrying a wicker table, and carrying it with difficulty and discomfort. He places it between the two wicker chairs in front of the screen and stands caressing his hands where the table has cut into them.*

MELL [*calls*]: Dwornitschek. [*To himself:*] Where is that man? [*Calls.*] Dwornitschek.

DWORNITSCHEK'S VOICE: Coming, sir, coming. [DWORNITSCHEK *enters from the hall, followed by a* LACKEY. *They are both in formal, full dress livery of white with knee breeches, and powdered wigs.* DWORNITSCHEK *carries a book, two letters, a scarf and a woman's hat. The* LACKEY *carries a tall brown hunting hat, whip, gauntlets and a large, luscious peach.*

MELL: Oh, there you are at last. Why are you so late?

DWORNITSCHEK: I fell downstairs, sir.

MELL: Well, that oughtn't to have taken you long. [*He fiddles with the screen.*]

DWORNITSCHEK: You should have let *me* carry those things, Mr Mell.

MELL: I couldn't wait. You are so slow.

DWORNITSCHEK: Slow but sure, sir. [*He puts things on table.*] When I was a lad, my aunt used to say –

49

MELL: I don't want to hear about your aunt.

DWORNITSCHEK: No, sir. Very few people do.

MELL: Have you got all the properties?

DWORNITSCHEK: Props, sir, is the more professional expression.

MELL: I was using the more technical term – Well, properties or props, have you got them?

DWORNITSCHEK: Yes, sir. Book –

MELL: – Peach –

DWORNITSCHEK: – Scarf –

MELL: – Whip –

DWORNITSCHEK: – Two letters and a pair of gloves.

MELL: Good. [*Mops his forehead.*] Oh, dear, what a headache I'm getting.

DWORNITSCHEK: What you need is an aspirin.

MELL: Have you an aspirin?

DWORNITSCHEK: No, sir.

MELL: You're a great help.

DWORNITSCHEK: Thank you, sir. If I might be allowed to say so, you let yourself get too nervous on these festive nights, sir. You *worry*.

MELL: How can I help worrying with all the responsibility there is on my shoulders?

DWORNITSCHEK: What I always say is – never worry too much today. Things may be worse tomorrow, and then you can worry twice as hard.

MELL: It does make me so nervous when people want to alter the programme at the last moment. First Miss Szabo says she's going to sing, then she says she's going to act – [*He breaks off as* ALMADY *enters.*] Good evening, sir, good evening. You are first in the field.

ALMADY [*grouchily*]: Good evening. The others will be here directly. They're dressing.

MELL: A wonderful shooting party today, sir. Capital sport, capital. There is nothing like a good brisk day out in the open with the guns. What a colour it has given you.

ALMADY: I wasn't there.

MELL: Eh? Oh! Not there?

ALMADY: No, I've been in my room all day, writing.

MELL: Pardon my curiosity, but may one ask what you were writing?

ALMADY: No, one may not.

DWORNITSCHEK: I think the gentleman does not wish to say what he was writing, sir.

MELL: Oh, you are still there?

DWORNITSCHEK: Yes, sir. Still here.

MELL: Then go away.

DWORNITSCHEK: Really, I shouldn't worry, Mr Mell. Look on the bright side, sir.

MELL: All very well for you. You have no responsibilities, and the guests give you big tips.

DWORNITSCHEK: That is the bright side, sir. [*He goes out followed by the* LACKEY.]

MELL: A secretary's life is a dog's life, Mr Almady. Work, work, work, from morning till night, and never a word of thanks. You are very silent, Mr Almady.

ALMADY: I sometimes find it soothing to be silent. Try it yourself one of these days. I take it the concert begins directly after dinner?

MELL: Immediately following the serving of coffee.

ALMADY: And when does this – this play of ours come on?

MELL: It is the last item on the programme. The place of honour.

ALMADY: Bah!

MELL: Sir?

ALMADY [*absorbed in his part which he is studying*]: Nothing.

MELL: Miss Szabo tells me that no scenery is required but two elegant chairs and one elegant table.

ALMADY: Is that an elegant table?

MELL: Well, really no. But what can one expect in a garden? Oh – if only the scene had been an interior, there's some perfectly lovely furniture in the Count's room – genuine Louis the Fifteenth. A very elegant period, Louis the Fifteenth.

ALMADY: I don't care a damn. They're all the same to me. Louis the Fifteenth or Louis the Fourteenth or Louis the Seventeenth.

MELL: But there isn't a Louis the *Seventeenth*, and I've often wondered why. Why, I've wondered, should there be a Louis the *Sixteenth* and a Louis the *Eighteenth,* but not a Louis the *Seventeenth?*

ALMADY: Oh, God. Ask a furniture dealer.

MELL: I did. I'm *always* asking furniture dealers. But they only know as far as Louis the *Sixteenth*. That's where the Louis stop for furniture dealers. Whenever I say Louis the *Seventeenth* they say you mean the *Sixteenth*, and I say no, I don't mean Louis the *Sixteenth*, I mean Louis the *Seventeenth* and – [*Breaks off and mops his brow.*] I'm afraid I'm talking a great deal, sir.

ALMADY: Oh, you've noticed that?

MELL: The fact is, Mr Almady, I'm all a-twitter.

ALMADY: What have *you* got to be nervous about?

MELL: I'm always like this on these big nights. You see I'm responsible for everything and it's terribly wearing on the nerves. I'm stage manager, property man and prompter. I turn the music, show the ladies to their seats, hand bouquets onto the stage – and I'm expected always to applaud at the right moment. I assure you I have often gone to bed after one of these entertainments with my hands so tender I could scarcely hold my toothbrush. You will pardon me for mentioning it, sir, but you don't seem quite your merry old self tonight.

ALMADY: I'm as cheerful as any man would be whose brain has been addled from studying an infernal part all day.

MELL: But I thought you said you had spent the day writing?

ALMADY: Yes, I – I always memorize a part by writing it out.

MELL: What energy! What enthusiasm! Have you a nice part?

ALMADY: No. Rotten.

MELL: Dear, dear, dear! You'll feel better when you hear the applause. We're great applauders here. We don't care how bad an actor is –

ALMADY [*offended*]: Thank you.

MELL: I beg your pardon. I – I don't mean it like that. [*Goes to door of* ILONA'S *room and knocks.*] Miss Szabo, please. Miss Szabo, please. Beginners, please.

[*Enter* ILONA *in evening dress. Enter* ADAM, *Right, in dress clothes.*]

ILONA: Well, we seem to be all here.

MELL: Good evening, Miss Szabo, good evening, good evening.

ILONA: Well, we may as well begin.

ALMADY: Wouldn't it be as well to wait for Mr Turai? [*Bitterly.*] Seeing that he is being so kind as to give us his invaluable assistance.

ILONA: He'll be here directly. Where is the prompter?

MELL: Present. Present.

ILONA: Here's the script.

MELL [*goes to stage*]: I hope this extempore set meets with your approval? [*Pointing to screen.*] A little idea quite my own.

ILONA: Charming. Albert – you seem – you seem – very quiet – this evening.

ADAM: Oh, no, not a bit. A little tired, that's all. We had rather a long motor drive and I didn't get much sleep last night – Please don't think – I'm afraid our friend the secretary is getting restive.

ILONA: What on earth is the matter?

MELL: I'm all a-twitter.

ILONA: Well, do simmer down. [*To* ADAM, *who has sat down:*] Surely you're not going to stay for this rehearsal?

ADAM: If you don't mind.

ILONA: Oh, I don't mind. But you'll be thoroughly bored. A silly little French piece. You'll be seeing it after dinner. I should have thought once would have been enough.

ADAM: Well, as a matter of fact, Mr Turai asked me to stay and help out till he came. And I promised him I would.

ILONA: Just as you please. [*Very nervous.*] Can't we begin? Are the props here?

MELL: Nothing is ever missing when I am the property man. There they all are – on the table.

ILONA [*takes the book and letter*]: Those are yours. [ALMADY *pockets the peach and the remaining letter.*] Now then – let's start. The Countess – that's me – discovered alone. Seated in chair, reading book. [*Sits down. To* ALMADY:) You're not on yet. [ALMADY *stalks off.*]

MELL: Do we go on now?

ILONA: Don't ask so many questions. Yes, go on.

MELL: Curtain rises on a glorious garden. Period Louis the Fifteenth.

ILONA: You don't have to read *that*.

MELL [*doubtfully*]: I always *have*.

ILONA: You only have to give the actors the spoken lines.

MELL: Now, I never knew *that* before. Now, that's very interesting. [*He looks stupidly at script.*]

ALMADY: What on earth's the matter now?

ILONA: I'm afraid Mr Mell is not much of a prompter.

ADAM [*taking script from* MELL]: It's all right – let *me* hold the book.

ILONA: No.

ALMADY [*simultaneously*]: No, no.

ILONA: You mustn't.

ADAM: What do you mean?

ILONA: I won't have it –

ADAM: Why not?

MELL: No doubt Miss Szabo means that it is beneath the dignity of such an important person. Please give *me* the book.

ADAM: Do stop fussing. Can't you see you make them nervous.

MELL: Make *them* nervous? What about *my* nervousness?

ADAM: I tell you *I'll* hold the book. And you can do it for the performance. Does that satisfy you?

MELL [*deeply offended*]: Oh quite. Oh, perfectly –

ILONA [*to* ADAM]: Now you've hurt the poor man's feelings. You've insulted him –

MELL: Madam, I'm a secretary. I spend all my time receiving insults.

ILONA: Oh? Well, let's begin. [*to* ALMADY:] You're off. [*Again* ALMADY *stalks off.*] Countess discovered seated in armchair, reading book. [*Takes up book.* ALMADY *is wearing the brown hat, gauntlets and carring the riding whip.*]

ADAM [*prompting*]: What a silly –

ILONA [*speaking her lines*]: What a silly story. [*Closes book.*] Just like all novels.

ADAM: What *can* I do –

ILONA [*yawning*]: What *can* I do to kill time? The Count is always

54

out riding. Paris seems very far away amidst these sleepy fields of Normandy.

ADAM: Hoofbeats heard off – [MELL *imitates hoofbeats by beating his thighs with his hands.*]

ILONA: Hark! I hear him coming. Can this be my husband? Surely he went off on his horse to visit our old tenant, honest Jacques Benoit. [MELL *makes the hoofbeats louder and louder.* ALMADY *comes into the scene dramatically, ominously, but his entrance is completely ruined by* MELL *continuing the hoof-beats.* ALMADY *stamps his feet impatiently and at last* MELL *stops.*]

ALMADY: So, madame!

ILONA: Why, what is the matter? Why do you frown, my dear Count?

ALMADY: Why do I frown? That, madame, you will learn – and speedily, as sure as my name is Count –, Count –

ADAM [*prompting*]: Maurice du Veyrier –

ALMADY: As sure as my name is Count Maurice de Veyrier de la Grande Contumace Saint Emilion.

ILONA: You frighten me, Maurice.

ALMADY: It is your guilty conscience that frightens you, madame.

ADAM: Traitress. [ILONA *starts and looks at him nervously.* ADAM *rises.*] Traitress! No doubt you supposed me a credulous imbecile whom it was simple to hoodwink. [*Enter* TURAI *and* MANSKY, *both in evening dress.* ILONA *and* ALMADY, *confused by their guilt, for the moment, believe that* ADAM *is accusing them.*]

ALMADY [*very embarrassed*]: No doubt – you – I –

ADAM [*still prompting*]: You thought that any story would do for me? You imagined that I was fool enough to swallow anything.

TURAI [*coming down, horrified, thinking that* ADAM *is making a scene*]: What!!!!

ADAM: Shhhh – [*Goes on prompting.*] No doubt you supposed me a credulous fool –

TURAI: O-oh [*Relieved; he grasps the situation. Takes the script from him.*] Let *me* have that script.

ADAM: Why? Aren't I prompting well?

ILONA: No.

ALMADY [*simultaneously*]: No.

ADAM [*ruffled*]: Nothing like being frank.

MELL: Don't take it to heart. Even *I* wasn't good enough for them.

ADAM: Perhaps you'll tell me where I went wrong?

TURAI: Don't ask so many questions. [*Seats himself in* MELL'S *place.*] I'll take on this job.

MELL: Everybody is so rude.

TURAI: All right. From where you stopped.

ALMADY [*glibly*]: Traitress, you have deceived me. I have long had my suspicions. I have now in my possession the proofs. No doubt you supposed me a credulous imbecile whom it was simple to hoodwink. You thought that any story would do for me. You imagined that I was a fool enough to swallow anything. Let me tell you, madame, that you are mistaken. For a long time I have suspected that there was something behind these rides of yours with our neighbor the Marquis Jean François Gelette de Tour d'Argent. Day after day, for hours at a time, you have made a practice of riding with him on the road from Dunernois Sur Saône to Saint Sulpice de la Grande Parmentiére – and slowly at that!

ILONA: It's a lie. Who told you?

ALMADY: Silence, woman! The proofs are in my pocket. Mon Dieu, is there no gratitude in this world? When I married you, who were you? A nobody. Your father, Brigadier-General Pierre Jean Bourmond de la Seconde-Chaumiere-Rambouillet, fell in battle at Grand-Lagruyere Sur Marne, and you eked out a scanty living as a seamstress at your mother's home in the village of Saint Genevieve, in the Department of Seine et Oise. So, madame! And then what happened? I came. I gave you name, rank and wealth such as you had never had dreamed of. You became Madame La Countess du Veyrier de la Grande Contumace Saint Emilion. I bestowed upon you not only my estates in Pardubien-Grand-Amanoir, but also my two castles in Challenges-Debicourt de la Romanée and at Rivalieux-Quandamouzieres Sur Vantera-aux Alpes Maritimes. [*He stops, exhausted.*]

TURAI: Don't stop. What's wrong?

[ALMADY *takes off his hat and gloves, puts the whip down on the table, and stepping out of character, comes down to* TURAI.]

ALMADY: It's these damned French names. They're perfectly frightful.

TURAI: I don't see what we can do about it.

ALMADY: You surely don't need them all?

TURAI: They're in the script.

ALMADY: But I'll go mad trying to memorize them. Titles with six hyphens in them and names of places with a dozen 'aux' and 'de la's' and 'surs'. And, damn it, they're all in *my* part. [*Choking with fury*] It's deadly. At least let's leave out that second castle.

TURAI [*coldly*]: My dear fellow, have you no sense of dramatic construction? If he had given her only one castle, the audience would think her perfectly justified in deceiving him. If he had given her three, they would look on him as a purse-proud fool who didn't deserve a faithful wife. No, two is exactly the right number. You can't beat Sardou when it comes to technique. Go on, please.

[ALMADY *goes up hopelessly and replaces his hat and gloves and takes up the whip.*]

ALMADY: I made you a countess and a wealthy woman. And what return do I get? You betray me – yes, madame, betray me – with my best friend and nearest neighbor, the Marquis Jean François Gelette de la Tour d'Agent, lord of Perigord des Champignons and Saint Sulpice de la Grand Parmentière. [*He breaks off and removes hat and gloves as before.*] My God, it's enough to give a fellow apoplexy.

TURAI [*surprised*]: I beg your pardon? That doesn't seem to be in the script.

ALMADY: I'm sorry. I can't help it. It's these names.

TURAI: Well, I'm always open to suggestions. What would you like to call the gentleman?

ALMADY: Foch or Briand – or something short like that.

TURAI [*sarcastically*]: Perhaps – Vichy! Get on, please.

ILONA [*nervously*]: Oh, do let's get on. Count, you have said enough.

TURAI: So *he* seems to think.

ILONA: I will not endure these shameful accusations. You are insulting the woman who bears your name.

ALMADY [*again taking off hat and gloves and putting down the whip*]: It's a damned shame.

TURAI: What is?

ALMADY: I always have to say the whole infernal thing from beginning to end, and she just says 'your name'.

TURAI [*coldly*]: We're wasting time.

ALMADY: Another word, madame, and I produce the proof.

ILONA [*laughing*]: The proof? One is amused. One smiles.

ALMADY: A smile which I will make to die upon your lips. Behold! The proof! [*He fiddles in his coat-tail pocket from which he belatedly takes the peach with sinister flourish.*]

ILONA [*with insincere terror*]: Ah, gracious heaven! The peach!

ALMADY [*lays the peach on table*]: Yes, madame, the peach. The first peach that ripened on the lovingly cherished, early-blooming, richly-bearing, East Indian dwarf peach trees in my orchard at Simarineux de la Pomme d'Api, making a triumphant entry into the world days ahead of any other peach in the whole of France. [*He turns and glares at* TURAI *resentfully.*] You know what a passionate fruit grower I am. You know that I have tended this peach from its first budding, cared for it, watched over it, wrapped it about with my love, kept a diary about it, and awaited its ripening like the coming of a Messiah. And what happens? This afternoon I go out riding. I am proceeding at a gentle jog-trot – [MELL *imitates hoof-beats as before.* ALMADY *is incensed by his stupidity.* MELL *subsides, abashed, and* ALMADY *resumes.*] I am proceeding at a gentle jog-trot from Duvernois Sur Saône to Saint Sulpice de la Grand Parmentière – [*He breaks off with an anguished look at* TURAI.]

TURAI [*coldly*]: Along the highroad –

ALMADY: Along the highroad. And whom should I see there, tripping along, but Juliette, your maid. I speak to her. She betrays embarrassment at seeing me. She stammers and ties her apron-strings in a knot. I ask her where she is going. Terrified, she bursts into tears and whispers, 'My lady sent me to the

Marquis Jean François Gelette de la tour d'Argent' – curse him!

TURAI: Right. This time that was in the script.

ALMADY: Why, I ask the girl, did your mistress send you to the Marquis? And then suddenly, happening to look closer, I see that she is trying desperately to hide a little parcel from me. I take it from her, I open it, and what do I see? [*Points to peach.*] That peach! The king of peaches, the apple of my eye – my pride and joy, my first born, the supreme peach from the orchards of Simarineux de la Pomme d'Api – the last word in stoneless fruit which I have been guarding since birth like a baby sister. And, as if this were not enough, wrapped round that glorious specimen of its kind, I discover a letter. [*He fiddles in his inside coatpocket, draws out a letter, sees it is the wrong one, replaces it hastily, and draws forth the proper one.*] This letter – [*He reads.*] – 'My beloved. This is the first peach that has ripened in France this year. I send it to *you*. Eat it reverently.' [*He holds the letter under her nose.*] There!

ILONA: Are you trying to make me smell it?

ALMADY: I am. For even if you were shameless enough to deny your writing you cannot deny your perfume. Or are you proposing to deny it?

ILONA: No.

ALMADY: Ha! Then you admit it?

ILONA: Yes.

ALMADY: You sent him this peach?

ILONA: Yes.

ALMADY [*again takes off his hat and gloves*]: It's simple rank injustice. I've got to say yardlong speeches at the top of my voice, and all her part conists of is little exclamations like 'oh!' 'no!' and 'yes!'

TURAI: Yes – I noticed that myself. These short crisp speeches are characteristic of Sardou's women! It can't be helped. Go on, please.

ALMADY [*goes back, puts on hat and gloves, more miserable than ever*]: So! You accept from me everything, love, name, rank, riches, estates – two castles – and then you go about the place sending my cherished fruit to your lover!

ILONA [*rises; tragically*]: No.

ALMADY: You have the effrontery to pretend that the Marquis is not your lover?

ILONA: Yes.

ALMADY: You mean he is?

ILONA: No.

ALMADY: You mean he is *not?*

ILONA [*triumphantly*]: Yes.

ALMADY [*with a theatrical laugh*]: A likely story, Madame. I am a fruit-grower, the leading amateur horticulturist in France and President of the Paris Peach Club. I know – I say, I know – that one does not give fruit like this save where one has first given – the heart. Madame, I despise you.

ILONA: You consider conduct like mine despicable?

ALMADY: I do.

ILONA: Good! Then I have one little question to ask you. In the early spring of the year there ripened in your orchard the first crop of whiteheart cherries. To whom did you send those cherries?

ALMADY [*turns away, embarrassed*]: To my mother. The Dowager Countess de la Grande Contumace Saint Emilion.

ILONA: Indeed? To your mother? Then permit me to show you something. You are not the only one who has discovered an interesting letter. [*Takes letter from table.*] Smell that! Do you recognize the perfume? [*Holds it under his nose.*]

MELL: What a *sensation!* Sardou at his best. There's no one like him.

ILONA: The perfume is of Mademoiselle Emilienne, première danseuse at the Folies Bergères, whom you honour with your friendship and protection.

ALMADY: How – how did you get this?

ILONA: Never mind. Always remember letters are like spent arrows. You never can tell where they are going to drop.

MELL [*applauds vigorously*]: An epigram.

ILONA: Read it, please.

ALMADY [*reading*]: 'My dearest. This morning that doddering old idiot of a count of mine – '

ILONA: You notice how your divinity writes of you? Go on.

ALMADY [*reading*]: – 'that doddering idiot of a count of mine sent me a basket of cherries. Did I tell you he was a famous fruit-grower? He says these are the first cherries that have ripened in France this year and he sends them to me as a token of his love. Drop in this evening, darling, and we'll eat the old fool's cherries together. Your loving Emilienne. P. S. Ring twice as usual!' [*He sobs.*]

ILONA: You see, what you do to me, I do to you. An eye for an eye, *a tooth for a tooth*, a peach for a cherry.

ALMADY [*brokenly*]: Yes. It's true.

ILONA: And now, leave my garden. This very afternoon I pack my boxes and go back to my mother. And if you will question my maid you will find that I told her to hang about till you came by – to blush and stammer – and finally to give you the letter *and* the peach. [*She breaks into stage laughter.*] Ha, ha, ha! Oh, ha, ha, ha, ha, ha!

ALMADY: Well, I must face it. I've lost.

ILONA: You've lost me.

ALMADY [*kneeling*]: Yvonne! Don't say that. See! I beg your forgiveness on my knees – overlook this one false step.

ILONA: The idea! A count and an *elderly* count – grovelling like that. [ALMADY *gets up and turns away.*] All the same, you have touched me. So I will forgive you. But you are not to get off without punishment. Firstly, I forbid you to eat this peach.

ALMADY: My God! Not that!

ILONA [*firmly*]: Yes.

ALMADY: So be it.

ILONA: Secondly, you will permit me to go to Paris alone.

ALMADY [*despairingly*]: Yvonne!

ILONA: Not a word. Either you trust me or you do not! If you do, I will return. If not, not.

ALMADY: Oh, heavens! And how long do you expect to stay in Paris?

ILONA: A week.

ALMADY [*suddenly bursting out*]: No! I can't live without you. I worship you. I adore you. I love you as the church steeple loves the cloud that settles on its summit, only to be wafted away by the first passing breeze. I can't live without you. Not a week, not a day. Not an hour.

ILONA: Just words.

[*At the words 'church steeple'* MANSKY *and* ADAM *have exchanged a glance of utter astonishment.*)

MANSKY [*rises*]: But – but – but – Just one moment – What was that you said?

ILONA: I beg your pardon?

TURAI: Now, listen, *please*. We can't have these interruptions. Don't pull them up the moment they've got nicely into the swing of it.

MELL: I can't wait to see how it all ends. Will she leave him? Or will the memory of their past love prove too strong?

MANSKY [*goes to* ADAM – *Aside to him*]: This is devilish queer.

TURAI: Quiet, please. All right. Go on. Better go back to 'Not a week! Not a day! Not an hour!'

ALMADY: *Not a week! Not a day! Not an hour!*

ILONA: Just words.

ALMADY: It's the truth. I'm crazy about you. And you – you have used me up and squeezed me like a lemon, and now you want to throw me away.

[*At the word 'lemon'* MANSKY *and* ADAM *again exchange glances.* MANSKY *gets up, deeply agitated.*]

MANSKY: Sandor –

TURAI: What is it?

MANSKY [*to* ILONA *and* ALMADY]: You'll excuse me? I have something very urgent to say to Mr Turai. [*He crosses to* TURAI *and drags him over to the corner below the fireplace.*] Do you hear what they're saying?

TURAI [*feigning non-comprehension*]: How do you mean, do I hear what they're saying?

MANSKY: I mean – didn't those last lines sound familiar to you?

TURAI: That's right. Now you mention it. I did notice something, only I thought it was my fancy.

MANSKY [*to* ADAM]: Come here. I give you my word, Sandor. Those lines were syllable for syllable the ones we heard last night through the wall.

TURAI [*looking at script*]: By Jove, you're right – This is uncanny.

MANSKY: Go on with the rehearsal, or they will be suspecting something. I want to hear some more.

[MANSKY *takes hold of* ADAM'S *arm.* ADAM *is very excited.* BOTH *listen intently.*]

TURAI: Well, let's get on. 'Now you want to throw me away.'

ILONA: I don't want to throw you away, silly. Oh, come on, then. Come here and let me kiss that beautiful classic brow.

MANSKY: Great heavens!

ILONA: What's the matter?

MANSKY [*whispering*]: Listen, you two. They're saying word for word what we heard them say last night. Do you grasp now what they were doing last night? *Rehearsing!* Simply going through their lines.

TURAI: I must admit this has come upon me as a complete surprise. Really, I'm quite shaken.

ADAM: Imitate me. If I can be perfectly calm, you can.

MANSKY [*pointing to* TURAI]: And he never recognized it!

ILONA: Mr Turai! What's going on?

ALMADY: Yes. What's all the discussion about?

TURAI: Well, it's like this. Mansky says – and I'm bound to say I agree with him – that for the actual performance tonight you will have to dig up a classic brow from somewhere.

ALMADY: Dig up a classic brow?

TURAI: You see, it's rather awkward. The script says – 'Kiss that beautiful classic brow.'

ALMADY: Well?

TURAI: Well, you'll have to get one somewhere.

ALMADY [*bitterly*]: You think my own would not be convincing?

MANSKY: My God, no!

ALMADY: It has been so described.

TURAI: In this play, yes. But, if you'll pardon my saying so, you wouldn't suggest that any woman of taste could say such a thing in *real* life?

ALMADY [*bitterly*]: Very good. No doubt the property man will be able to supply me with a face. [MELL *is appalled at the prospect of having to get a 'face' but he dutifully makes a notation of it in his little book.*]

TURAI: Oh – my dear fellow.

[*ALL go back to their places.*]

ADAM [*impatiently*]: We're wasting time. Let's get on.

TURAI: Sh! Sh! We've only a few minutes more.

ADAM: No more interruptions.

MELL: Thank God!

ILONA: Where were we? Oh, yes. Come here and let me kiss that beautiful classic brow. [*Kisses him on the forehead.*]

ALMADY: That's not a kiss. That's a tip.

MANSKY: Surely that line is a trifle vulgar.

TURAI: It's vulgar because it's spoken by a vulgar man.

MANSKY: The speaker is a count.

TURAI: But a dull-witted bounder, for all that. He's the sort of man who would say things like that. Don't you start trying to teach Sardou how to write dialogue.

ALMADY [*furious*]: For God's sake, are we going to rehearse?

TURAI: Yes. Go on, please.

ALMADY: That's not a kiss. That's a tip.

ILONA: Don't shout like that.

ALMADY: I will shout. I'm a squeezed lemon. That's what I am – a lemon. [*Falls sobbing at her feet.* MANSKY *whispers something to* ADAM. ADAM *smiles happily and whispers back. They shake hands.*]

TURAI: Please – please – What's the matter?

MANSKY: Nothing. I was merely saying to Adam that I think that word 'lemon' is all wrong.

TURAI: I think it's excellent. Absolutely in character. The speaker is a big lemon-and-peach man from Saint Sulpice de la Grande Parmentière, and he naturally goes to the orchard for his similes. Try to realize that he's practically an imbecile with virtually no vocabulary. [ALMADY *looks up from* ILONA'S *lap and registers indignation Prompting:*] 'Please, please' – [*To* ILONA:] From you, my dear. [*To* ALMADY:] You're crying. [ALMADY *sobs.*]

ILONA: Please, please. Don't cry. I can't bear it. You know how fond I am of you. [*She goes to table where peach is.*]

ALMADY: Those nights of love – those flaming, wonderful nights! Have you forgotten them so completely? [*He stands up, and starts to touch the peach.*]

ILONA: Stop! Control yourself.

ALMADY [*gazing at peach*]: You ask me to control myself – when I look at *that*? At that perfect shape. The rose flush of that skin. [*Starts to touch peach.*] Just to stroke it –

ILONA: Hands off.

ALMADY [*snatching up the peach, holds it in one hand and with the other strokes it voluptuously*]: My God! How round it is! How smooth, how velvety – and how fragrant! [*Raises it to his mouth.*]

ILONA: You mustn't bite it.

[*She snatches his hand.* MANSKY *gives a shriek and goes into fits of laughter.* ADAM *stretches his arms out to* MANSKY *and roars.* ADAM *slaps* MANSKY *on the back,* MANSKY *laughing uninterruptedly.* ALMADY *turns away furiously.* ILONA *turns away, ashamed.*]

MANSKY: Heavens! What fools we've been!

ADAM: Haven't we?

MELL [*eagerly*]: Won't you tell me the joke?

ADAM: You wouldn't understand.

ILONA: What are you two so amused about?

TURAI [*curtly*]: Come, come. We're wasting time. Let's get on.

MANSKY: Yes, get on. I want to hear this. Round, smooth, velvety and fragrant.

ADAM: And you mustn't bite.

ILONA: You mustn't bite it.

ALMADY: I must – I am so hungry.

[ADAM *and* MANSKY *go on laughing.* MELL *laughs too, but with a puzzled look, as much to say 'I'm joining in, but I really don't understand.'*]

ALMADY: Ah, well! I see I am nothing to you any more.

ILONA: Oh, for goodness' sake! I swear that no man – [*Breaks off, unable to go on.*]

TURAI [*prompting*]: No man who has ever come into my life –

ILONA: – has meant so much to me as you. From the top of your head to the soles of your feet you are a man.

TURAI: I think we might cut that last bit.

ALMADY: Why?

TURAI: Well, I mean to say – A little too explicit, don't you think? Rather too obvious a sexual implication. A wee bit coarse, perhaps, yes? We must consider the feelings of the audience. [*To* MELL:] Will there be any young girls there tonight?

MELL: Oh, yes, indeed.

TURAI: Then we must cut it. They may bring their parents. Instead suppose we say 'I love you, even though you are only a poor imitation of a man.' [ALMADY *registers rage.*] Go on. [*To* ALMADY:] 'My God! I suffer –'

ALMADY [*bitterly*]: My God! I suffer like a sick horse. [*To* TURAI:) Look here, that ought to come out.

TURAI: Why?

ALMADY: How could anyone speak of himself so vulgarly?

TURAI: We went into all that just now. Just what a cattle-raiser would say.

ALMADY: But he's a fruit-raiser!

TURAI: Cattle, too. Cattle as a side line.

ILONA: Don't look so pathetic. Well, come here. Kiss me. You donkey.

ALMADY [*furiously to* TURAI]: It's too much – horse and donkey.

ADAM [*aside to* MANSKY]: This is where I went out. How funny it seems now.

TURAI [*looks at script*]: We're getting near the end now. They kiss here.

  [ALMADY *starts to kiss* ILONA.]

ILONA [*pushing him away*]: Oh, never mind the kiss. Kiss over.

ALMADY [*offended*]: Just as you please. I want you to remember that kiss forever.

ILONA: Your kiss is revolting to me.

ALMADY [*despairingly*]: Does that stay in?

TURAI: My dear fellow, we can't cut everything.

ALMADY: But a line like that's so damned personal. The audience will loathe me.

MANSKY: It beats me why on earth you ever chose a part like this.

TURAI [*with subtle mockery*]: Yes. It's no business of mine, but I must say I can't understand that, either. It doesn't help to cut lines here and there. It's the whole part. The character's a bounder and a fool.

MANSKY: The author must have loathed this fellow. You notice that, Sandor, don't you?

TURAI [*ironically*]: Of course, I noticed it.

ILONA: Do let's get to the end. Mademoiselle Emilienne describes you as an old fool.

TURAI [*prompting*]: 'And so I am.'

ALMADY: And so I am, Yvonne. [*Furious*] So I am.

MANSKY: You certainly are.

ILONA [*sincerely*]: It's disgusting that a man of your age should persecute a woman, and by playing on her sense of gratitude seek to obtain a love which she would never bestow as a free gift.

ADAM [*crossing down to* TURAI *and whispering*]: Uncle Sandor, will you give me your word of honour that Ilona shall never know how shamefully I suspected her?

TURAI: Don't be childish.

ADAM: If ever she found out she'd never look at me again.

TURAI: I'll never tell her.

ILONA: Please don't interrupt any more.

ADAM [*bows elaborately and says with meaning*]: Forgive me.
[ILONA *accepts his apology with an affectionate gesture, and when his back is turned it is she who is mutely asking forgiveness.*]

TURAI: Go on!

ILONA: Think of your wife. Think of your children.

ALMADY [*turns away*]: My children!

ILONA: What would your son say? Your son, a highly respected colonel in the Dragoons.
[*This is too much. The actor in* ALMADY *is crushed. He comes down to* TURAI *brokenly and speaks supplicatingly.*]

ALMADY: Mr Turai.

TURAI [*amiably*]: Yes?

ALMADY: It's just a suggestion, but couldn't we say lieutenant there?

TURAI: I'm afraid not. You see it was 'general' in the text.

ALMADY [*wildly*]: My son a general?

ILONA [*to* TURAI]: How far back can I go?

TURAI: At the most a major.

ILONA [*quickly*]: Very well. Your son, a highly respected major in the Dragoons.

ALMADY: You are right, Yvonne. The shock would kill him.

[ALMADY *breaks off, evidently unwilling to speak his next line. But* TURAI *prompts him relentlessly.*]

TURAI: 'A ridiculous old petticoat-chaser.'

ALMADY [*speaking the lines almost sotto voce in a casual offhand manner*]: A ridiculous old petticoat-chaser, that's what I am. Bah!

TURAI: Oh, come, Mr Almady. Not so tamely please. More *life.* Once more.

ALMADY [*with petulance and irritation*]: A ridiculous old petticoat-chaser, that's what I am. Bah!

TURAI [*relentlessly*]: Still not quite strong enough. More gusto. More sincerity.

ALMADY [*shouts the line to relieve his fury*]: A RIDICULOUS OLD PETTICOAT-CHASER, THAT'S WHAT I AM. BAH!

TURAI [*coldly*]: Once more, please.

ALMADY [*shouting to the full limit of his vocal chords in wild desperation*]: A RIDICULOUS OLD PETTICOAT-CHASER, THAT'S WHAT I AM. BAH!

TURAI [*with approval*]: Fine – *that's* it. Now read it that way at the performance.

[ALMADY *is completely crushed and beaten.*]

ALMADY [*genuinely*]: I promise you I shall never again make myself obnoxious to this woman who loves another man and is sick and tired of me. Never, never again.

ILONA [*briskly*]: Never again?

ALMADY [*briskly*]: Never again.

ILONA: Then, Maurice, I will be generous. I will not go to Paris, and you may eat the peach.

ALMADY [*hurls himself at the peach*]: My God! At last! [*Gnaws the peach.*]

TURAI [*rising*]: Curtain.

MANSKY: The end?

TURAI: The end.

MANSKY: He really should have given his wife the peach. That would have made a much prettier finish.

TURAI: Oh, my dear fellow! Where's your sense of character? The man's selfish to the core. He'd never give his wife peaches.

MANSKY: A very unsympathetic part. Still, he played it well.

TURAI: It fitted him.

MELL [*dancing about in anguish, pointing to* ALMADY, *incoherent with agitation*]: Oh! Oh!

TURAI: What's the matter with you?

MELL: He's eating the peach! He's eating the peach! I never dreamed he was going to *eat* the peach. I shall have to dash out and get another. [*He rushes off to the hall.*]

ILONA [*takes off scarf. To* ADAM, *who stands overcome with happiness*]: Well, how do you like me in this part?

ADAM: Oh, darling, you were wonderful, simply wonderful. And, if you want to know what I think – this little comedy is worth all Shakespeare put together. [*He kisses her hands.*]

MANSKY: Oh, no, no, no. The thing dates terribly. When did Sardou write it?

TURAI: I don't know. What period Sardou is this, Mr Almady?

ALMADY: I should imagine it was his last work.

MANSKY: Then he must have been a very old man at the time. It's terrible. He probably wrote it just before he died.

TURAI: Or just after. [*To* ILONA:] Can I have a minute? Just a few things I'd like to tell you about your part.

ILONA: Yes, yes, I shall be very grateful. [*To* MANSKY *and* ADAM:] Go along. We shan't be a moment.

MANSKY: What beats me is why an actor who has always played heroes picked a part like that for himself. He must be terribly fond of acting.

[MANSKY *and* ADAM *go out.*]

TURAI [*to* ALMADY, *who is sitting dejectedly*]: You seem upset.

ALMADY [*miserably*]: Not at all. [*He glares at* TURAI.]

TURAI: So you've decided to take the midnight express directly after the performance?

ALMADY: Yes.

TURAI: I think you're wise. A good, fruity train highly spoken of by connoisseurs. Well, just to show you the sort of fellows we Turais are, I'll let you off the major. Ilona, you can say lieutenant.

ALMADY: Even lieutenant seems a little –

TURAI: Good God! We can't make him a drummer boy.

ALMADY [picks up his part]: Very well, So be it. I suppose I ought to be thankful for small mercies. [Goes towards the door to the hall.]

TURAI: Where are you off to?

ALMADY: I'm going to have another go at those infernal French names. But in spite of everything – thank you.

[ALMADY bows and then goes out.]

ILONA: Sandor, you're an angel. Was it awfully difficult, writing that play?

TURAI: Oh, no. That damned peach stumped me for a while. Smooth, round, velvety and fragrant, and you mustn't bite. It wasn't easy to get round that. Believe me, there are very few things in this world that are round, smooth, velvety – and respectable.

ILONA [turns her head away]: Oh – he was talking about my shoulder.

TURAI [with delicate irony and gazing at her shoulder, then kissing it]: Really? I thought it was your forehead.

ILONA: You're an old devil; that's what you are.

TURAI: Just what I expected. Now that it's all over, everybody else is a gentleman and I'm an old devil. But somehow I don't think I am. My little Ilona, I have saved a young man a bad heartache. It's a negative kindness, but is there a positive one that's better? Yes, on the whole, I think I'm fairly well satisfied with myself. And there's a little old woman looking at me from somewhere – probably from hell – and her eyes seem to be twinkling, as if she was satisfied, too. It's unfortunate, that you won't have me always on hand to –

[Re-enter MANSKY and ADAM.]

MANSKY [on the landing, to ADAM]: Poor old Turai's feeling awfully sore about all this. He had a wonderful scheme for bringing you two together, based on what he calls psychology. And now he's furious because that won't be needed.

[*Enter* DWORNITSCHEK *from hall.*]

ADAM: Sh! Ilona will hear you. Let's drop the subject.

DWORNITSCHEK: Dinner is served.

ADAM *meets* ILONA. *They embrace and kiss lovingly and go out arm in arm.*]

MANSKY [*with self-satisfaction to* TURAI]: So, my friend, it comes down to this. There are many clever writers, but the most successful of them all is still old man life himself.

TURAI: That's because he doesn't have to collaborate with you.

[*He takes* MANSKY'S *arm. As he passes* DWORNITSCHEK *he stops and looks at him.*]

DWORNITSCHEK [*smiling*]: Dwornitschek, sir.

TURAI: Now, look here – that really is your name, isn't it?

DWORNITSCHEK: Oh, yes sir.

TURAI: I just wondered. Thank you.

[TURAI *and* MANSKY *go out.*]

DWORNITSCHEK: Thank you sir.

CURTAIN

Good Morning, Bill

A three-act comedy (based on the Hungarian of
Ladislaus Fodor) by P. G. Wodehouse

CHARACTERS

[*In the order in which they appear*]

MARIE, *Lottie's maid*

LORD TIDMOUTH

LOTTIE

BILL PARADENE

PAGE-BOY

SALLY SMITH M.D.

SIR HUGO DRAKE, *Bill's uncle*

Good Morning, Bill was first staged on 28 November 1927 at the Duke of York's Theatre, London.

SCENES

ACT ONE

The scene is the sitting-room of a suite at a big seaside hotel on the South Coast of England. There is a door at the right which leads into the passage and thence to the main staircase. Another, at the left, is the door of the bedroom from which LOTTIE *will presently emerge. Opposite this is a window with a balcony.*

The time is five o'clock on an April afternoon, and MARIE, LOTTIE's *maid, is setting the tea-table. From somewhere below – presumably from the Winter Garden or Lounge, where Swiss waiters prowl among potted palms – come the strains of a Jazz band, playing* MARIE's *favourite tune. She hums it as she sets the table, and even goes to the length of dancing a few steps. So absorbed, indeed, is she that a knocking on the outer door does not penetrate to her consciousness.*

The knocking is repeated, and LOTTIE's *voice calls through the open door of the bedroom.*

LOTTIE: Marie.

MARIE [*pausing immediately, for* LOTTIE's *is one of those voices which impress themselves on the most preoccupied*]: Yes, Moddom?

LOTTIE: Are you deaf, you poor fish? Somebody at the door.

MARIE: Very good, Moddom.

   [*She goes to the door and opens it, and there trickles in an immaculate and yet somehow subtly battered individual who is wearing in addition to his spats and beautifully cut suit an eyeglass and – till he removes it – a white bowler hat. He carries a large umbrella. He comes down into the room, sights the tea table and, with a slight diminution of his customary quiet gloom, approaches it and picks up a sandwich.*]

LOTTIE [*still a disembodied voice*]: Is that you, Bill?

MARIE: It is not Mr Paradene, Moddom. It is – [*She looks at the visitor inquiringly. He is now well into his second sandwich, but can*

77

still speak and does so. He says that his name is Lord Tidmouth, and Marie relays the information through the door.] It is Lord Tidmouth, Moddom.

LOTTIE: Who the dickens is Lord Tidmouth?

[TIDMOUTH, *feeling that he ought to enter into the spirit of this long-distance conversation, approaches the bedroom door and speaks, raising his voice.*]

TIDMOUTH: Hullo! What ho! I'm a friend of Bill Paradene's.

LOTTIE: Oh? I'll be out in a minute.

TIDMOUTH: Right ho. [*To* MARIE, *confidentially, lowering his voice.*] I say, what *is* that in there?

MARIE: That is Moddom, your lordship. [*Exit* MARIE.]

[TIDMOUTH, *wandering to the table again, starts on another sandwich.*]

LOTTIE [*off*]: I shan't be long now.

TIDMOUTH: Right ho.

LOTTIE: Have a sandwich.

TIDMOUTH: I am.

LOTTIE: You're what?

TIDMOUTH: A sandwich. I mean, I'm having one. I say, these are extraordinarily good. Sardine or my senses deceive me. [*He tests this theory by taking another, and all doubts are removed.*] Yes, absolutely sardine. I read an interesting thing in the paper the other day. It said the sardine's worst enemy was the halibut, and I give you my word that until I read it I didn't know the sardine *had* an enemy. And I don't mind telling you my opinion of the halibut has gone down considerably. Very considerably. Fancy anything wanting to bully a sardine.

[*A good deal moved by this thought, he returned to the table, and while his back is towards the bedroom door* LOTTIE, *enters. She is wearing a rather vivid suit of pyjamas.*]

LOTTIE: Here I am at last.

[LOTTIE *is extremely pretty, but in the more obvious style. The sound of her voice causes* TIDMOUTH, *to turn: and, turning, he sees the pyjamas, and is visibly affected.*]

TIDMOUTH: Holy Smoke! – [*recovers himself*] – I mean, hullo !

LOTTIE: Hullo!

TIDMOUTH: Hullo!

LOTTIE: That's what I said. Take a chair or a sofa or something.

TIDMOUTH: Thanks. [*He sinks a little bonelessly on to the sofa, and* LOTTIE, *seats herself beside him.*]

LOTTIE: Bill ought to be looking in any minute. He's taking me out to dance. Sorry to keep you so long. I was shaving.

TIDMOUTH: Shaving?

LOTTIE: My neck, you silly ass.

TIDMOUTH: Oh!

LOTTIE: So you're a friend of Bill's?

TIDMOUTH: Yes. Haven't seen him for ten years, though.

LOTTIE: That's a long time.

TIDMOUTH: Yes. I just looked in to return his umbrella.

LOTTIE: His umbrella?

TIDMOUTH: He lent it me ten years ago. I was at his flat one afternoon, and it was raining, and I was in a great hurry to get away because I wanted to go and have a row with my fiancée, so I borrowed Bill's umbrella.

LOTTIE: I see. And did you have a row with your fiancée?

TIDMOUTH: Oh, rather.

LOTTIE: Who won?

TIDMOUTH: She did. She married me. And it was only when we were half-way through the honeymoon that I found I'd taken Bill's umbrella along. We went to live in Paris. She ran away with a Frenchman.

LOTTIE: Did you get a divorce?

TIDMOUTH: Yes. And married again. And on the honeymoon I noticed Bill's umbrella among the luggage. My second wife ran away with a Spaniard.

LOTTIE: Too bad.

TIDMOUTH: When I married my third wife, we spent the honeymoon at Le Touquet. It rained the whole time – But, of course, I had the umbrella.

LOTTIE: And who did your third wife run away with?

TIDMOUTH: A Brazilian.

LOTTIE: Your home during the last ten years seems to have been a sort of Meeting Place of the Nations.

TIDMOUTH: Yes. So I've come to bring the umbrella back – I don't think the damn thing's lucky.

[*There is a pause. The pyjamas have had a stunning effect on* TIDMOUTH, *and he is obviously nervous at being shut up in this room with them.*]

LOTTIE: What –

TIDMOUTH [*simultaneously*]: Have you – [*Stops.*] Sorry.

LOTTIE: Go on. Shoot.

TIDMOUTH: I was only going to say, have you been readin' anything lately?

LOTTIE: Oh, yes. I've just read the funniest book.

TIDMOUTH: Who by?

LOTTIE: That awfully funny man who writes things – I never can think of his name.

TIDMOUTH: What's it called?

LOTTIE: Some awfully funny title – I can't think of it for the moment.

TIDMOUTH: What's it about?

LOTTIE: I can't remember. But I think his books are awfully good, don't you?

TIDMOUTH: Whose?

LOTTIE: This man whose name I've forgotten.

TIDMOUTH: Oh, absolutely. [*There is a pause.*] Think old Bill's going to be long?

LOTTIE: I couldn't say. Why, am I boring you?

TIDMOUTH: No, no. But I'm afraid I'm not frightfully good at conversation.

LOTTIE: Then let's dance.

TIDMOUTH: That's an idea. [*Listens.*] Music and everything.

LOTTIE [*listening to music from below*]: I love that tune.

TIDMOUTH: Topping, isn't it?

[*They start to dance, and it is plain that* TIDMOUTH'S *embarrassment has been removed. As a conversationalist he has his limitations, but on the dancing floor he is at home. He revives like a watered flower. His spirits soar to such an extent that after about half a minute of the invigorating exercise it suddenly strikes him that it is silly not to kiss* LOTTIE, *so he does so. And at this moment the door*]

*opens, and there enters a young man in a flannel suit. His agreeable
face, at the moment of his entry, was wearing a preoccupied look.
This, as he observes* TIDMOUTH *and* LOTTIE, *changes to one of
grim disapproval. He eyes them in silence for a moment, then in a
cold voice he says 'Good afternoon!'*

It is the first intimation TIDMOUTH *and* LOTTIE *have received
that they are no longer alone, and they fly apart. There is one of those
embarrassing pauses, then* LOTTIE *speaks.*]

LOTTIE: Bill! [BILL PARADENE *continues to eye her stonily.*] I didn't
hear you come in.

BILL: So I imagined. Take off those pyjamas!

TIDMOUTH [*shocked*]: No, I say, my dear old chap! Gentlemen
present!

BILL: How many times have I told you not to run round the place
in pyjamas? Go and get dressed.

LOTTIE [*indicating* TIDMOUTH]: This gentleman . . .

BILL: I'll attend to him.

LOTTIE: Oh, all right.

[*Obviously a little hurt at what she considers his unreasonable
attitude, she goes into the bedroom, and* BILL *turns on* TIDMOUTH.]

BILL: Now then, you! Who are you? And what do you mean by it?

[*He is surprised to see* TIDMOUTH *advancing on him with
outstretched hand and a beam of welcome.*]

TIDMOUTH: Bill, old man! Have you really forgotten me?

BILL: Eh?

TIDMOUTH: Your ancient pal. Name of Tidmouth.

BILL: What! [*He stares.*] For heaven's sake! Squiffy?

TIDMOUTH: That's me.

BILL: Well, well, well. Old Squiffy! I would never have recognized
you. The last time I saw you, you were going off to meet your
fiancée. Did you ever get married?

TIDMOUTH [*with feeling*]: Did I ever get married! And that
reminds me, Bill, old man, how do you feel on the subject of
rocking-horses?

BILL: What on earth are you talking about?

TIDMOUTH: You see, to-morrow is my first wife's second son's
third birthday . . .

BILL: How many wives have you got?

TIDMOUTH: None at the moment. The supply has sort of petered out. But my first wife's second son has his third birthday next week, and I've just bought him a rocking-horse. I told the man at the shop to send it round here till my train went. You don't mind?

BILL: Of course not.

TIDMOUTH: Thanks. Well, tell me all about yourself, Bill. You're looking very fit. Still got that place of yours in the country – Woollam what was its name?

BILL: Woollam Chersey. Yes. You must come and stay there.

TIDMOUTH: Well, I'd love to, Bill, old man, but the fact is – what with my domestic troubles and so forth – I'm more or less of a broken man these days, and don't feel quite up to country-house parties.

BILL: It won't be a country-house party. Just you and me and my uncle.

TIDMOUTH: Which uncle is that?

BILL: I've only one. Sir Hugo Drake, the nerve specialist.

TIDMOUTH: I never met him. Nice chap?

BILL: Oh, not so bad. He'd be all right if he could get it into his head that I'm a grown-up man and not still a kid in knicker bockers. He will fuss over me like a hen, and it drives me crazy. But he won't worry you. What are you doing about two weeks from now?

TIDMOUTH: Nothing in particular. Just beetling around.

BILL: Well, I'll expect you then.

TIDMOUTH: Right ho. Thanks.

[*There is a pause.*]

[*Embarrassed:*] I say, Bill, old man.

BILL: Hullo?

TIDMOUTH: Touching on that little contretemps, if I may so express it, which occurred just now, I should like . . .

BILL: Oh, don't apologize.

TIDMOUTH: Carried away, don't you know. What with the music and the sardine sandwiches . . .

BILL: It's quite all right. Best thing that could have happened. It gives me an excuse for getting out of an entanglement which has been on my nerves for weeks. Squiffy, old man, have you ever felt a sort of strange emptiness in the heart? A sort of aching void in the soul?

TIDMOUTH: Oh, rather.

BILL: What do you do about it?

TIDMOUTH: I generally take a couple of cocktails.

BILL: Cocktails aren't any good. Nothing's any good. I've read books, gone in for sport, tried work. No use whatever.

TIDMOUTH: What sort of work?

BILL: Stock-farming. And what's the result? I have a thousand pigs, and my heart is empty.

TIDMOUTH: What you want is a tonic.

BILL: No. I know what I want, Squiffy. I want love.

TIDMOUTH: Don't you believe it. Love? Listen, old boy. The amount of love I've had in the last ten years, if placed end to end, would reach from London to Paris. And look at me!

BILL: Ah, but I've found the right woman.

TIDMOUTH [*jerking a thumb towards bedroom door*]: Um?

BILL [*with a shudder*]: No. The girl I mean is everything that Lottie is not.

TIDMOUTH: Who is she?

BILL: I don't know.

TIDMOUTH: What's her name?

BILL: I don't know.

TIDMOUTH: Where does she live?

BILL: I don't know.

TIDMOUTH: You aren't an Encyclopaedia, old boy, are you?

BILL: I saw her out there on the links last week. I've seen her several times since then. She's a poem, Squiffy – all health and fresh air and wholesomeness.

TIDMOUTH: Ever spoken to her?

BILL: No. I hadn't the nerve. She's so far above me.

TIDMOUTH: Tall girl, eh?

BILL: Spiritually, you ass.

TIDMOUTH: Oh, I see.

[*Re-enter* LOTTIE, *partially clad in a dancing-dress.*]

BILL: She's like a breath of clean wind, Squiffy, blowing across the fields in Springtime.

LOTTIE: Who, me? How do you like this dress?

BILL [*sourly, looking at it*]: What dress?

LOTTIE: I'm ready to go dancing.

BILL: I don't want to go dancing.

LOTTIE: But you said you would.

BILL: I can't. I've made up my mind to stay in.

LOTTIE: Well, I've made up my face to go out.

BILL: In any case, I wouldn't take you out looking like that. You've got nothing on.

LOTTIE: Naturally. You told me to go and get dressed.

BILL: Look here, Lottie, I may as well tell you straight out. I'm never going to dance with you again.

LOTTIE [*dangerously polite*]: Oh? Sprained your ankle or something?

BILL: I'm going home.

LOTTIE: Indeed?

BILL: I've got to go home some time, haven't I? There's the estate to look after and . . . Well, that's all there is to it, I think it's time I went home.

TIDMOUTH: A thousand pigs are pining for him.

LOTTIE: And what's the matter with taking me along?

BILL: I don't think you would be quite in the picture.

LOTTIE: I'm not fit to associate with your beastly vicars and farmers and ploughboys, eh?

[BILL *is trying hard to be soothing.*]

BILL: I never said that. I only meant that you would not mix in well with the life of a small village. Good heavens, there's nothing offensive in that. Be reasonable. Lots of the world's most wonderful women would be out of place in a sleepy little spot like Woollam Chersey. Queen Elizabeth . . . Catherine of Russia . . . Cleopatra . . . dozens of them.

TIDMOUTH [*aside to* BILL, *approvingly*]: The right note, old boy. Stick to it.

BILL: Besides, if I can't go out for a couple of minutes without coming back and finding you kissing . . .

LOTTIE: So that's the trouble? You know as well as I do that this man means nothing to me. I look upon him just like some low, creeping thing.

TIDMOUTH: Awfully nice of you to put it like that. That's exactly what my second wife said to me in the summer of '21. The very words.

LOTTIE: You know perfectly well there's no need for you to be jealous.

BILL: I'm not jealous.

LOTTIE: Oh, aren't you? And *why* aren't you, may I ask? I see it all now. There's somebody else.

BILL: There isn't.

LOTTIE: Yes, there is. There is. There is. I know perfectly well there's another woman stealing you from me. [*Growing louder and louder.*] Who is she? What's her name? Tell me her name. Who is she?

TIDMOUTH [*struck with an idea*]: I say, have you any Spanish blood in you?

BILL: Now, Lottie, listen . . .

LOTTIE: I won't listen.

TIDMOUTH: My second wife was half Spanish. How well I remember. . . .

LOTTIE [*turning on him*]: Shut up!

BILL [*simultaneously, turning on him*]: Shut up!

TIDMOUTH: Oh, rather. I merely spoke.

LOTTIE [*returning to the attack on* BILL]: So you want to get rid of me, do you? You want to throw me aside like a – like a –

TIDMOUTH [*prompting*]: Worn-out glove.

LOTTIE: Like a worn-out glove. You think you're going to discard me like an –

TIDMOUTH [*prompting*]: Old tube of tooth-paste.

LOTTIE: Shut up!

TIDMOUTH: Oh, rather.

LOTTIE: Let me tell you you're mistaken if you think you can get rid of *me* so easily.

BILL: Lottie, please.

TIDMOUTH: Lottie, please.

LOTTIE: Lottie, please! Lottie, please! Lottie, please! [*Working up to a crescendo.*] If you want a row, you shall have it. [*She snatches up a cup.*] There! [*She hurls the cup down with a crash.*]

 [PAGE-BOY *enters from right.*]

PAGE-BOY: Did you ring, sir?

LOTTIE: And there! [*She breaks a second cup.*]

MARIE [*enters from left*]: Did you call, Moddom?

LOTTIE: And there! And there! And there! [*She breaks more cups.*]

BILL: Lottie, pull yourself together.

TIDMOUTH: Cups cost money, what?

BILL: Stop it. [*He catches hold of* LOTTIE.]

LOTTIE: I won't. Let me go. Let me go . . .

 [*Screams.*] Oh! Oh! Oh! I'm dying . . . [*She sinks down, fainting.* MARIE *catches her. General confusion.*]

TIDMOUTH: She's fainted.

MARIE: Water!

PAGE-BOY: Vinegar!

MARIE: Eau-de-Cologne!

TIDMOUTH: Pepper!

MARIE: Give her air.

PAGE-BOY: Slap her hands.

TIDMOUTH: Sit on her head.

BILL [*furiously*]: Will you be quiet!

 [*The noise subsides.*]

 Now then. [*To the* PAGE-BOY:] Go for a doctor.

PAGE-BOY: Yes, sir. [*Exit* PAGE-BOY.]

BILL [*to* MARIE]: Take her into the bedroom, lay her on the bed and undress her.

TIDMOUTH [*eagerly*]: Me?

 [*He realises that* BILL *is talking to* MARIE, *and drops back disappointed.* MARIE *starts to lead* LOTTIE *into bedroom, babbling.*]

MARIE: Poor lamb . . . It's a shame. . . .

 [*Exit* MARIE *with* LOTTIE.]

BILL [*to Tidmouth*]: What are you hanging about for?

TIDMOUTH: Well, honestly, old chap, I don't quite know. Just lending sympathy and moral support, as it were.

BILL: Get a doctor.

TIDMOUTH: But the boy's getting one.

BILL: Well, get another. Get a dozen.

TIDMOUTH: I know just how you feel, old boy. In the winter of '23 – a very similar situation arose when I told my second wife her new hat looked like nothing on earth. She . . .

BILL: Get *out*!

TIDMOUTH: Absolutely!

[*Exit* TIDMOUTH.]

BILL [*calls*]: Marie.

[*Re-enter* MARIE.]

MARIE: Sir?

BILL: How is she?

MARIE: Still unconscious, sir. And I don't like her breathing. If you ask me, it's storterous.

BILL: Storterous?

MARIE: Sort of puffy. Like this. [*Puffs.*]

BILL [*sharply*]: Marie.

MARIE: Sir?

BILL: When I want any farmyard imitations from you, I'll ask for them.

MARIE [*wounded*]: Very good, sir. [*Exit* MARIE *into bedroom.*]

[*Re-enter* PAGE-BOY.]

PAGE-BOY: The doctor, sir.

BILL: Ask him to come in.

PAGE-BOY: This way, please.

[*He stands aside, to allow the doctor to enter, and she enters. For it is a She, a young and becomingly dressed girl in the early twenties. She carries a small black bag about the size of a vanity case, and at the sight of her* BILL *starts violently and stares in amazement. The* PAGE-BOY *reluctantly withdraws.* BILL *swallows convulsively:*]

BILL: ?

[*The girl – her name is* SALLY SMITH – *looks at him with polite inquiry.*]

SALLY: I beg your pardon?

BILL: It can't be!

SALLY: I don't quite understand.

BILL: I-er-I mean to say . . . that is to say . . . I mean I . . . What I mean is I've seen you out on the golf-links.

SALLY: Yes? I play a good deal, when I have time.

BILL: Yes . . . I saw you there . . . Out on the links . . . I saw you several times out on the links. [*He pauses a moment, wishing to make his meaning clearer, then sees how this can be done.*] You were out on the links, and I saw you.

SALLY: I was told that someone here wanted a doctor.

BILL: Yes, but-I mean-I don't-I can't-I mean –

SALLY: If you're the patient, I should diagnose you as a bad case of aphasia.

BILL: You-you don't mean to say-? You aren't a doctor?

SALLY: Certainly. Smith is my name. Doctor Sally Smith.

BILL: Good heavens!

SALLY: I beg your pardon?

BILL: Er-nothing.

SALLY: You said 'Good heavens!' And I don't like people saying 'Good heavens!' to me.

BILL [*contritely*]: I only said 'Good heavens!'

SALLY: Yes – in the voice a small boy would use if he were being introduced to a Barnum and Bailey freak.

BILL: I assure you –

SALLY: You know that's just how you said it.

BILL: I'm sorry.

SALLY: Fine! Now everything's all right. You'll excuse me for biting your head off, won't you? I always have to start an interview with a new male client by sitting on him hard. The male mind doesn't seem able to grasp immediately and without assistance the fact that a woman doctor need not of necessity be a gargoyle with steel-rimmed spectacles and wash-leather complexion . . . Would you mind telling me who you are?

BILL: My name is Paradene. [*Earnestly:*] *William* Paradene.

SALLY: Thank you. Now where is the patient?

BILL: Just a moment. If you wouldn't mind sitting down. . . .

SALLY: Why?

BILL: I-I mean, she can't see a doctor now.

SALLY: Why not?

88

BILL: She isn't well.

SALLY: So she can't see a doctor? My dear good man, are you always like this, or is this one of your bad days?

BILL: I know I'm a fool . . .

SALLY: Ah! A lucid moment.

BILL: It's the shock of seeing you walk in like this . . .

SALLY: Why shouldn't I walk in? You sent for me.

BILL: Yes, but you don't understand. I mean, I've seen you out on the golf-links . . .

SALLY: So you said before.

BILL: You see – Mrs . . .

SALLY: Miss.

BILL: Thank God!

SALLY: I beg your pardon?

BILL: Nothing, nothing. I-er-that is to say . . . or, putting it rather differently . . .

SALLY: Does your keeper share this suite, or is he in another part of the hotel?

BILL [*mopping his forehead*]: Oh, my goodness.

SALLY: What's the matter? There seems to be something on your mind – such as it is. What is troubling you?

BILL: You take my breath away.

SALLY: For shortness of breath try a jujube. And now, please, my patient.

BILL: Oh, yes – Do you mind excusing me for a moment? [*Goes to door of bedroom and calls softly:*] Marie!

MARIE [*appearing in doorway*]: Yes, sir?

BILL: How is she?

MARIE: Asleep, sir.

BILL [*brightening*]: Fine! See that she doesn't wake up.
[*Exit* MARIE.]
[*Coming back to* SALLY.] The maid says the patient has fallen asleep.

SALLY: Quite natural. Sleep often follows violent hysteria.

BILL: How do you know it was hysteria?

SALLY: By the broken china. Long-distance diagnosis. Well, let her have her sleep out.

BILL: I will.

SALLY: And will you please stop looking at me like that.

BILL: I'm *not* looking at you like that. At least, I'm not trying to.

SALLY: Automatic, eh? Very interesting. Unconscious reaction of the facial and labial muscles at sight of a pretty woman.

BILL [*goaded*]: I wish you would stop treating me as if I were something under a microscope.

SALLY: Well, I'm glad I have my vascular motors under control.

BILL: Your – what did you say?

SALLY: Of course. You're a layman. By vascular motors we mean the nerves that regulate the flushing and paling of the skin. I can control them. So, whatever the provocation, I never either blush or turn pale. I keep my decent, ordinary, healthy colour.

BILL: It's a beautiful colour. It's amazing that you've such a complexion.

SALLY: Indeed? Why?

BILL: Well, working as hard as you do . . .

SALLY: You seem to have an entirely wrong conception of me. You appear to look on me as a poor, faded laboratory plant, spending a life of drudgery between books and invalids. I'm as fit as a fiddle, thank Heaven, and enjoy every minute of my life. I have a good practice, and quite enough money. I go to theatres and concerts. I play games. I spend my holidays travelling. I love my work. I love my recreations. I love life.

BILL: You're wonderful.

SALLY: And why shouldn't I? Who has a better right to everything there is in life than I? I enjoy pleasure, and I earn every bit of pleasure I enjoy. And it's because I earn it that I enjoy it. I love jolly suppers – because I pay for them myself . . . Nice clothes, nice shoes, silk stockings – because I buy them myself. I'm like the Village Blacksmith – I owe not any man. I wonder if you've the remotest idea how happy it can make a woman feel just to be a worker and *alive* – with good nerves, good circulation and good muscles. Feel my arm. Like iron.

BILL [*touching her arm in a gingerly way*]: Wonderful!

SALLY: And my legs. Hard as a rock. Prod 'em.

BILL [*drawing back, embarrassed*]: No really . . .

SALLY: Go on. [*Stares at him.*] You're blushing.

BILL: Yes. I'm afraid my vascular motors aren't as well controlled as yours.

SALLY: Can't you admire a well-rounded, highly perfected leg in a purely detached spirit as a noble work of Nature?

BILL: No, I'm afraid I've never quite managed to do that.

SALLY: Why, in some countries the women go bathing with nothing on.

BILL: And the men buy telescopes.

SALLY: Don't snigger.

BILL: Forgive me. I laugh, like Figaro, that I may not weep.

SALLY: What do you want to weep about?

BILL: I'm feeling a little depressed. In the life you have outlined – this hard, tense, independent, self-sufficing life with its good nerves and good circulations and muscles of the brawny arm as strong as iron bands – don't you think – there's something just a little *bleak*?

SALLY: Bleak?

BILL: Well, frankly . . .

SALLY: Always be frank.

BILL: Frankly, then, it reminds me of the sort of nightmare H. G. Wells would have after cold pork. It seems to leave out the one thing that makes life worth living.

SALLY: You mean love?

BILL: Exactly. I grant you one hundred per cent on nerves and circulation and general fitness. I admire your biceps, I'm sure your leg-muscle is all it should be, and I take off my hat to your vascular motors. But doesn't it strike you – it's the merest suggestion – that you're just a trifle lacking in *sentiment*?

SALLY: Nothing of the kind. All I'm lacking in is sentimentality. I don't droop and blush and giggle . . .

BILL: No, I noticed that.

SALLY: . . . But naturally I don't intend to exclude love from my life. I'm not such a fool.

BILL: Ah!

SALLY: Why do you say 'Ah?'

BILL [*with dignity*]: Listen! You're the lovelist girl I ever met, but you've got to stop bullying me. I shall say 'Ah!' just as often as I please.

SALLY: I merely asked because most people, when they stand in front of me and say 'Ah!' expect me to examine their throats. Are you hinting that you've fallen in love with me?

BILL: Yes.

SALLY: Never hint. Always say just what you mean. I hate people who beat about the bush.

BILL: I'm sorry. I was trying to break it gently.

SALLY: It's not such a shock as all that.

BILL [*eagerly*]: You mean – ?

SALLY: I don't mean anything, except that your symptoms aren't so unique as you seem to imagine.

BILL: You've heard them before – from a patient?

SALLY: Dozens of times.

BILL: I might have known it. [*Gloomily.*] Just my luck. And I suppose – ?

SALLY: No. You're wrong.

BILL [*eagerly again*]: You mean there's nobody else?

SALLY: Nobody.

BILL: Then do you think . . . do you suppose . . . might it happen . . . would it be . . . or, putting it another way, is it possible . . .

SALLY: Crisper, crisper. And simpler. What you're trying to suggest now is that perhaps I might one day love you? Am I right?

BILL: You take the words out of my mouth.

SALLY: I had to, or they would never have emerged at all. Well, if ever I love a man, I shall inform him of the fact, simply and naturally, as if I were saying good morning.

BILL: Tell me, have you often – er – wished a man good morning?

SALLY: No. That experience has yet to come.

BILL [*joyfully*]: Wonderful!

SALLY: Not so very wonderful. It simply means I haven't met the right man.

BILL: Yes, you have. You don't know it yet, but you have. [*He goes to her ardently.*] I feel as if a great weight had rolled off me. I had always hoped in my heart that women like you existed, and now it's all come true. Don't laugh at me. It's come upon me like a whirlwind, this. I never expected it. I never guessed. I never . . .

[*He breaks off as* MARIE *enters.*]

[*Irritably:*] Well, what is it?

MARIE: If you please, sir, she's awake now.

BILL: Awake? What on earth are you talking about? Who's awake?

MARIE: Why, Moddom, sir.

BILL [*blinking like an awakened somnambulist*]: Moddom?

SALLY: I think you had forgotten our patient, hadn't you?

BILL: But . . .

SALLY [*briskly to* MARIE]: Ask her to come in, please. I will examine her at once.

LOTTIE [*off*]: I'm coming, doctor.

[MARIE *stands aside to allow her to enter – then goes.*]

[*Entering.*] Sorry to have kept you waiting . . .

[*She sees* SALLY *and stops. She stands with her hands on her hips, glaring at her. Dangerously:*] Oh? And who may this be?

SALLY: Don't be absurd. I'm the doctor.

LOTTIE: You think I'm going to swallow that?

SALLY: Can you read?

LOTTIE: Of course I can read.

SALLY [*producing her card*]: Then read that.

LOTTIE [*reading the card*]: Doctor Sally Smith. Well, I suppose it's all right. Still, it looks funny to me. [*Starts to work herself up into a fury.*] And let me tell you that if there *is* any hanky-panky business going on between you two, I'll very soon . . .

SALLY [*calmly*]: Quiet, please.

LOTTIE [*stopping as if she had run into a brick wall*]: Eh?

SALLY: I wish to make an examination.

BILL: Perhaps I'd better leave you.

SALLY: Just as you like.

BILL: I'll go for a stroll on the Front.

SALLY: All right. I shan't be long.

[*Exit* BILL. SALLY *puts her stethoscope together.*]

LOTTIE [*getting rather refined*]: You'll forgive me, I'm sure, Doctor – [*Pauses.*] Isn't that too silly of me, I've forgotten your damn name.

SALLY [*busy with stethoscope*]: Quite a simple one to remember. Smith.

LOTTIE: Oh, thank you. I was saying, Doctor, that I was sure you'd forgive me for flying off the handle a little just now. The fact is, I've been having a bit of a row with my gentleman friend, and coming in and finding you two together like that, naturally I said to myself . . .

SALLY: Take off the bath-robe.

LOTTIE [*taken aback*]: Eh? Oh, all right. [*She throws off her bath-robe.*] Let me see, where was I? Oh yes. What started it all was him saying to me as cool as a cucumber that he wasn't ever going to take me dancing again. Oh, I said to him, and why not, if I may ask? I said. Well, he said to me, I'm going home, he said. Going home? I said. Yes, he said. So naturally I said I know what the trouble with *you* is, I said, you want to cast me off like a worn-out glove, I said. But if you think, I said, that for one moment I'm going to stand anything like that, I said, you're mistaken, I said. You see, it's not as if I were just an ordinary girl. A palmist once told me that I was full of fineness and individuality and sensitiveness, and what I do say is, I have a right to a little bit of consideration.

SALLY: The lungs appear sound. Take a deep breath. [*She listens through stethoscope.*] Well, the heart is all right. Now for the reflexes. Cross your legs. [*She tests the reflexes.*] Nothing the matter with them. All right, that's all.

LOTTIE: Examination over?

SALLY: Yes.

LOTTIE: What's wrong with me?

SALLY: Nothing much. You need a rest.

LOTTIE: Aren't you going to look at my tongue?

SALLY: I can tell, without looking at it, that that needs a rest, too. What you want is a few weeks in a nice quiet sanitorium.

LOTTIE: You're going to send me to a sanitorium?

SALLY: Yes. You'll get cold baths and plain food, and no cigarettes and no cocktails.

LOTTIE: I believe it's a trick.

SALLY: A trick?

LOTTIE: I believe you're just trying to get me out of the way so that you can have him to yourself.

SALLY: Him? [*Astounded.*] You can't mean . . .? Do you really imagine for one moment that I'm in love with Mr Paradene?

LOTTIE: You aren't?

SALLY: Of course I'm not.

LOTTIE: And you want me to go to a sanitorium?

SALLY: I do.

LOTTIE: Well, it all looks funny to *me*.

[*Enter* TIDMOUTH.]

TIDMOUTH: I say, I've snaffled a medicine-man. [*Sees* SALLY.] Hullo!

SALLY: I have already examined the patient. My name is Doctor Smith.

TIDMOUTH: I'm Lord Tidmouth. I say, this is rather awkward. Old Bill told me to get a doctor, and I grabbed one in the lobby.

SALLY: I'm afraid there is nothing for him to do here.

TIDMOUTH: But he's apt to be a bit shirty, isn't he, if he finds I've lugged him up here for nothing. He wasn't any too pleased at having to come at all. He was on his way to the links.

SALLY: Oh, well, as you've called him in, we can have a consultation, if he likes. Where is he?

TIDMOUTH: Navigating the stairs. Stout old boy, not very quick on his pins. [*Goes to door.*] This way, Doc. Oh, there you are. [*He stands aside to allow* SIR HUGO DRAKE *to enter.* SIR HUGO *is a stout, red-faced man, carrying a bag of golf-clubs, and dressed in a violent suit of plus-fours. He is puffing a good deal from the stairs.*]

SALLY: Good afternoon, Doctor.

SIR HUGO: Afternoon. [*Puffing.*] You the patient?

SALLY: No. I'm afraid I am a doctor myself. There seems to have been a little misunderstanding.

SIR HUGO: You mean no need for me to come at all?

SALLY: I'm afraid not.

TIDMOUTH: The whole trouble was, you see, old Bill got the wind up and sent the entire strength of the company out scouring the town for medicos. It begins to look like a full house.

SALLY: I thought that as you were here, Doctor . . .

SIR HUGO: Drake.

SALLY: Not sir Hugo Drake, the great specialist?

[SIR HUGO *nods*.]

This is a proud moment for a mere general practitioner, Sir Hugo.

SIR HUGO: Nice of you to say so.

SALLY: I am Doctor Smith.

SIR HUGO: Oh, yes. Heard of you. You're at St Luke's.

SALLY: Fancy your knowing!

SIR HUGO: All say you're thoroughly capable. No need for me, then. Patient in excellent hands.

SALLY: It would be a great honour and privilege, Sir Hugo, if you would consent to a consultation.

SIR HUGO: Consultation? All right. If you wish it. Can't take long, though. Most important appointment. This young lady the patient?

LOTTIE: Yes, sir.

SIR HUGO: Well, step into the bedroom, young lady, while we go into your case.

LOTTIE: She says I've got to go into a sanitorium.

SALLY: Subject to Sir Hugo's opinion.

SIR HUGO: Oh, we'll thresh the whole thing out, never fear. We'll go into your case minutely. Run along, my dear.

LOTTIE: Well, I ought to be all right between the two of you.

[*Exit* LOTTIE *into bedroom.*]

TIDMOUTH: Then I'll leave you to it, what? I've often wondered what you doctors talk about when you hold consultations. Lot of deep stuff, I expect.

[*Exit* TIDMOUTH.]

SIR HUGO: Well, nothing the matter with her, I suppose?

SALLY: Nothing but a little nerves.

SIR HUGO: I imagined from the way that young fellow snatched me up and carried me off that it was a matter of life and death. [*Grumbling.*] Silly idiot. Now I shall be late for my golf match.

SALLY: What a shame, Sir Hugo. You don't get much time for golf, either, I suppose?

SIR HUGO: Very little, very little. Just ran down here for the week-end. You play?

SALLY: Oh, yes.

SIR HUGO: What's your handicap?

SALLY: Six.

SIR HUGO [*stunned with admiration*]: Good God! I'm twenty-four. How do you manage it?

SALLY: Oh, I keep my head down, keep my eye on the ball, and don't press.

SIR HUGO: I'm not so bad off the tee. It's the short chip shots that bother me.

SALLY: Shanking?

SIR HUGO: No, topping principally.

SALLY: I believe I could put you right.

SIR HUGO [*eagerly*]: You could?

[TIDMOUTH *pops his head in.*]

TIDMOUTH: How are you getting on?

SIR HUGO [*testily*]: Kindly leave us alone, young man. We are at a very difficult point in the diagnosis.

TIDMOUTH: Oh, right ho. Pip pip. [*Exit* TIDMOUTH.]

SIR HUGO: You were saying, Doctor . . .?

SALLY [*takes up* TIDMOUTH'S *umbrella, which is lying on a chair*]: So much depends on the right grip. Do you use the Vardon?

SIR HUGO: I used to, but lately I've gone back to the double-V.

SALLY: Well, the great thing is not to grip too tight.

SIR HUGO: But I should have thought the tighter you gripped the more force you would get into the shot.

SALLY: You don't want force for a chip. It's all direction. Grip firmly but lightly.

SIR HUGO: How right you are. Firmly but lightly.

SALLY: The hands should be kept low, and, above all, should finish low. So many people finish their iron shots with the hands up as if they were driving.

SIR HUGO: I see.

SALLY: At the finish of a chip shot the club should be very little above the horizontal. Not like in the drive.

SIR HUGO: I see. Talking of driving, it may interest you to hear of a little experience I had the other day . . .

SALLY: A rather similar thing happened to me . . .

SIR HUGO: There was the ball, lying –

SALLY: My caddie said: 'You're out of bounds.' I said: 'I'm not out of bounds.' And, would you believe it . . .

SIR HUGO: . . . Right at the bottom of a rabbit-scrape . . .

SALLY: . . . What do you think I found?

SIR HUGO: What do you think I did?

SALLY: I just . . .

SIR HUGO: I simply . . .

[*Re-enter* LOTTIE, *in travelling costume.*]

LOTTIE: Haven't you two finished yet?

SIR HUGO [*embarrassed*]: Oh, quite, quite. We were just about to call you. We've examined your case from every angle . . .

SALLY: And Sir Hugo agrees with me . . .

SIR HUGO: Exactly. That your trouble . . .

SALLY: . . . Is a slight matter of nerves . . .

SIR HUGO: Nothing of any consequence, though disagreeable . . .

SALLY: And you must be kept in a sanitorium . . .

SIR HUGO [*toying absently with the umbrella*]: Firmly but lightly. Er-just so.

SALLY [*scribbing on a card*]: I can recommend this one. It is only a short distance from here.

LOTTIE [*takes card*]: Oh, all right. I'm not particular.

SALLY [*calls*]: Lord Tidmouth.

[*Enter* TIDMOUTH.]

TIDMOUTH: Hullo? Consultation over?

SALLY: Yes. Sir Hugo agrees with me that the patient should go to a sanitorium. Is Mr Paradene outside?

SIR HUGO: Mr Paradene?

TIDMOUTH: No. He's not out there. He's probably on the Front somewhere.

LOTTIE: I don't want him. I've nothing to say to Mr Paradene. Even if he was here, I wouldn't so much as say good-bye to him. [*To* TIDMOUTH:] You'll escort me to this looney-bin they're pushing me off to, won't you?

TIDMOUTH: Charmed.

SALLY [*looks out of window*]: It's started to rain. You'd better take your umbrella. [*She holds it out.*]

TIDMOUTH: That's not mine. It belongs to old Bill.

SALLY: Well, I'm sure he won't mind, so long as you don't lose it.

TIDMOUTH: Lose it? Lose *this* umbrella? Dear lady, not in a lifetime. Well, toodle-oo, everyday.

[*Exit* TIDMOUTH *with* LOTTIE.]

SIR HUGO: Curious.

SALLY: I beg your pardon, Sir Hugo?

SIR HUGO: Paradene. An unusual name Bill . . .

SALLY: Not so unusual.

SIR HUGO: But the two names in conjunction. William Paradene. I have a nephew, William Paradene.

SALLY: Really?

SIR HUGO: His poor mother was my sister, and since her death I have regarded myself *in loco parentis* to the boy. Causes me a great deal of anxiety. It seems incredible that he could be staying here – under his own name – with . . . Just show me that grip once more, will you?

SALLY: Certainly. But Lord Tidmouth seems to have taken away our mashie-niblick.

SIR HUGO [*taking a club from his bag*]: Use this.

SALLY: All right. Now, give me your hands. [*She takes his fingers and clasps them round the handle of the club.*] That's right. Not so much over, or you'll hook.

[*They are standing like this when the door opens and –* BILL *enters.*]

BILL: Is the examination finished?

SIR HUGO: William!

BILL: Good Lord! Uncle Hugo!

SIR HUGO: So this is where you have been all these weeks. William, I am inexpressibly shocked. A boy of your age dancing attendance on a young woman of flashy appearance . . .

BILL: Uncle, please.

SIR HUGO: This is a pleasant surprise for a man who stands to you *in loco parentis*, is it not! I come here for a little golf, and before I can so much as put a ball down on the first tee . . .

BILL: Uncle, really!

SALLY: Boys will be boys, Sir Hugo.

SIR HUGO: Not while I'm *in loco parentis* to them, they won't. [*Looks at his watch.*] Good God, is that the time? I must fly. [*To* SALLY] I'll remember what you told me about that grip.

SALLY: I'm sure you will find it will help you.

SIR HUGO: Firmly but lightly. [*To* BILL:] The idea! [*To himself:*] Firmly but lightly. [*To* BILL:] I'm surprised at you! [*To himself:*] Firmly but lightly. Fingers not too far over . . . [*Exit* SIR HUGO *babbling.*]

BILL [*staring at the door*]: How on earth did he get here?

SALLY: Lord Tidmouth found him in the lobby and dragged him up. Poor Mr Paradene, you don't have much luck with your medical advisers, do you? Oh, my prophetic soul, my uncle!

BILL: Never mind him. Has Lottie really gone?

SALLY: yes.

BILL: What a relief. [*Opens window.*] I feel like a new man . . . April weather. Fresh air . . .

SALLY: Yes. Jolly stuff, fresh air, isn't it? Smells so much better than perfume. Will you be leaving here now?

BILL: Sally, you're like the fresh air yourself. And like the sunshine and the clean feel of the breeze coming up off the sea . . .

SALLY: If you are leaving, don't forget to give me your address.

BILL [*eagerly*]: You want to write to me?

SALLY: No. I just want to know where to send my bill.

BILL: Good Heavens!

SALLY: What's the matter?

BILL: It's enough to drive a man mad. Whenever I say anything – anything with any sentiment in it, you immediately become the doctor . . .

SALLY: I don't become the doctor – I *am* the doctor.

BILL: . . . And freeze me with a cold douche.

SALLY: What do you expect me to do – swoon in your arms?

BILL [*sulkily*]: You haven't an atom of feeling in you.

SALLY: Oh yes, I have. And some day the right man will bring it out. [*She touches his arm.*] Cheer up. You look just like a sulky baby that's been refused its bottle.

[*He scowls.*]

I think your uncle is right, and you're still a small boy.

BILL: Indeed? I'll prove to you some day that I'm grown up.

SALLY: Oh, I'm not saying you may not grow up some day. But at present you're just a child.

BILL: I'm not.

SALLY: You are.

BILL: I'm not.

SALLY: Yes, you are.

[*Enter* PAGE-BOY.]

PAGE-BOY: Please, sir, your rocking-horse has arrived.

SALLY: There!

BILL: My rocking-horse? What do you mean, my rocking-horse?

PAGE-BOY: Well, all I know is, there's a rocking-horse outside. Shall they bring it in?

SALLY: Yes, yes, yes. Of course bring it in. And if Mr Paradene's teddy-bear is there, bring that, too.

[TWO MEN *bring in the rocking-horse and go.*]

PAGE-BOY: The bill, sir.

[*He gives* BILL *an envelope and goes.* SALLY *is laughing, leaning against the table.* BILL *opens the envelope.*]

BILL: It's for Tidmouth. I remember now – confound him!

SALLY: Oh, don't abuse the poor man. You owe him a lot.

BILL: Indeed!

SALLY: Yes, indeed. That rocking-horse seems to make me all of a sudden feel quite differently towards you. Kindly . . . Sympathetic. . . . I can see you sitting on one of those with your little fat legs dangling down . . .

BILL: Go on. Laugh at me.

SALLY: Well, why not? Don't you like people you can laugh at?

BILL: You mean – ?

SALLY: Yes, I find I quite like you now. It's the rocking-horse that has done it. Look, see it's rocking between us now.

BILL: I'll move it.

SALLY: Don't you dare do anything of the kind. Don't you see it's a magic rocking-horse? Directly it came into the room, passion flew out of the window. You can't be wild and passionate and emotional now, can you? Stroke the little mane, and you'll feel all you can do is laugh – simply, naturally, freely, like a child.

BILL: By Jove, you're right.

[*Both laugh.*]

SALLY: There you are. We're all children at heart. All that's needed to make us simple and wholesome and childlike again is the talisman. A rocking-horse may not have wings but one can fly on it – fly right away into a world which is clean and simple, a world where a man and a woman can be friends. Do you agree?

BILL: I think I do.

SALLY: Splendid. [*She holds out her hand and he takes it.*] Well, I must be going.

BILL: No, don't.

SALLY: I must. Do you think you are my only patient?

BILL: Do you treat the others as you've treated me?

SALLY: Oh no, I believe in the individualistic method. With you, I have accomplished quite enough for a first visit. You have laughed – laughed as only children and clean-hearted people laugh. I think I'm a good doctor.

BILL: When can I see you again?

SALLY: We'll think about that later. Meanwhile, here is the prescription. Lead a regular life . . . Go in for sport and the open air. Dine early and lightly and before going to bed take a three-mile walk. It'll make you sleep well. Good-bye.

BILL: But wait.

SALLY [*at door*]: Well?

BILL: Suppose I can't sleep? Suppose I lie in bed, staring into the darkness, thinking of you, yearning for you, aching for you . . .

SALLY [*thoughtfully*]: Oh, in that case . . .

BILL [*eagerly*]: Yes?

SALLY: Get up and walk another three miles. Good-bye. [*She goes quickly.*]

BILL [*starting forward*]: Sally . . .

[*He bumps up against the rocking-horse, and stands staring at it as the curtain falls.*]

CURTAIN

ACT TWO

The living-hall at The Manor, Woollam Chersey, BILL'S *ancestral home in Hampshire. At the back, a wide entrance from the outer hall. At right and left front, doors – the one at the right leading to the guest room, that at the left into* BILL'S *room. A bookcase, large arm-chairs, a desk, a telephone, a piano.*
It is half-past ten in the evening.
[*As the curtain rises* BILL *and* TIDMOUTH *are discovered.* BILL *is lying back in one of the arm-chairs, down stage and facing the footlights. He is smoking, and is in a reverie, his eyes fixed on the ceiling.* TIDMOUTH *is at a table further up stage, playing Patience. For a moment after the rise of the curtain there is silence.* BILL *blows a cloud of smoke.* TIDMOUTH *uncovers a card, holds it in the air for a moment, then puts it on one of the piles, removes another card from one of the piles and puts it on another, then uncovers another card. While he plays, he bursts into absentminded song.*]

TIDMOUTH[*sings*]: I fee-ar naw faw in shee-ining arrmour,
    Though his lance be swift and – er – keen.
        [BILL *stirs uneasily.*]
    But I fee-ar, I fee-ar the glarrmoor
    Ther-oo thy der-ooping larr-shes seen,
    I fee-ar, I fee-ar the GLAR-moor . . .
BILL [*sitting up, irritably*]: Oh, shut up.
TIDMOUTH [*starting*]: Eh? Sorry, old top, I thought you were
    dead.
BILL: What are you doing?
TIDMOUTH: Playing patience, laddie. [*Absently bursting into song
    again, as he fiddles with the cards. Sings:*] Just play-ing PAT-i-
    ence . . .
BILL: Stop it.

TIDMOUTH: Oh, right ho.

BILL [*getting up and looking at him*]: Do you mean to say you really get any pleasure out of that rotten game?

TIDMOUTH: Darned good game. [*Speaking as he fiddles with cards.*] Did you ever hear the story of the ventriloquist who played patience. He used to annoy his wife by holding long conversations with himself in his sleep. It became such a trial to the poor woman that she had thoughts of getting a divorce. And then one evening . . . [*Pauses and plays a card*] . . . by the greatest good luck, he caught himself cheating at patience and never spoke to himself again.

BILL: Silly idiot.

TIDMOUTH: Harsh words, old man, from host to guest. Nice place you've got here, Bill.

BILL: Glad you like it. Where's my uncle?

TIDMOUTH: Out in the corridor, practising putting into a tooth-glass.

BILL: Thank God, that'll keep him occupied for a while. Squiffy, there's something I want to tell you.

TIDMOUTH: Carry on, old boy.

BILL: To-night, I . . . [*He breaks off as –* SIR HUGO *enters.* SIR HUGO *is wearing a mauve smoking-jacket and carries a putter.*]

SIR HUGO [*joyfully*]: It's coming.

TIDMOUTH: It's come.

SIR HUGO: The knack is coming. I'm getting it. Four out of my last seven shots straight in the glass.

TIDMOUTH: I think *I'll* take a shot in a glass. [*Gets up and mixes himself a whisky and soda.*]

SIR HUGO: I fancy I have at last found out what has been wrong with my putting.

TIDMOUTH [*drinking*]: Happy days.

SIR HUGO: William.

BILL: Yes?

SIR HUGO: I say I think I have at last found out what has been wrong with my putting.

BILL: Oh?

SIR HUGO: I've been gripping too tight. How right that girl was.

Grip firmly but lightly, she said, that's the secret. It stands to reason . . .

BILL: Excuse me. [*Exit abruptly*.]

SIR HUGO: Did you see that?

TIDMOUTH: Eh?

SIR HUGO: That boy. Ever since he got home he has been like that – nervous, rude, jumpy, abrupt.

TIDMOUTH: He does appear a bit jumpy, now you mention it.

SIR HUGO: What do you suppose is the matter with him?

TIDMOUTH: I know. He's not eating enough yeast.

SIR HUGO: He's in love.

TIDMOUTH: You think so?

SIR HUGO: I'm sure of it. I noticed it the day I arrived here. I had begun to tell him about the long brassie-shot I made at the sixteenth hole, and he gave a sort of hollow gasp and walked away.

TIDMOUTH: Walked away?

SIR HUGO: Walked away in the middle of a sentence. The boy's in love. There can be no other explanation.

TIDMOUTH: I'll tell you how we can prove it.

SIR HUGO: How?

TIDMOUTH: When he comes back, I'll sit down at the piano and sing him something sentimental . . . something really mushy. Watch how he reacts.

SIR HUGO: An excellent idea.

TIDMOUTH: Sh. [*He goes to the piano, as* BILL *re-enters*.]

SIR HUGO: What made you leave us so suddenly, William?

BILL [*gruffly*]: Went to fetch something.

SIR HUGO: You seem very restless to-night.

BILL: I'm not.

TIDMOUTH [*at piano*]: 'Remembah the day
                      I said to you
                      "I lurve you!"'

[BILL *winces,* TIDMOUTH *pauses and looks quickly at him, catches* SIR HUGO'S *eye and nods. He goes on singing the rest of the song,* BILL *and* SIR HUGO *registering the while, and finally reaches the last line, which he gives out in a raucous bellow*.]

'But you for-got
TO RE-MEM-BAH.'

[*As he sings this line,* BILL *utters a stifled exclamation and rushes out.* TIDMOUTH *comes away from the piano, and he and* SIR HUGO *look at one another.*]

SIR HUGO: There! You observed?

TIDMOUTH: Absolutely.

SIR HUGO: My suspicions were correct. William is pining for that young woman.

TIDMOUTH: What young woman?

SIR HUGO: The flashy young person in the Sanitorium.

TIDMOUTH: You mean Lottie?

SIR HUGO: Exactly. We thought the episode was concluded, but evidently the infatuation still persists.

TIDMOUTH: What are you going to do about it?

SIR HUGO: Rather ask, what *have* I done about it?

TIDMOUTH: All right. What *have* you done about it?

SIR HUGO: Never mind.

TIDMOUTH: Then why did you tell me to ask?

SIR HUGO: Young man, have you ever studied psychology?

TIDMOUTH: Well, no, not to any great extent. They didn't teach me much at school except the difference between right and wrong. There *is* some difference, but I've forgotten what.

SIR HUGO: Have you ever asked yourself what is the secret of the glamour which this young woman exercises over William?

TIDMOUTH: No.

SIR HUGO: It is due to the fact that he has encountered her so far only in the gaudy atmosphere of hotels and dance-halls – her natural setting. But suppose he should see her in the home of his ancestors, where every stick and stone breathes of family traditions, beneath the eyes of the family portraits? What then?

TIDMOUTH: I'll bite. What?

SIR HUGO: She would disgust him. His self-respect would awaken. The scales would fall from his eyes, and his infatuation would wither and decay. Whatever his faults, William is a Paradene.

TIDMOUTH: In that case, it might be a sound scheme to ask her down here for a visit.

SIR HUGO: Ha, ha! Young man, can you keep a secret?

TIDMOUTH: I don't know. I've never tried.

SIR HUGO: H'm. Well, let me tell you this, Lord Tidmouth. I have the situation well in hand. Youth may fancy it can control its own destiny, but Age, with its riper wisdom, is generally able, should the occasion arise, to lay it a stymie. Excuse me, I must go and putt. [*Exit* SIR HUGO.]

[*Re-enter* BILL.]

BILL: Has he gone?

TIDMOUTH: Just oozed off. Want me to call him back?

BILL: Good heavens, no. Squiffy, listen to me. We're pals, aren't we?

TIDMOUTH: Absolutely. Bosom is the way I should put it.

BILL: Very well then. I want you to do me a great service. You must get my uncle out of the way to-night.

TIDMOUTH: Murder him?

BILL: If you like. Anyway, go to his room with him and see that he gets to sleep. To-night I want to be alone.

TIDMOUTH: Bill, old man, you're being very mysterious this p.m. You shimmer about and dash in and out of rooms and make dark, significant speeches. All you need is a mask and false whiskers, and you could step into any mystery play and no questions asked. What's up?

BILL: I'll tell you.

TIDMOUTH: You forgot to say 'Hist!'

BILL: I have got a very big thing on, and I must not be interrupted. To-night, Squiffy, I put my fate to the test – to win or lose it all, as the poet says.

TIDMOUTH: What poet?

BILL [*irritated*]: What the devil does it matter what poet?

TIDMOUTH: I merely asked.

BILL: Montrose, if you really want to know.

TIDMOUTH: I don't.

BILL: Squiffy, I'm in love.

TIDMOUTH: Good Lord! Uncle was right.

BILL: So much in love that I could howl like a dog . . . [*Looks sharply at* TIDMOUTH.] I suppose you're going to say 'What dog?'

TIDMOUTH: No, no.

BILL: It's awful. It's killing me.

TIDMOUTH: Bill, old man, this is serious news. So your old uncle was actually right.

BILL: What do you mean?

TIDMOUTH: I felt all along that something like this would happen. I wanted to warn you at the time. 'Bill, old man,' I came within a toucher of saying, 'pause before it is too late.' And now she's in the sanatorium, and you're pining for her. Oh, for the touch of a vanished hand . . .

BILL: What are you talking about?

TIDMOUTH: Lottie, of course.

BILL: Lottie? Are you really idiot enough to suppose I'm in love with Lottie? If you had twice as much sense, you'd be half-witted.

TIDMOUTH: Who are you in love with, then?

BILL [*rapturously*]: Sally Smith . . .

TIDMOUTH: The lady doctor?

BILL: Yes.

TIDMOUTH: Well, this is all new stuff to me. But if you miss her so much, why did you come down to the country?

BILL: I couldn't stay near her, either. It was driving me mad.

TIDMOUTH: Why?

BILL: She wouldn't let me tell her how much I loved her. Once I went to see her, at her office, absolutely determined that this time I would ask her to marry me, and before I could even speak she said 'Put out your tongue.'

TIDMOUTH: What did you do?

BILL: I put it out. 'Coated,' she said, and prescribed a mild tonic. Now, could I have followed that up by asking her to be my wife?

TIDMOUTH: It wasn't what you would call a good cue.

BILL: I left, cursing. Cursing everything – myself, my luck and the fate that ever brought us together. I came down here, hoping I'd get over it. Not a chance. I'm worse than ever. I've tried to dull the pain by reading. I've read every author who ever wrote about love . . . Shelley . . . Swinburne . . . everything in the whole damned language from 'Come Into the Garden, Maud,' to 'Romeo and Juliet.'

TIDMOUTH: 'Romeo and Juliet?'

BILL: A play. By Shakespeare.

TIDMOUTH: Good Lord! Is that fellow still writing?

BILL: It was only this afternoon that I finally found a book that really had a helpful idea in it. The telephone directory. [*Goes to table and picks it up.*] I'll read you what it said. It said 'Smith, Doctor S., Sixty-One Alderney Street, S.W. Telephone Number, 7525 Grosvenor.' All through the afternoon I stared at that telephone directory and it stared back at me. At five o'clock I said to myself: 'Why not?'

TIDMOUTH: You don't mean? –

BILL: She's a doctor, I said to myself. If I were ill, she would fly to my side. At six o'clock I gave in and . . .

TIDMOUTH: Good Lord! Telephoned?

BILL: Yes. I pretended to be my valet. I said that Mr Paradene was seriously ill. We were sending the car and would she come at once.

TIDMOUTH: Well! You certainly won't mind taking a chance.

BILL: Not when there's something worth taking a chance for. It's a two hours ride in the car. The chauffeur left at half-past six. He should have reached London between half-past eight and nine. She ought to get here just about eleven.

TIDMOUTH: It's nearly eleven now.

BILL: Yes. So can you wonder I'm a little jumpy? [*Goes to telephone. Into 'phone:*] Hullo. I want trunks. A London call. Grosvenor 7525. Put it through as quick as you can, will you. It's urgent. Thanks.

TIDMOUTH: What's the idea?

BILL: I want to know if she has left.

TIDMOUTH: Why? Do you think she hasn't?

BILL: I don't know . . . I can't help fearing . . . No! She *must* come. She must. And we will stand here face to face . . . alone . . . all alone in the great, deep, endless night. I shall have it out with her to-night, fairly and squarely. No more dodging and evasion. She shan't put me off this time . . . So now perhaps you understand why you've got to keep my infernal, snooping, blundering, fussing busybody of an uncle out of the way.

TIDMOUTH: But – it's just a suggestion – won't he hear her drive up in the car?

BILL: A Rolls Royce doesn't make any noise. I told the chauffeur not to sound his horn.

TIDMOUTH: You certainly seem to have thought of everything. Well, I'm glad I'm not you.

BILL: Why?

TIDMOUTH: Because it is my firm and settled belief, old top, that, when she gets here and finds it was all a put-up job, this female is going to cut up rough.

BILL: Don't call her a female.

TIDMOUTH: Well, she *is*, isn't she? I mean, that's rather what you might call the idea, I should have thought.

BILL: She won't suspect. I shall convince her that I'm a sick man.

TIDMOUTH: By the time she has done with you, you probably will be. Hell hath no fury like a woman who's come eighty miles to be made a fool of.

BILL: Don't be such a pessimist.

TIDMOUTH: Oh, all right. Have it your own way. All I can say is, may the Lord have mercy on your soul.

[*Enter* SIR HUGO]

SIR HUGO: A very marked and sustained improvement.

TIDMOUTH: Isn't that nice!

BILL: You off to bed, uncle?

SIR HUGO: Yes. Off to bed now. Early to bed, early to rise, nothing like it for keeping the eye clear and the hand steady.

BILL: Tidmouth wants to come up with you and have a chat.

SIR HUGO: Delighted.

BILL: Tell him that excellent story of yours about the caddie and the indiarubber tee.

SIR HUGO: Certainly.

BILL [*To* TIDMOUTH]: You'll roar with laughter.

TIDMOUTH: How jolly.

SIR HUGO: Well, come along, my boy. You coming, Bill?

BILL: No, I think I'll sit up a little longer.

SIR HUGO: Good-night, then. See you in the morning.

[SIR HUGO *goes*.]

TIDMOUTH: Is that a long story, Bill?

BILL: Longish. But to help a pal, Squiffy . . .

TIDMOUTH: Oh, all right. We Tidmouths never desert a pal. [*He starts to go, pauses at the exit in the attitude of Sidney Carton.*] 'It is a far, far better thing that I do than I have ever done . . .' Well, honk honk!

[*Exit* TIDMOUTH.]

BILL [*left alone, looks round nervously. The telephone rings. He goes to it*]: Hullo? . . . Grosvenor 7525? . . . Doctor Smith's house? . . . This is Mr Paradene's valet speaking. Can you tell me if the doctor has left? . . . Just before nine? [*He sighs.*] Thank you . . . Hullo . . . The doctor will probably not be returning tonight . . . Yes, very serious. She will have to sit up with the patient . . . Yes . . . Goodnight.

[*He hangs up the receiver. There is a silence. He hums to himself the tune played in Act One. He lights a cigarette, looks round, obviously very excited, then goes off. The stage remains empty for a short time.* BILL *returns. He is wearing a dark silk dressing-gown. He arranges a pillow and lies down on the sofa. There is a pause. The clock strikes eleven in slow, regular strokes.* BILL *puffs at his cigarette, staring at the ceiling.*

Enter SALLY. *She is wearing a motoring coat. She comes forward without a sound and looks down at* BILL *with a smile. He is not aware of her entry.*]

SALLY [*suddenly and loudly*]: Good-evening.

BILL [*starting up*]: Good Lord! You made me jump.

SALLY: Weren't you expecting me?

BILL: Yes.

SALLY: Well, here I am.

BILL: yes.

SALLY: Well, don't stand staring at me as if I were a ghost.

BILL: Yes – I mean – it's like a dream. You here . . . in my home . . . it all seems so strange.

SALLY: You're right. Strange is the exact adjective. For a man who has brought a doctor a night journey of eighty miles at fifty miles an hour, you look surprisingly well.

BILL [*quickly*]: But I'm not. I'm desperately ill. You can't tell how a man's feeling just by looking at him.

SALLY: I don't intend to. We'll have a thorough examination. What are the symptoms?

BILL: The-er-did you say the symptoms?

SALLY: I did – But if they're too horrible to mention, never mind. I'll soon find out for myself.

BILL: Won't you let me help you off with your coat first?

SALLY: Thanks.

[*He helps her take off her coat. Sally looks at him.*] Hullo! You're shivering.

BILL: Am I?

SALLY: Do you feel chilly?

BILL: No. Hot all over.

SALLY: Let me feel your pulse. [*She feels his pulse.*]

BILL: I think . . .

SALLY: A hundred and ten. Very interesting. And yet you haven't a temperature. A pulse of a hundred and ten without fever. Quite remarkable. Do you feel dizzy?

BILL: Yes.

SALLY: Then sit down.

BILL: Thanks. Won't you?

SALLY: Thanks. [*They sit.* SALLY *puts her stethoscope together.*] Now we can get on.

BILL [*doubtfully*]: Yes.

SALLY: What seems to be the trouble?

BILL: The trouble? Oh yes-er- Won't you have something to eat and drink? The drive must have tired you.

SALLY: Later. Business first. The symptoms, please.

BILL: Must we talk about my symptoms?

SALLY: Might I mention that I've driven eighty miles simply in order to talk about them.

BILL: But surely there's not such a desperate hurry as all that. I mean, can't we have just five minutes conversation . . .

SALLY: You're the weirdest patient I've ever attended. You send out an S.O.S. for a doctor, and all you want to do when the doctor comes is to chat.

BILL: But you don't seem to understand how tremendously happy it makes me – to see you sitting there. I can scarcely believe it even now. Are you really there?

SALLY: Prod me if you like.

BILL: Now I know it's really you. Only you would have said that.

SALLY: And the symptoms?

BILL: Oh, hang the symptoms! Why must we begin straight away to talk about my health?

SALLY: It may seem eccentric to you, but when I get an urgent call to visit an invalid I find my thoughts sort of straying in the direction of his health. It's a foolish habit we doctors have. Tell me, when did you first notice that there was anything wrong with you?

BILL: Three weeks ago.

SALLY: About the time you first met me.

BILL: Yes.

SALLY: An odd coincidence. What happened?

BILL: My heart stood still.

SALLY: It couldn't.

BILL: It did.

SALLY: Hearts don't stand still.

BILL: Mine did. It then had strong palpitations.

SALLY: Throbbed?

BILL: Like a motor-cycle. And it has been getting worse ever since. Sometimes I feel as though I were going to suffocate. It is as if I were being choked inside by an iron hand.

SALLY: Probably dyspepsia. Go on.

BILL: My hands tremble. My head aches. My legs feel like lead. I have floating spots before the eyes and I can't sleep. Dawn comes and finds me still awake. I stare before me hopelessly. Another night has passed, and in the garden outside the roosters are crowing.

SALLY: Anything connected with roosters you had better tell to a vet.

BILL: Is that all you can do to a patient – laugh at him?

SALLY: If you think I am finding this a laughing matter, you're wrong. [*Casually*:] Undress, please.

BILL [*appalled*]: What . . . what did you say?

SALLY: Undress.

BILL: But . . . but I can't.

SALLY: Would you like me to help you?

BILL: I mean – is it necessary?

SALLY: Quite.

BILL: But, Sally . . .

SALLY: Doctor.

BILL: But, doctor, I . . . really . . .

SALLY: I notice the vascular motors are still under poor control. Why do you blush?

BILL: What do you expect me to do – cheer? Look here, do you mean to tell me this is the first time any of your male patients has jibbed at undressing in front of you?

SALLY: Oh, no. I had a case last week.

BILL: I'm glad somebody has a little delicacy besides myself.

SALLY: It wasn't delicacy. He didn't want me to see that he wore detachable cuffs . . . Well . . .?

BILL: Oh, if I must . . . [*He throws off his dressing-gown.*]

SALLY: I can't think what you were making such a fuss about. Your cuffs aren't detachable . . . Now, please. [*She begins the examination by listening at his chest through the stethoscope.*]

BILL [*emotionally*]: I wonder if you realize what this means to me, to see you here – to feel that we two are alone together at last . . .

SALLY: Did you ever have any children's diseases?

BILL [*annoyed*]: No. [*Returning to the emotional mood.*] Alone together at last . . .

SALLY: Mumps?

BILL: No.

SALLY: Measles?

BILL [*shouting*]: No!

SALLY: I merely asked.

BILL: It's too bad. Here I am, trying to pour out my soul to you, and you keep interrupting with questions about mumps and measles.

SALLY: My dear man, I'm not interested in your soul. My job has to do with what the hymn-book calls your 'vile body'.

[*There is a pause, while she continues the examination.*]

BILL [*breaking out emotionally again*]: Can't you understand that the mere sight of you sets every nerve in my body tingling? When you came in I felt like a traveller in the desert who's dying of thirst and suddenly comes upon an oasis. I felt . . .

SALLY: Any retching or nausea?

BILL: Oh, my God!

SALLY: Now tell me about your sex-life.

BILL: My – ? [*Exploding.*] Good heavens! Don't you know the meaning of the word 'reticence'?

SALLY: Of course not. I'm a doctor.

BILL [*huffily, and trying to be dignified*]: Well, naturally I have had experiences, like other men.

SALLY [*listening at stethoscope*]: Um-hum?

BILL: I admit it. There *have* been women in my life.

SALLY [*at stethoscope*]: Say ninety-nine.

BILL [*quickly*]: Not half as many as that.

SALLY: Say ninety-nine, please.

BILL: Oh? Ninety-nine.

SALLY: Thank you. Well, your lungs appear to be all right. Remove the rest of your clothes, please.

BILL: What!!!

SALLY: You heard.

BILL: I won't do it.

SALLY: Just as you like. Then the examination is finished. Tell me, Mr Paradene, just to satisfy my curiosity, what sort of a fool did you think I was?

BILL: I beg your pardon?

SALLY: I'm glad you have the grace to. Did you imagine that this was the first time I had ever been called out into the country?

BILL: I . . . I . . .

SALLY: Let me tell you it is not. And do you know what usually happens when I am called to the country?

[BILL *chokes wordlessly.*]

I see you don't, or you might have stage-managed the thing a little better. When I am sent for to visit a patient in the country, Mr Paradene, the road is lined with anxious relatives, watching for the car. They help me out and bustle me into the house. They run around like chickens with their heads cut off – and everybody who isn't having hysterics on the stairs is in the kitchen brewing camomile tea.

BILL: Camomile tea?

SALLY: People who get ill in the country are always given camomile tea.

BILL: I never knew that before.

SALLY: You'll learn a lot of things if you stick round with me. And one of them, Mr Paradene, is that I am not a complete idiot. From the moment I got your telephone call this thing seemed most suspicious to me. And now my suspicions are confirmed. I arrive here, and what do I find? No one about. Everything hushed and quiet. And when I see my patient, who is obviously trying to look his most interesting and romantic in a silk dressing-gown, the first thing he says is: 'I'm desperately ill, doctor, but let's forget it and talk of love.' Really, Mr Paradene!

BILL: No – honestly –

SALLY: You'll excuse my slight warmth. I've driven eighty miles on a fool's errand, and somehow I find it a little irritating.

BILL: But I tell you you're wrong.

SALLY: What! Have you the nerve to pretend there's anything whatever the matter with you?

BILL: Certainly there is. I-I'm not myself.

SALLY: I congratulate you.

BILL: I'm a very sick man.

SALLY: And I'm a very angry woman.

BILL [*with dignity*]: Of course, if you don't believe me, there's nothing more to say.

SALLY: Oh, isn't there? I'll find plenty more to say, trust *me*.
[*There is a pause.*]

BILL: I see. So you have found me out, and you've been amusing yourself at my expense?

SALLY: You might say – getting a little of my own back.

BILL: You've had a lot of fun with me, haven't you?

SALLY: Quite a good deal, since you mention it.

BILL: And now, I suppose, you're going?

SALLY: Going? Of course I'm not. I shall sleep here. You don't expect me to drive all night, do you?

BILL: I beg your pardon. [*Points.*] That will be your room.

SALLY: Thank you.

BILL: Well, it's something, I suppose, that you have consented to sleep under my roof.

SALLY: You could hardly have expected me to go to the garage.

BILL: But think of me – feeling that you are so near me, only a few feet from me . . .

SALLY: That will not disturb my sleep.

BILL [*bitterly*]: I suppose nothing on earth could do that?

SALLY: I'm sure nothing will – tonight at any rate. I shall not even bother to lock my door. I am afraid of no one and nothing in the world.

[*She goes to door of room and opens it.*]

BILL [*following*]: Not even yourself?

SALLY: Myself least of all. Good night. [*She goes into the room, closing the door behind her.*]

[BILL *stands looking at door. Enter* TIDMOUTH.]

TIDMOUTH: Hullo, Bill, old man.

BILL [*turns*]: Oh, it's you?

TIDMOUTH: What's left of me after an hour's *tête-à-tête* with the old relative. I say, Bill, that uncle of yours waggles a wicked jaw-bone.

BILL: Does he?

TIDMOUTH: He talked and talked and talked. And then he talked some more. Mostly about his mashie shots. I got him off to bye-bye at last, and I've tottered down here to restore the tissues with a spot of alcohol.

BILL: Help yourself. So you got him off to sleep?

TIDMOUTH: Yes. At infinite cost to life and limb. I feel a perfect wreck. However, I've left him slumbering like a little child, one hand still clutching James Braid's *Advanced Golf*. So that's that.

BILL: Much obliged. Well, I'll be turning in.

TIDMOUTH: Oh, don't go. I say, isn't it about time that lady doctor of yours rolled up? Allowing two hours for the journey –

that is, assuming she had no puncture or blow-out or breakdown or engine-trouble or lost the way or . . .

BILL: Oh, go to blazes!

TIDMOUTH [*looking after* BILL *as he goes*]: Not one of our good listeners.

[TIDMOUTH *during the last few speeches has gone to the table and poured whisky into a glass. He now starts to work the syphon.* LOTTIE *enters softly behind him. She carries a suitcase.*]

LOTTIE [*loudly and breezily*]: Hullo!

[TIDMOUTH *gets involved in a Niagara of soda-water.*]

TIDMOUTH: If you know me a thousand years, never do that again. [*He turns and sees her.*] Great God of Battles! You!!!

LOTTIE: Yes. I got a telegram from Bill's uncle asking me to come.

TIDMOUTH: Good Lord! So that's what the old boy was hinting at. [*To* LOTTIE:] Did he specify that you were to come beetling in at midnight?

LOTTIE: Oh, I'm a quick starter. I came directly I got the telegram. When someone sends for me, I don't stop to pick daisies.

TIDMOUTH: Oh? [*There is a pause.*] Well, welcome to the Manor and all that sort of rot.

LOTTIE: Is Bill expecting me?

TIDMOUTH: No, he's *not*.

LOTTIE: Oh? Then I shall come on him as a surprise?

TIDMOUTH: Surprise is *right*.

LOTTIE: Do you know why Sir Hugo sent for me?

TIDMOUTH [*embarrassed*]: I couldn't tell you.

LOTTIE: I'm telling *you*. I thought it all out on the train. Bill has discovered that he can't get on without me.

TIDMOUTH: Well . . .

LOTTIE: I knew it would happen. He's pining for me.

TIDMOUTH: Well, you can put it that way if you like.

LOTTIE: It stands to reason he must be pretty crazy about me to make his old uncle wire for me in such a hurry.

TIDMOUTH: Full information will no doubt be supplied tomorrow by the aged relative. But, if you'll take a pal's advice, you'll biff off at the earliest opportunity.

LOTTIE: What!

TIDMOUTH: At the very earliest opp.

LOTTIE: What are you talking about?

TIDMOUTH: Oh, my sainted aunt! That old boy has made a proper mess of things. Look here, old thing, you just tuck yourself away in there – [*Points to a room off.*] – till tomorrow morning, and then we'll smuggle you off.

LOTTIE: I think you're cuckoo. What do I want to go away for? Bill's in love with me and can't live without me.

TIDMOUTH: Absolutely. Of course. Yes. Beyond a question. Indubitably. Only . . .

LOTTIE: Well?

TIDMOUTH: Nothing, nothing. You toddle into that room and get your eight hours. I'll tote the suit-case. [*He reaches for it, sees the umbrella strapped to it, and recoils.*] Holy Smoke! How did that umbrella get here?

LOTTIE: You forgot it when you left me at the sanitorium.

TIDMOUTH: Am I never to get rid of this beastly umbrella as long as I live?

LOTTIE [*suddenly*]: Say, listen.

TIDMOUTH: Hullo?

LOTTIE: Is anything the matter?

TIDMOUTH: The matter?

LOTTIE: You're acting sort of mysterious, it seems to me, and I'm wondering if there's any funny business going on. Are you trying to keep Bill and me apart?

TIDMOUTH: No, no.

LOTTIE: Well, you better hadn't, that's all. If I find you're pulling any smooth stuff, I'll murder you. Nothing could be fairer than that, could it?

TIDMOUTH: Absolutely not.

LOTTIE: Well, good-night, then.

TIDMOUTH: Tinkerty-tonk.

[*LOTTIE goes into the room.* TIDMOUTH *stands, mopping his forehead. Then he returns slowly to the table and starts mixing himself another drink. Enter* BILL. *He sees* TIDMOUTH, *and utters a loud exclamation of annoyance.* TIDMOUTH *starts violently, splashing himself with soda-water again.*]

BILL: You still up? Why the devil don't you go to bed?

TIDMOUTH: Bill, listen. I've something to tell you.

BILL: Keep it for the morning.

TIDMOUTH: But it's serious. Bill, we have a little visitor.

BILL: I know. I know.

TIDMOUTH: Oh, you *know*? I thought you didn't. But how do you know? She only just . . .

BILL: Stop babbling and go to bed.

TIDMOUTH: Yes, but, Bill . . .

BILL: Shut up.

TIDMOUTH: Lottie . . .

BILL: Don't talk to me about Lottie.

TIDMOUTH: I was merely saying that Lottie . . .

BILL: Stop it.

TIDMOUTH: I just wanted to mention that Lottie . . .

BILL: Will you get out!

TIDMOUTH: Oh, all right. [*He starts to go.*] Bung-oh! [*He pauses at the exit.*] And I came down here for a rest-cure! [*Exit* TIDMOUTH.]

   [*As soon as he has gone,* BILL *begins to pace the floor restlessly. He pauses at* SALLY'S *door, as if to knock, then resumes his pacing. Finally, as if he had come to a decision, he walks firmly and quickly to her door and knocks on it.*]

BILL [*in a choking voice*]: Sally.

SALLY [*off*]: What is it? Who's there?

BILL: Come out. I want to talk to you.

   [*Enter* SALLY.]

SALLY: well?

   [*There is a pause.*]

BILL: Have you got everything you want?

SALLY: Yes, thank you. I find that you have given me your room.

BILL: Yes.

SALLY: Where are you going to sleep?

BILL: I shall manage.

SALLY: Oh? Well, it's very kind of you. [*There is a pause.*] Was that all you wanted to say to me?

BILL [*urgently*]: No.

SALLY: Well?

BILL: Don't stand in that doorway. Come out here.

SALLY: Just as you like. [*She closes door and comes down.*] Well?

BILL: I've been walking about in the garden.

SALLY: Yes?

BILL: Thinking.

SALLY: Yes?

BILL: Trying to get a grip on myself

SALLY: I hope you were successful.

BILL [*grimly*]: I wasn't.

SALLY [*lightly*]: Too bad. Well, good-night. [*She starts to go.*]

BILL: Come back.

SALLY [*coming down again*]: Sorry. I thought you had finished.

BILL: I haven't begun.

SALLY: Good gracious! Don't you country folk ever go to bed? I had no idea you wandered about the house all night, knocking at people's doors and engaging them in long conversations.

BILL: You seem amused.

SALLY: I am.

BILL: Oh? Well, let me tell you that we have now finished with the amusing part of this business. I now propose to call your attention to the fact that this little farce, which seems to entertain you so much, has a serious side. I'm going to have it out with you here and now.

SALLY: Proceed. You interest me strangely.

BILL [*goaded*]: Don't laugh at me.

SALLY: What else do you expect me to do?

BILL: In the first place, I admit that I did get you down here by a trick.

SALLY: A contemptible trick.

BILL: That's as it may be. Anyway, you're here, and you've got to listen to me.

SALLY [*yawning*]: And to make a long story short . . .?

BILL [*furious*]: I'll make it short enough. Three words will be sufficient. I love you.

SALLY: This is wonderful news.

BILL: That's right. Laugh! But let me tell you no woman ever made a fool of me.

SALLY: Who did, then?

BILL: You women are all alike . . .

SALLY: Please don't include me under the heading of 'You women'. I dislike being grouped. I am an individual – Doctor Sally Smith.

BILL: And I mean to conquer that individual. You think you can play the fool with a man as much as you please – hold him off with a raised eyebrow when he becomes too pressing – keep him under control with a laugh . . .

SALLY: Why, this is eloquence! The Boy Orator!

BILL: Oh, you may sneer, but you know in your heart you're afraid.

SALLY [*freezing*]: Afraid? I? You flatter yourself.

BILL: I may not be your match at fencing, but the bludgeon is quite as handy a weapon as the rapier.

SALLY: From the insight you've given me into your character to-night, I should have thought your favourite weapon was the black-jack.

BILL: You and I are going to settle things tonight. You have known right from the start that I love you, and from our first meeting you have fought me. All right! Tonight shall decide which of us two is the strongest.

SALLY: *Stronger*. Didn't they teach you that at school? Even when insulting a woman, always be grammatical.

BILL: So I'm insulting you? By offering you my love?

SALLY: No – by suggesting that, if I refuse it, you will employ force. For that is what you are suggesting, is it not?

BILL: Yes. It is.

SALLY: Good. Then excuse me for a moment.

BILL: Stop.

SALLY: I was merely going to fetch my bag and prepare a soothing injection. I should think two centigrams of morphia would be sufficient.

BILL [*goes to her and seizes her wrist*]: Stop fooling.

SALLY: Oh! You're very strong.

BILL: I'm glad you're beginning to realize it. Come here. [*He pulls her to him.*]

SALLY: Let me go.

BILL: I won't. Never again. Well? Here you are, in my arms. How do you like it? Now try to be aloof and superior. Now try to hold me off with your matter-of-fact-ness.

SALLY: You beast!

BILL: Beast, eh? I'm improving. Just now I was only a poor fool – just something for you to laugh at. Laugh at me now – if you can.

SALLY [*suddenly ceasing to struggle*]: Oh, well. They always warned me it was dangerous to be a doctor.

BILL [*holding her*]: Now then!

SALLY [*conversationally*]: Do you know, the last man who treated me like this was a lunatic. In the violent ward of an asylum.

[*BILL starts, and in a spasm of revulsion lets her go. She sinks on to a sofa.*]

But he was more decent than you. He merely wanted to murder me.

[*There is a pause.*]

BILL [*abruptly, with a changed manner*]: All right. All over. You win.

[*He walks away from her – formally.*] I beg your pardon.

SALLY: Don't mention it. You might just as well apologize for having rheumatism.

BILL: What!

SALLY: It wasn't your fault. The thing was purely pathological. But I shall have to cure you.

[*She goes to the desk.*]

BILL: Only you can do it.

SALLY: I'll write you a little prescription.

BILL [*starting*]: For God's sake!

SALLY [*writing*]: Kalii bromati . . . Natrii bromati . . . Grammata quinque . . . Misce fiat pulvis . . . divide in doses aequales numero quindecim . . . Detur sigentur . . . One powder three times a day after meals. [*Hands him the prescription and gets up.*] There you are. Any chemist will make that up for you.

BILL [*bitterly*]: You are very kind.

SALLY: In addition there will be hygienic regulation of your mode of living. Avoid excitement and mental strain.

BILL: Thanks. That's a great help.

SALLY: Take plenty of fresh air, do physical jerks every morning, and eat lots of vegetables. Good night. [*She strokes his face softly.*]

BILL: Sally!

SALLY: What's the matter?

BILL: You stroked my face.

SALLY: Yes.

BILL: Gently.

SALLY: Yes.

BILL: Almost – lovingly.

SALLY: Yes.

BILL [*overjoyed*]: Darling!

SALLY: Don't jump to conclusions. The gesture was purely automatic. We doctors often stroke our patient's faces when they have passed the crisis.

BILL: Oh? . . . So you think I have passed the crisis?

SALLY: I think so. You see, you had the sense to call in a good doctor. Good night. [*Exit* SALLY.]

[BILL *stands staring at her door. There is a moment's pause. Then* LOTTIE *comes out of the other room.*]

LOTTIE: Bill! [*She rushes at him and flings her arms round him.*]

BILL: Good God! You! You here?

LOTTIE: I knew you loved me all the time. [*Loudly.*] Bill!

[*The door of* SALLY'S *room opens, and* SALLY *stands in the doorway.*]

SALLY [*gives a sharp cry*]: Oh! [*She goes in, closing the door with a bang.*]

[BILL, *turning at the sound of her voice, is just in time to see the door close. He shakes* LOTTIE *off and rushes at the door. He bangs on it. Then he tries the handle, but the door is locked. He stands there, shouting.*]

BILL: Sally! . . . Sally! . . .

CURTAIN

ACT THREE

The scene is the same as Act Two.
Time: Next morning.
[*The stage at the rise of the curtain is apparently empty, but* BILL *is asleep in a deep arm-chair that has its back to the audience.*
As soon as the curtain is up, SIR HUGO *enters. He is dressed in plus-fours and carries a putter. His mind is evidently occupied with golf, for he stops and stoops down, adopting a putting stance and going through a motion of putting. Then he takes a ball from his pocket, puts it on the floor, and aims carefully at the leg of a chair. He is just going to make the putt, when the sound of a loud yawn breaks the silence.*
SIR HUGO *starts violently and looks up. Two clenched fists rise above the back of the arm-chair, as its occupant stretches himself. Then* BILL'S *head appears.* BILL *gets up, yawns and stretches himself again, and finally sees* SIR HUGO.]

BILL [*sleepily*]: Oh, hullo, uncle.
SIR HUGO: William! What on earth are you doing there?
BILL [*yawns*]: Eugh . . . [*Sleepily:*] What?
SIR HUGO: That's what I said – What?
BILL: What?
SIR HUGO: Yes, what?
BILL [*drowsily*]: What what?
SIR HUGO: Good God, boy, wake up!
BILL [*yawns*]: Eugh . . . [*Awake now.*] What did you ask me?
SIR HUGO: Have you been sleeping in that chair all night?
BILL: Yes. Oo, I'm stiff.
SIR HUGO: But why?
BILL: Well, wouldn't *you* be stiff if you slept all night in a chair?
SIR HUGO: I'm not asking you why you're stiff. I'm asking you why you slept in the chair.
BILL: I gave up my room to a lady.

SIR HUGO: You gave up your room to a lady?

BILL: Yes, I . . . Oh, heavens, need we do this cross-talk stuff so early in the morning?

SIR HUGO: But I don't understand. Did a lady arrive last night?

BILL: Yes. About half-past eleven.

SIR HUGO: Good God! [*Half to himself.*] She didn't waste time. Did you see her?

BILL: Of course I saw her.

SIR HUGO: I mean – you spoke to her? You had a talk – a conversation – an interview with her?

BILL: Yes. All three.

SIR HUGO: And then you sent her off to bed by herself, while you remained coldly and austerely out here on a chair? Splendid! Splendid!

BILL: What are you talking about?

SIR HUGO: Capital! Excellent! Precisely as I foresaw. When the test came, you found that you were a Paradene after all. I knew it. I knew it.

BILL: Uncle, you're gibbering. And the one thing a man does not want to meet, when he's slept all night in a chair and hasn't had breakfast, is a gibbering uncle.

SIR HUGO: I am *not* gibbering. I repeat that you have proved yourself a true Paradene. Directly you saw this woman in the home of your ancestors, beneath the gaze of the family portraits, the scales fell from your eyes, and your infatuation withered and died.

BILL: It did not wither.

SIR HUGO [*incredulously*]: It did not wither?

BILL: It did not wither.

SIR HUGO: You say it did not wither?

BILL: Damn it, uncle, you're back to the cross-talk stuff again.

SIR HUGO: You mean to tell me that, even after you have seen this woman in your ancestral home, you still love her?

BILL: More than ever.

SIR HUGO: Good God!

BILL: And I'm not going to rest till I have made her my wife.

SIR HUGO: Your wife?

BILL: My wife.

SIR HUGO: Your – ?

BILL [*warningly, as he scents the return of the cross-talk note*]: Uncle!

SIR HUGO: You want to *marry* her?

BILL: Yes.

SIR HUGO: But . . . Good God, boy! . . . Have you reflected?

BILL: Yes.

SIR HUGO: Have you considered?

BILL: Yes.

SIR HUGO: Have you gone off your head?

BILL: Yes. No. What do you mean?

SIR HUGO: You – a Paradene – want to marry this woman!

BILL: Yes. And I'm going to find her now and tell her so – again.

SIR HUGO: Again?

BILL: This will make the eleventh time. [*He hurries out.*]

SIR HUGO [*following him to door*]: But, William . . . Reflect . . . Consider . . . [*He mops his forehead and stares gloomily into the future.*] All this is going to put me right off my game. I know it is. I shan't go round in under the hundred today.

[*He is brooding on this when the door of the guest-room opens and* LOTTIE *comes out.*]

LOTTIE: Good morning, doc.

SIR HUGO: Good morning.

LOTTIE: You don't seem surprised to see me.

SIR HUGO: No. I heard that you had arrived. I have just been talking to William, and he has told me the appalling news.

LOTTIE: What's that?

SIR HUGO: He is resolved to marry you.

LOTTIE: *Marry* me? You mean – cake and wedding presents and rice and everything?

SIR HUGO: Yes.

LOTTIE: Well, this opens up a new line of thought. [*Suddenly:*] What do you mean by 'appalling news'?

SIR HUGO: It is appalling.

LOTTIE: You think I'm not good enough for him?

SIR HUGO: Precisely.

LOTTIE: Listen! What's the earliest in the morning you ever got a sock right on the side of the head? [*She advances threateningly.*]

SIR HUGO [*taking refuge behind chair*]: Now, now, my good girl . . .

LOTTIE: Don't you call me a good girl.

SIR HUGO [*hastily*]: No, no, you're not, you're not. But, my dear Miss . . . Miss . . .

LOTTIE: Burke is the name.

SIR HUGO: My dear Miss Burke, cannot you see for yourself how impossible this match is?

LOTTIE: Honest, I owe it to my womanly feelings to paste you one.

SIR HUGO: No, no, be reasonable.

LOTTIE: How do you mean it's impossible? If Bill's so crazy about me . . .

SIR HUGO: But William is a Paradene.

LOTTIE: What of it?

SIR HUGO: And you . . . After all – in the kindliest spirit of academic inquiry – who *are* you?

LOTTIE: I haven't a card on me at the moment . . .

SIR HUGO: I mean, what is your family?

LOTTIE: If anybody's been telling you I've got a family, it's not true.

SIR HUGO: You misunderstand me. But the whole thing is impossible, quite impossible. I must act . . . I must act . . . [*Exit* SIR HUGO *hurriedly.*]

    [*Enter* SALLY *from the other bedroom. She sees* LOTTIE, *and stops.*]

LOTTIE [*cheerfully*]: Hello.

SALLY [*coldly*]: Oh, it's you? I wanted to see you.

LOTTIE: Yes?

SALLY: To tell you that you leave this house immediately.

LOTTIE: Who, me?

SALLY: Yes, you.

LOTTIE: I like your nerve. Who are you, anyway?

SALLY: I'm Mr Paradene's doctor.

LOTTIE: And I'm Mr Paradene's medicine.

SALLY: And, as his doctor, I forbid him whatever I think fit. So out you go . . . this morning.

LOTTIE: One moment. Just one moment. You evidently haven't heard the news.

SALLY: What news?

LOTTIE: Cast your eye upon the future mistress of the house. From now on, the whole works belongs to me and what I say goes. Bill's going to marry me.

SALLY: It's not true.

LOTTIE: Oh, isn't it? I've just had it straight from the horse's mouth.

SALLY: It can't be true.

LOTTIE: Well, ask his old uncle. He'll tell you. And listen. Let me remark that the first thing I mean to do, once I've taken charge and settled in, is to see that Bill changes his medical adviser. This is certainly the last time I let him tell his troubles to a lady doctor – even one as plain as you are.

SALLY [stung]: I like that. I must say, if it's a question of good looks, I can give you a pretty large handicap . . . [Recovering herself.] . . . Er – not that it matters, of course.

LOTTIE: Well, it's no use your trying to come between us. Love's love, isn't it? If it isn't, what is it? I know you had an eye on Bill yourself . . .

SALLY: I? You're quite mistaken. I wouldn't marry Mr Paradene if he were the last man in the world. I-I dislike Mr Pardene very much . . . [Violently, unable to control her feelings.] I hate Mr Paradene . . . I hate him . . .

[Re-enter SIR HUGO. He is carrying in his right hand a roll of bank-notes.]

SIR HUGO: Doctor Smith!

SALLY [recovering herself]: Good morning, Sir Hugo.

SIR HUGO: I had no notion you were here.

SALLY: I was sent for – last night – professionally.

SIR HUGO: Somebody ill?

SALLY: Not now.

SIR HUGO: Are you making a long stay?

LOTTIE: No. Very short. She's leaving right away. [To SALLY, *very much the grande dame*:] No doubt you would like a car to take you back to London? I believe my futu-ah husband has several.

SIR HUGO [*wincing*]: Future husband!

LOTTIE [*dangerously*]: That's what I said. Have you anything to remark?

SIR HUGO [*hastily*]: No, no. [*To* SALLY:] Has Miss Burke . . . has this young lady told you the appall- . . . the-er-interesting news?

SALLY: She told me that she was going to marry Mr Paradene. But I can't say I considered that very interesting. If you will excuse me, I will go and pack. I have to be in London by eleven for my hospital rounds. [*Exit* SALLY]

SIR HUGO [*looking after her*]: Now, how in the world could a man, knowing a girl like that, want to marry a . . . [*He catches* LOTTIE'S *eye and stops abruptly*.] I forget what I was going to say.

LOTTIE: Yes, you forgot just in time. Tell me, doc, in the course of your medical work, have you ever seen a cauliflower ear?

SIR HUGO: Never.

LOTTIE: Well, if you aren't careful you will – next time you look in the mirror. What have you got there?

SIR HUGO: Money.

LOTTIE [*eagerly*]: Money?

SIR HUGO: For you – if you will give my nephew up.

LOTTIE: Oh, that's it, is it?

SIR HUGO: Yes. Tell me, my dear young lady, have you really reflected what marriage to William would be like? My nephew, you must remember, my dear Miss Burke, is a Paradene. He belongs to a very ancient family. There were Paradenes in Woollam Chersey before the Wars of the Roses.

LOTTIE: And there were Burkes in Balham before they built the first cinema.

SIR HUGO: Yes, yes. But, without meaning to be in any way offensive, I think you will admit that your social position is scarcely equal to that of a Paradene. I fear the County would resent it bitterly if William should be considered to have married beneath him. Can't you see how unpleasant it would be for you, received by nobody, ignored by all? Your proud, generous spirit would never endure it.

LOTTIE: Then what's the answer?

SIR HUGO: Give him up. [*Shows money.*] And take this.

LOTTIE: You offer me money to give up the man I love? You think that I can be bribed with money to relinquish my life's great happiness? You imagine that I will sell my dreams – for *money*?

SIR HUGO: Yes.

LOTTIE [*briskly*]: And you're dead right. How much?

SIR HUGO: I have two hundred pounds here.

LOTTIE: And very nice, too – just for busfare. But what's your real offer?

SIR HUGO: I will write you a cheque for five hundred pounds.

LOTTIE: Five hundred pounds? A measly five hundred for giving up my life's great happiness? Haven't you any romance in your soul, or are you a Scotchman in disguise?

SIR HUGO: A thousand.

LOTTIE: Make it two.

SIR HUGO: Very well. Two.

LOTTIE: And if you should feel tempted to stop the cheque . . .

SIR HUGO: My dear young lady . . .

LOTTIE: You won't get the chance, that's all. I'll come with you and we'll cash it hand in hand over the counter. [*She takes the money from him.*]

SIR HUGO [*with a deep breath of relief*]: Then that's settled.

LOTTIE: Yes.

SIR HUGO: What a relief! [*Exit* SIR HUGO.]

[LOTTIE *stands counting the money. Enter* TIDMOUTH.]

TIDMOUTH: Hullo! Money?

LOTTIE: That's right.

TIDMOUTH: Where did you get that from?

LOTTIE: The old chap just gave it to me.

TIDMOUTH: Sir Hugo?

LOTTIE: Yes. I've given Bill up.

TIDMOUTH: No, really?

LOTTIE: Yes. And the thought crossed my mind . . .

TIDMOUTH: Well?

LOTTIE: It just occurred to me as a passing idea . . .

TIDMOUTH: What?

LOTTIE: Well, you and me . . .

TIDMOUTH: What about us?

LOTTIE: Don't you think we'd suit each other?

TIDMOUTH [*impressed*]: Now, you know, that's rather an idea. I've had a sort of floating feeling on those lines myself from time to time.

LOTTIE: I think I could love a poor fish like you quite a lot.

TIDMOUTH: Awfully nice of you to say so.

LOTTIE: After all, what are brains?

TIDMOUTH: Quite.

LOTTIE: Or looks?

TIDMOUTH: Exactly.

LOTTIE: Kiss me.

TIDMOUTH: Right ho. [*They kiss.*]

LOTTIE: Nice?

TIDMOUTH: Fine!

LOTTIE: Have another?

TIDMOUTH: Thanks. [*They kiss.*]

LOTTIE: How simple these things are.

TIDMOUTH: Aren't they! And some silly asses say that love is complicated.

[*Enter* BILL.]

BILL [*seeing* LOTTIE]: Oh, there you are.

LOTTIE: Yes, here I am.

TIDMOUTH: Morning, Bill.

BILL: Shut up.

TIDMOUTH: Right ho.

BILL [*to* LOTTIE]: Do you propose to stay long?

LOTTIE: No. I'm going off to London with my futu-ah husband.

BILL: Your–who?

TIDMOUTH: Me.

BILL: Oh? Well, a fat lot of good that is – now.

LOTTIE: Bill! I believe you're cross with me.

BILL: Cross!

LOTTIE [*to* TIDMOUTH]: Isn't he cross?

TIDMOUTH: Yes, I think he's cross.

BILL: You've only ruined my life, that's all.

TIDMOUTH: Oh, don't say that, old top.

BILL: I just met her in the garden, and she wouldn't look at me. [*To* LOTTIE:] Breakfast is ready in there. I should be much obliged if you would get yours quick – and go.

LOTTIE: Well, I must say you're a jolly fine host.

BILL: Oh, get along.

LOTTIE: All right. I'm going.

TIDMOUTH: Save the brown egg for me.

　　[*Exit* LOTTIE.]

　　You're very hard on that poor little girl, Bill. You show a nasty, domineering, Sheik-y spirit which I don't like to see.

BILL: I'd like to wring her neck. What did she want to come here for – and last night of all nights?

TIDMOUTH: But be fair, old man. She was sent for.

BILL: Sent for?

TIDMOUTH: Yes. By the aged relative. He wired to her to come.

BILL: My uncle did?

TIDMOUTH: Yes.

BILL: Why on earth?

TIDMOUTH: Well, it was like this . . .

BILL [*with growing fury*]: I'd like to wring his neck. Where is he? I'll go and have a heart to heart talk with that old fool. What the devil does he mean by it? *I'll* talk to him. [*Exit* BILL.]

TIDMOUTH: Steady, old man. [*Following* BILL.] Be judicious. Exercise discretion. [*He realizes that* BILL *has passed out of earshot, and comes down, as* SALLY *enters from the garden.*] Oh, hullo. Good morning.

SALLY: Good morning.

TIDMOUTH: Nice day.

SALLY: Is it?

TIDMOUTH [*persevering*]: Bill was in here a moment ago.

SALLY: Oh?

TIDMOUTH: Yes. He said he'd seen you.

SALLY: Would you mind not talking about Mr Paradene.

TIDMOUTH: Right ho.

SALLY: Lord Tidmouth.

TIDMOUTH: On the spot.

SALLY: That girl . . . That-that girl . . . How long has she been here?

TIDMOUTH: She arrived late last night.

SALLY: What! Is that true?

TIDMOUTH: Absolutely. The old uncle sent for her.

SALLY: Sir Hugo? Sir *Hugo* sent for her?

TIDMOUTH: Yes.

SALLY: But why?

TIDMOUTH: Yes.

SALLY: But why?

TIDMOUTH: Well, as far as I could follow him, it was something to do with psychology and all that sort of rot.

SALLY: I don't understand you.

TIDMOUTH: Well, it was this way. I gather that he thought old Bill was pining for her, and he fancied it would cure him if he saw her in the old ancestral home. Old Bill had nothing to do with it. He got the shock of his life when he saw her.

SALLY [*drawing a deep breath*]: Oh! Well, that's a relief. I thought my patient had had a relapse, which, after I had been working on him for three weeks, would have been too bad.

TIDMOUTH: I see. So that's that, isn't it? I mean, now you see all, so to speak, what?

SALLY: Yes.

TIDMOUTH: And you *will* marry the poor old blighter, won't you? Old Bill, I mean. He's pining for you. I give you my honest word he's been giving the finest exhibition of right-and-left-hand pining I've ever witnessed. Marry him, old thing, and put him out of his misery.

SALLY: Lord Tidmouth, mind your own business.

TIDMOUTH [*plaintively*]: I say, you needn't bite a fellow's head off like that.

SALLY [*laughing*]: Poor Lord Tidmouth! I oughtn't to have snubbed you, ought I?

TIDMOUTH: Don't apologize. I'm used to it. My second wife was a great snubber.

SALLY: I was only annoyed for a moment that you should think I could possibly be in love with Mr Paradene.

TIDMOUTH: Don't see why you shouldn't be. Bill's an excellent chap.

SALLY: A rich waster . . .

TIDMOUTH: Handsome . . .

SALLY: Mere conventional good looks.

TIDMOUTH: Kind to animals.

SALLY: Well, I'm not an animal. If ever I fall in love, Lord Tidmouth, it will be with someone who is some use in the world. Mr Paradene is not my sort. If he had ever done one decent stroke of work in his life . . .

TIDMOUTH: You're pretty strong on work, aren't you?

SALLY: It's my gospel. A man who doesn't work is simply an excrescence on the social fabric.

TIDMOUTH: Pardon me while I wince once more. That one found a chink in the Tidmouth armour.

SALLY [*laughing*]: Oh, you! You know perfectly well, Lord Tidmouth, that you are a mere butterfly.

TIDMOUTH: Pardon me. I may be a butterfly, but I am not mere.

SALLY: All the same, you're not a bad sort.

TIDMOUTH: Dear lady, your words are music to my ears. Exit rapidly before you change your mind. Teuf-Teuf! [*Exit* TIDMOUTH.]

[*Enter* SIR HUGO.]

SIR HUGO: Oh, Doctor Smith. Have you seen my nephew, William?

SALLY: He was out in the garden a little while ago.

SIR HUGO: I am most anxious to find him. I have something of vital importance to say to him.

SALLY [*not interested*]: Yes?

SIR HUGO: I have mercifully succeeded in saving him from making a ghastly blunder and ruining his whole life. He was on the very verge of taking a step which could only have resulted in the most terrible disaster . . . By the way, I knew there was something I wanted to ask you. When you putt, which leg do you rest the weight on?

SALLY: I always putt off the left leg.

SIR HUGO: Indeed? Now, that's most interesting.

SALLY: Some people say the right.

SIR HUGO: Yes. J. H. Taylor says the right.

SALLY: But Walter Hagen prefers the left.

SIR HUGO: He ought to know.

SALLY: Yes.

SIR HUGO: I remember seeing Walter Hagen hole a remarkable putt. He was fully thirty feet from the hole on an undulating green. He . . .

　　[*Enter* BILL]

Ah, William. I was looking for you.

BILL: And I was looking for *you*. What's all this that Tidmouth tells me?

SIR HUGO: Tidmouth tells you?

BILL: Yes, Tidmouth tells me.

SIR HUGO: Tidmouth tells you?

BILL: Yes . . . Will you stop that cross-talk stuff.

SIR HUGO: What did Tidmouth tell you?

BILL: That you've got some asinine idea that I'm in love with Lottie.

SIR HUGO: What!

BILL: There's only one woman in the world that I love or ever shall love, and that's Sally.

SIR HUGO: Sally?

SALLY: I'm Sally.

SIR HUGO: You love this girl?

BILL: Yes.

SIR HUGO [*overjoyed*]: My dear boy! My dear young lady! This is the most wonderful news I have ever had. Bless you, bless you. My dear Doctor, take him! Take him, I say, and may he be as happy as I should be in his place. I'll leave you. Naturally you wish to be alone. Dear me, this is splendid news. William, you have made me a very happy man. [*To* SALLY:] What did you say your handicap was?

SALLY: Six.

SIR HUGO [*rapturously*]: Six! Wonderful! What the Paradenes need is a golfer like you in the family. [*Exit* SIR HUGO.]

BILL [*laughing nervously*]: I'm afraid Uncle was a little premature.

SALLY: A little, perhaps.

BILL: But don't you think . . .?

SALLY: No, I'm afraid not.

BILL: You understand that I had nothing to do with Lottie being here last night?

SALLY: Yes.

BILL: And doesn't it make any difference?

SALLY: No.

BILL: But, Sally . . .

SALLY: No – I'm afraid you're not my sort of man.

BILL: I love you.

SALLY: Is love everything?

BILL: Yes.

SALLY: No. Respect matters, too.

BILL: I see. You despise me?

SALLY: Not despise. But I can't take you seriously.

[*There is a pause.* BILL *goes to desk and sits down.*]

BILL: I see.

SALLY: I'm sorry.

BILL [*coldly*]: Don't mention it. You will excuse me now, won't you?

SALLY [*coldly*]: Certainly. [*She starts to go, then sees that he is taking papers from a drawer.*] What are you doing?

BILL: I thought of doing a little work.

SALLY [*astounded*]: Work?

BILL: Yes. Business connected with the estate. I've been neglecting it.

SALLY [*Drawing a deep breath*]: Work!

BILL: You won't think me rude? I've got rather behindhand. I've been a little worried lately.

SALLY: Do you mind if I sit here? I won't disturb you.

BILL: Please do.

[SALLY *settles herself in arm-chair, and watches him.* BILL, *ostentatiously ignoring her presence, starts to busy himself with the papers. There is a pause.*]

SALLY: How are you getting on?

BILL: All right, thanks.

SALLY: I won't disturb you.

BILL: That's all right.

[*There is a pause.*]

SALLY: You don't mind my sitting here?

BILL: Not at all.

SALLY: Just go on as if I were not here.

BILL: Very well.

[*There is a pause.*]

SALLY: I would hate to feel I was disturbing you.

BILL: Kind of you.

SALLY: So I won't say another word.

BILL: All right.

[*There is a pause.*]

SALLY [*gets up and slowly goes and stands behind him*]: What are you working at?

BILL: Well, if the information conveys anything to you, I am writing out an order for some new Alpha separators.

SALLY: Alpha . . . what?

BILL: Separators. They are machines you use to separate the cream from the milk.

SALLY: How interesting. Why do you want Alpha separators? [*She comes close to him.*]

BILL: Because I happen to own a dairy farm.

SALLY: You do? . . . Tell me more.

BILL: More what?

SALLY: More about your dairy farm.

BILL: Why? Does it interest you?

SALLY: Tremendously . . . An Alpha separator; it sounds awfully complicated.

BILL: Not so very. It's based on centrifugal force.

SALLY [*eagerly*]: Yes?

BILL: Here's a diagram . . . [*Ardently:*] That thing there is the reservoir.

SALLY [*her voice trembling slightly*]: I see . . .

BILL: Below it is the regulator with a float-valve . . .

SALLY [*excited*]: Go on.

BILL [*very ardently*]: As soon as the regulator is full, the float-valve shuts off the influx.

SALLY: How frightfully clever of it!

BILL [*growing still more ardent*]: Shall I tell you something?

SALLY: Do.

BILL [*impressively*]: That machine can separate two thousand seven hundred and twenty-four quarts of milk in an hour.

SALLY: Two thousand . . .

BILL: . . . Seven hundred and twenty-four.
  [*They look into each other's eyes.*]

SALLY: It's the most wonderful thing I ever heard.

BILL: I thought you'd be pleased.

SALLY: Oh, I *am*! [*Points.*] And what's that little thingummy?

BILL [*passionately*]: That . . . is the Holstein butter-churner.

SALLY [*swaying*]: The butter-churner? . . . O-h!

BILL [*alarmed*]: Is anything the matter?

SALLY: No, no. Go on talking.

BILL: About milk?

SALLY: Yes. I never knew it could be so exciting. Do you get your milk from contented cows?

BILL: Well, they haven't complained to *me*. [*Points.*] See that thing? The sterilizer.

SALLY [*overjoyed*]: The sterilizer!

BILL: That's the boiler there. At seventy degrees centigrade the obligatory and optional bacteria are destroyed.

SALLY [*with growing excitement*]: Do you mean to say you are familiar with the bacteria of milk?

BILL: I am.

SALLY: But this is wonderful. [*Gleefully.*] The cavillus acidi lactici . . .

BILL: The bacillus lactis acidi . . .

SALLY: The bactorium koli . . .

BILL: The bacillus erogenes . . .

SALLY: The proteus vulgaris . . .

BILL: The streptococci . . .

SALLY: The colosiridium butiricum . . .

BILL: The bacillus butiricus, the bacillus sluorovenus, *and* the penicilium glaucum.

SALLY: Great heavens!

BILL: What's the matter?

SALLY: It can't be possible!

BILL: What?

SALLY: That you actually do know something about something, after all? You really do do work – decent, honest, respectable work!

BILL: I do. And from now on I'm going to do it harder than ever. Don't you imagine, just because you've turned me down, that I'm going to sit moaning and fussing over my broken heart. I'm going to *work*, and not think about you any more.

SALLY: That's the stuff.

BILL: I shall forget you.

SALLY: Fine!

BILL: Completely.

SALLY: Splendid!

BILL: Put you right out of my mind for ever.

SALLY: Magnificent!

BILL: As soon as you have left this house, I shall order new tractors.

SALLY: Yes, do.

BILL: New harrows.

SALLY: Bravo!

BILL: And fertilizers.

SALLY: Fertilizers, too!

BILL: Also Chili saltpetre and Thomas tap-cinders . . .

SALLY: *Not* Thomas tap-cinders?

BILL: Yes. Thomas tap-cinders.

SALLY: I never heard anything so absolutely glorious in my life. [*The telephone rings.*]

BILL: Hullo! Who can that be? [*Goes to 'phone.*] Hullo. This is Mr Paradene . . . The doctor? . . . [*To* SALLY:] You're wanted.

SALLY [*goes to 'phone*]: Hullo . . . Yes, speaking . . . Now? . . . Quite impossible, I'm afraid . . . You might try Doctor Borstal. He substitutes for me . . . I can't possibly leave here now. The case I am attending is very serious. Much more serious than I thought . . . Good-bye. [*She rings off.*]

BILL: Sally . . .

SALLY: One moment. [*She opens her bag.*]

BILL: What are you looking for?

SALLY: My thermometer. [*She produces thermometer.*]

BILL: Are you feverish?

SALLY: That's just what I want to find out.

BIPL: Sally . . .

SALLY: Go on. [*She puts the thermometer in her mouth.*]

BILL: I love you. I can't help saying it. I love you. I love you.

SALLY [*nods*]: M'hm.

BILL: And today it seems to me as though my real life were beginning . . .

SALLY [*nods*]: M'hm.

BILL: Starting from today, I shall ride each morning through the fields. The clean, fresh wind will blow in my face.

SALLY [*nods*]: M'hm.

BILL: All around me there will be life and movement . . . things growing . . . human beings like carved statues against the morning sky . . . And in the sky clouds . . . beautiful, happy clouds . . .

SALLY [*nods*]: M'hm.

BILL: Strong arms . . . Straining muscles . . . The good smell of the earth . . . Animals . . . Benzine and crude oil . . . Benzine and crude oil, Sally!

SALLY [*nods enthusiastically*]: M'hm.

BILL: The machines get under way. The flywheels spin. Summer is here, Sally. Summer is here. The fields gleam like gold. The sun sparkles. Harvest time. Ripe wheat. Do you understand, Sally? [*Enthusiastically*] Ripe wheat shining in the summer sun.

SALLY [*very softly*]: M'hm. [*She takes the thermometer from her mouth.*] I have no fever.

BILL: But you're trembling.

SALLY: I know. And my pulse is a hundred and ten . . .

BILL: Like mine.

SALLY: And yet I have no fever. And – do you know? –

BILL: What?

SALLY: I've lost control of my vascular motors.

BILL: Sally!

SALLY: One moment. I am faced with the most difficult diagnosis of my whole career.

BILL: Sally!

SALLY [*holding up her hand*]: Wait. [*At first objectively, then with more emotion, interrupting herself again and again. At the end she merely breathes the words.*] I ascertain the following. The organs are intact. I have no pain. No fever. But the pulse is a hundred and ten. The reflexes are heightened. On the periphery of the skin I note a strong radiation of warmth. A slight twitching in the nape of the neck. The hands tremble. The heart action is quickened. Every symptom points to something serious . . . something very serious indeed.

BILL: What?

SALLY: Acute love.

BILL: Sally!

SALLY: Do you remember what I said to you that day we met? If ever I found a man I could love I would tell him so as frankly as if I were saying good morning.

[*She goes to him.*]

Good morning, Bill!

[*They come into each other's arms as the curtain falls.*]

CURTAIN

Leave It To Psmith

A comedy of youth, love and misadventure, in three acts by
Ian Hay and P. G. Wodehouse

Leave It To Psmith was first staged at the Shaftesbury Theatre, London, on 29 September 1930, with the following cast:

THE EARL OF MIDDLEWICK	Clive Currie
BELLOWS	Roger Maxwell
FREDDIE BOSHAM	Reginald Gardiner
RUPERT BAXTER	Edward Chapman
PHYLLIS JACKSON	Nonnie Taylor
LADY MIDDLEWICK	Eileen Munro
A LIFT MAN	Edward Chapman
CYNTHIA MCTODD	Thea Holme
EVE HALLIDAY	Jane Baxter
RONALD EUSTACE PSMITH	Basil Foster
EDDIE COOTES	Aubrey Mather
GLADYS RUMBELOW	Joan Hickson
CHRISTOPHER WALDERWICK	John Charlton
RALSTON MCTODD	Jack Lambert
AGATHA CROFTON	Blanche Adele
ETHELBERTA FITZWIGGIN	Kathleen James
AILEEN PEAVEY	Olive Blakeney
VISCOUNT CHIPSTEAD	Arthur Vezin

The Play produced by Frank Cellier

SCENES

ACT ONE

SCENE ONE—The Oak Gallery, Blandings Castle. (Morning.)
SCENE TWO—The Exterior of Green Park Tube Station. (Midday.)
SCENE THREE—The Morpheus Club, W.1. (Afternoon.)

ACT TWO

The Oak gallery, Blandings Castle. (The following evening.)

ACT THREE

A Keeper's Cottage, Blandings. (The next morning.)

ACT ONE

SCENE ONE

The Oak Gallery at Blandings Castle. The gallery is really the anteroom to the castle library, which is entered by large double doors on the right. On the left is a door leading to the outer hall. At the back are wide open French windows revealing a balustraded terrace. There are pots of hydrangeas at intervals along the top of the balustrade. Landscape beyond. Family portraits on the walls. In the centre, a settee, circular and with a stiff cylindrical cushion fixed upright in the centre, making a 'back' to lean against wherever one sits. Near the windows a writing-table, with chair for same. A stone seat on the terrace. Small round table with two chairs also on the terrace.

LORD MIDDLEWICK, *an elderly peer of rather scholastic appearance, enters from the terrace, calling 'Bellows, where are my glasses?' and searching about in a short-sighted way under the settee, etc.*
BELLOWS, *the butler, enters and advances slowly, then coughs.*
LORD MIDDLEWICK *comes to meet him, and peers into his face.*

LORD MIDDLEWICK: Who's that?
BELLOWS: It is I, my lord – Bellows.
LORD MIDDLEWICK: Have you found my glasses?
BELLOWS: Not yet, my lord.
LORD MIDDLEWICK [*testily*]: You can't have looked.
BELLOWS: I have searched assiduously, my lord, but without avail. Thomas and Henry also announce non-success.
LORD MIDDLEWICK: Well, tell the fools to look again. I am as blind as a dam' bat without my glasses.
BELLOWS: I suppose, my lord, that you do not remember where you saw them last?
LORD MIDDLEWICK [*angrily*]: No, I don't! Would I be listening to your conversation if I did? Go and hunt in the smoking-room. I was there after breakfast.
BELLOWS: Very good, my lord. [*Moving to the door.*] A telephone

147

message has come through from London, my lord, to announce that her ladyship has caught the morning train from Paddington, and will be home for luncheon.

LORD MIDDLEWICK: Thank you for warning me. All right. Go away!

BELLOWS: Very good, my lord. [*Exit* BELLOWS.]

[LORD MIDDLEWICK *groes his way out on the terrace, along the balustrade, still searching. He trips over a bag of golf clubs, which is lying against the stone seat. Trying to save himself, he knocks one of the hydrangeas off the parapet into the garden below: there is a crash. In a fit of anger* LORD MIDDLEWICK *picks up the golf clubs and throws them over the parapet after the pot. Glass crash.* FREDDIE BOSHAM, *his son, appears on the terrace. He is in white flannels.*]

FREDDIE [*cheerfully*]. Hallo, Dad! Tossing the caber?

LORD MIDDLEWICK [*peering up*]: Who's that?

FREDDIE: Your remaining unmarried son – your Frederick. I hear you have lost your glasses.

LORD MIDDLEWICK: Of course I have lost my glasses! That's why I fell over those cursed things.

FREDDIE: Nuisance, what?

LORD MIDDLEWICK [*sarcastically*]: It is slightly inconvenient.

FREDDIE: Can you see me?

LORD MIDDLEWICK: No. There are compensations for everything, thank God! [*Coming down and searching round the circular settee.*]

FREDDIE: I'm sorry. I am looking my debonairest this morning. You haven't noticed a slim girlish figure tripping this way along the Yew Walk, have you? [*Sitting on the settee.*]

LORD MIDDLEWICK: I couldn't see a charging rhinoceros without my glasses.

FREDDIE: Oh, of course, you've lost your glasses, haven't you? I say, why don't you put on your spare ones?

LORD MIDDLEWICK [*trying to keep calm*]: I have broken my spare glasses.

FREDDIE: Tough luck! And you've lost the other pair?

LORD MIDDLEWICK: Yes.

FREDDIE: Why don't you look for them? They must be somewhere, you know. Bustle about!

[*His father clenches his fists and stamps about.*]

– I have it! Can you remember where you saw them last?

LORD MIDDLEWICK [*exploding*]: Go away!

FREDDIE: Away? But I wanted to have a word with you about something.

LORD MIDDLEWICK [*slowly*]: Go away!

FREDDIE: Right away? [*Rising.*]

LORD MIDDLEWICK: Yes.

FREDDIE: Righto!

LORD MIDDLEWICK: And send Baxter to me.

[*Enter* RUPERT BAXTER *through the double doors from the library, with a bundle of papers. He is* LORD MIDDLEWICK'S *secretary. He wears pince-nez, and seems to regard the whole world with suspicion. He puts the papers on his desk.*]

FREDDIE: You ask for Baxter, and Baxter's there! Efficient Baxter! So long. [*He disappears on to the terrace.*]

LORD MIDDLEWICK: Baxter, I have lost my glasses. Where are they? I want them at once. And if you ask me where I saw them last, I will not be responsible for the consequences.

BAXTER: They are hanging down your back, Lord Middlewick.

LORD MIDDLEWICK: God bless my soul! [*He begins to fumble for them.*]

BAXTER: Allow me. [*Pulling them round to the front, and* LORD MIDDLEWICK *puts them on.*]

LORD MIDDLEWICK [*becoming quite genial again*]: Ah! That's better. What a lovely morning. [*Doing exercises.*] I am afraid I was rather short with Mr Frederick a moment ago. Never mind! Have you unpacked that black-letter missal which came from Christie's this morning? I should like to examine it.

BAXTER: I am afraid you have not very much time to spare for reading this morning. You mustn't miss your train.

LORD MIDDLEWICK: What train?

BAXTER: The one-fifty to London, Lord Middlewick. You have to take the chair at the Annual Festival of the Medieval Manuscripts Association tonight.

LORD MIDDLEWICK: Where?

BAXTER: In the Marble Hall, Ptomani's Restaurant, Soho.

LORD MIDDLEWICK: I though that was on Saturday.

BAXTER: On Saturday you are due at Great Waffleden, to lay the foundation-stone of the Diddlecombe Institute.

LORD MIDDLEWICK: Baxter, you possess a quite unique gift for making undesirable public engagements for me. Have I to speak tonight?

BAXTER: Yes. Here is your speech.

LORD MIDDLEWICK: You are sure it's the right one? You remember what happened at the Ponder's End Temperance Rally a fortnight ago. You gave me a speech which was meant for the Licensed Victuallers' Defence Association, and I read half of the beastly thing before I realized what it was about.

BAXTER: Lord Middlewick, I have always maintained that we were the victims of a practical joke upon that occasion.

LORD MIDDLEWICK: Who was the joker?

BAXTER: I suspect Mr Frederick.

LORD MIDDLEWICK: My son? He hasn't the brains. You are getting too suspicious of everybody, Baxter: it's a disease with you. Do you remember that housemaid you suspected of being a man in woman's clothes – and she wasn't? Eh? You landed yourself that time, Baxter.

BAXTER: It was a most embarrassing episode, Lord Middlewick.

LORD MIDDLEWICK: But was it a lesson to you? No! You are getting less efficient and more officious every day.

BAXTER: Lord Middlewick! I resign!

LORD MIDDLEWICK: Resign? Don't talk dam' nonsense! Who else would give you a job? Now, if I am really going up to town, somebody had better pack my bag.

BAXTER: I have already given instructions to that effect.

[FREDDIE *appears again on the terrace. He enters and is about to telephone, but sees his father and desists.*]

FREDDIE: Hallo, Dad! Found your glasses?

LORD MIDDLEWICK: Yes, Frederick. I have them on.

FREDDIE: So you have. I suppose they were there all the time.

LORD MIDDLEWICK: Go –
[LORD MIDDLEWICK *is about to lose his temper again, when* BAXTER *intervenes.*]

BAXTER: Speaking of the library, I really think it will have to be re-catalogued.

LORD MIDDLEWICK: What, again! When was it done last?

BAXTER: In eighteen-forty-three.

LORD MIDDLEWICK: Yesterday! Besides, who can do it?

BAXTER: I have advertised for a suitable person. Here is her application. [*Giving letter to* LORD MIDDLEWICK.] She is highly recommended, and her charges are moderate.

LORD MIDDLEWICK [*to* BAXTER, *reading the signature*]: What is this lady's name?

BAXTER: Miss Eve Halliday. I have instructed her to call at your Club about one o'clock tomorrow.

LORD MIDDLEWICK: My luncheon-hour! Of course – you would!
[*Enter* BELLOWS. *Coughs.*]
– What is it now?

BELLOWS: The Secretary of the Diddlecombe Institute, my lord.

LORD MIDDLEWICK: Curse him! Very well, I'll see him in the Estate Office.

BAXTER: Has the car gone to the station for her ladyship?

BELLOWS: Yes, sir.
[*Exit* BELLOWS.]

FREDDIE: The car? They ought to have sent an armour-plated omnibus. Remember what our lady-mother is bringing with her. The doings!

BAXTER: Will her ladyship be bringing the Dulworthy diamonds here?

LORD MIDDLEWICK: Yes, she will! It's the sort of thing a woman would do – inherit valuable jewels, and then wear them, instead of putting them safely into a bank. We shall have half the burglars in London camping round the estate when the news gets out.

FREDDIE: We must reserve the film rights!

LORD MIDDLEWICK: Bah! [*Exit* LORD MIDDLEWICK *with* BAXTER.]

[FREDDIE *goes into the library, then returns. He sits at the desk, and takes up the telephone.*]

FREDDIE: Hallo! Good morning! What a lovely view this is, isn't it? . . . Perhaps you're right. And how is the Beauty Chorus at the Telephone Exchange this morning? What? . . . Oh, what *number.* Great Waffleden, two-oh, please. Waffleden Grange – you know. Where Phyllis lives.

[PHYLLIS JACKSON *has appeared on the terrace. She is a pretty girl of about 20. She wears a leather motoring-coat, and is swinging her hat in her hand.*]

PHYLLIS [*calling softly*]: Freddie!

FREDDIE [*turning and seeing her*]. Darling! [*Into the telephone.*] No – not you! [*He bangs down the telephone.*] . . . Phyllis! Angel! I was just ringing up to find out what had become of you. How did you get here?

PHYLLIS: In the old two-seater. I left it at the end of the Yew Walk, by the empty keeper's cottage. Is that all right?

FREDDIE [*gazing at her fondly*]: Absolutely.

[*She puts her hands in his waistcoat-pocket and takes out a cigarette-case and helps herself.*]

. . . Now, what about slipping over to Great Waffleden for a spot of lunch and a movie?

PHYLLIS: Why the haste? Where is everybody?

FREDDIE: My Dad is in the Estate Office, being measured for a foundation-stone. My sainted stepmother is speeding back from London, flushed with victory after the battle.

PHYLLIS: Don't talk like a village idiot, darling. What battle?

[*Taking a light with* FREDDIE' *automatic lighter.*]

FREDDIE: The battle of Lincoln's Inn Fields, rendered inevitable by the decease of my great aunt Calpurnia, Dowager Duchess of Dulworthy, who passed away in full possession of her faculties and a nice little packet in the Post Office Savings Bank, three months ago.

PHYLLIS [*sitting on settee*]: And who took part in the battle?

FREDDIE [*walking about*]. Practically everybody who was still on speaking terms with the dear old lady at the time of her demise.

[PHYLLIS *powders her nose.*]

All concerned acquitted themselves with credit, second cousin Ethelberta Fitzwiggin being especially prominent in the forward rushes. However, science told in the end, and as the whistle blew my stepmother emerged from the scrimmage with the Dulworthy diamonds in her right hand and a fragment of Ethelberta's scalp in her left. She's bringing the Dulworthy diamonds home now. The scalp has been returned.

PHYLLIS: What about my Freddie? Isn't there anything for you?

FREDDIE: I hear rumours of a legacy.

PHYLLIS [*rising and going to him*]: Darling! How much?

FREDDIE: I don't know. I was her godson; it might be quite a juicy one.

PHYLLIS: This may mean a lot to us. That's why I came over this morning. I had a long talk with Father last night.

FREDDIE: What about?

PHYLLIS: About you.

FREDDIE: You lucky pair! And what was the old boy's reaction to me as a matrimonial proposition?

PHYLLIS: He wasn't very complimentary, darling.

FREDDIE: Oh, that's all right. I know him. One of those stern, flint-like Englishmen who crush down their emotions. What did he say?

PHYLLIS: He said you were utterly brainless, insufferably conceited, and bone idle.

FREDDIE: But otherwise he likes me? And is he prepared to welcome me as a son-in-law?

PHYLLIS: He says that if you really want me you must do one of two things.

FREDDIE [*gloomily*]: A deep V-shaped depression is reported from Iceland. All right, tell me the worst!

PHYLLIS: Either you must go to work –

FREDDIE: In the jam factory?

PHYLLIS: Yes.

FREDDIE: 'Jackson's Jams and Jellies. Made from Fresh Fruit and Refained Sugar.' Good! 'Adhesive labels attached by the Honourable F. Bosham in person'. [*Shakes his head.*] Not so good!

PHYLLIS: Freddie, don't be an old snob. Our family has made jam for fifty years, and we're proud of it.

FREDDIE: Our family has made nothing at all for five hundred years, and we're tickled to death about it. No – one moment! I was forgetting Great-Uncle Rupert.

PHYLLIS: Great-Uncle Rupert?

FREDDIE: He helped to make a road in the Isle of Wight.

PHYLLIS: The Isle of Wight?

FREDDIE: The Isle of Wight! – near Parkhurst. It took him three years.

PHYLLIS: Three years?

FREDDIE: Three years, less a small remission for good conduct. [PHYLLIS *looks puzzled.*]

A little matter of a stumer cheque. Of course, we never mention him. [*Sitting by* PHYLLIS.] But what was your pop's alternative to the job? I think you mentioned one.

PHYLLIS: Yes. You must put five thousand pounds into the business. Then he'll give you an allowance and let us get married. Can you do it? Is the legacy juicy enough?

FREDDIE: We'll ask stepmother when she gets back from town.

PHYLLIS: Why not ask your father now, before she comes back?

FREDDIE: A sound idea. I was going to try to touch him for a trifle anyhow. We might as well make a wholesale order of it.

[*Enter* LORD MIDDLEWICK. *He has dressed to go to London, with his hat and umbrella.*]

LORD MIDDLEWICK: Ah, Frederick. Have you nothing to occupy your time, my boy?

FREDDIE: Hallo, Dad! You know Phyllis, don't you? Dear little Phyllis!

PHYLLIS [*with her best smile*]. Good morning, Lord Middlewick.

LORD MIDDLEWICK: Good morning, my dear. Well, Frederick, you want me?

FREDDIE: Yes. H'm! First of all, Dad, I want to thank you – by acclamation – for all your kindness and generosity.

LORD MIDDLEWICK [*blankly*]: When?

FREDDIE: From my birth until the present date.

LORD MIDDLEWICK: What are you vapouring about, my boy? Come to the point.

FREDDIE: Righto, Dad! Will you lend me ten thousand pounds?

LORD MIDDLEWICK [*incredulously*]: Will I lend you ten thousand what?

[PHYLLIS *holds up the fingers of one hand to indicate five.*]

FREDDIE [*turning towards her, then to his father*]: Ten thousand pounds. Yes, Dad, will you?

LORD MIDDLEWICK: No!

FREDDIE: Then how much will you lend me?

LORD MIDDLEWICK: Nothing.

FREDDIE: Right! Now we're getting down to business. I ask for ten thousand pounds; you offer me nothing. Let's be reasonable and split the difference. I'll take five thousand. [*Smiling proudly towards* PHYLLIS.]

LORD MIDDLEWICK: Don't be a bigger imbecile than you can help, my boy.

FREDDIE: You're sure you won't lend me five thousand pounds?

LORD MIDDLEWICK: I was never so sure of anything in my life.

FREDDIE: That's final?

LORD MIDDLEWICK: Utterly!

FREDDIE [*giving a deep sigh and looking resignedly towards* PHYLLIS, *then turning to his father again*]: Very well, then. Can you lend me a pound till Saturday?

LORD MIDDLEWICK: What for?

FREDDIE: I want to take Phyllis over to Great Waffleden, to break bread at the County Arms, and then see a super film I hear well spoken of. It's called 'Blood on the Bathroom Floor.'

LORD MIDDLEWICK [*losing all patience*]: Bah!

[BELLOWS *enters.*]

BELLOWS: Her ladyship has returned, my lord.

LORD MIDDLEWICK: Oh, has she? Where is her ladyship?

BELLOWS: In the hall, my lord.

LORD MIDDLEWICK: Then I'll go into the library.

[*Exit* LORD MIDDLEWICK *to the library. Exit* BELLOWS.]

FREDDIE [*turning to* PHYLLIS]: Crashed!

PHYLLIS [*coming to him, over his shoulder*]: Never mind,

darling; you did your best. Lady Middlewick may have some good news for us.

FREDDIE: My dear stepmother never brings us good news. All she ever brings is a frequent nasty surprise – in the shape of a guest.

PHYLLIS: What sort of guest?

FREDDIE: Something queer – something literary or artistic. We are much exposed to people like that in this house. She's always discovering them, behind ferns and under large flat stones, and bringing them down for the week-end.

LADY MIDDLEWICK'S VOICE [off]: Go and find his lordship and tell him I want him at once.

PHYLLIS: Here is Lady Middlewick.

[LADY MIDDLEWICK enters – a handsome, middle-aged woman in travelling-dress. At the same time LORD MIDDLEWICK appears on the terrace, with the black-letter missal already mentioned, and sits at the table. Enter BELLOWS, who hands him a magnifying-glass and goes. LORD MIDDLEWICK begins to examine the missal, and is soon absorbed.]

LADY MIDDLEWICK: Ah, Freddie, my dear boy!

FREDDIE: Hallo, Mother! [Embracing her.] Welcome home from the front. Here's little Phyllis Jackson.

PHYLLIS [again with her best smile]: Good morning, Lady Middlewick.

LADY MIDDLEWICK [bowing stiffly]: How do you do?
[Looking up at her husband.] Eustace, what have you got there?

LORD MIDDLEWICK: A black-letter missal of the early fourteenth century. I have just secured it.

LADY MIDDLEWICK: You seem to have waited a long time for it.
[Going on to the terrace, and looking over his shoulder.]

LORD MIDDLEWICK [absently]: Yes, dear.

PHYLLIS [to FREDDIE]: Ask her now, about the legacy.

FREDDIE: Righto! [To LADY MIDDLEWICK:] And how did you leave them all at Waterloo?

LADY MIDDLEWICK: Do you mean Paddington?

FREDDIE: No, I was referring to the well-known battle of that name. The stricken field. Have the tumult and the shouting died? Peace with honour? Blood wiped up, and everything?

LADY MIDDLEWICK: Don't be disgusting, Freddie.

FREDDIE: How's second cousin Ethelberta?

LADY MIDDLEWICK: In bed, I am glad to say – with a temperature.

FREDDIE: She really thought she was going to get the diamonds?

LADY MIDDLEWICK: She did!

FREDDIE: No one had told her about the famous Middlewick left hook, poor girl.

LADY MIDDLEWICK: Freddie, don't talk like a potboy!

FREDDIE: Right, Mother. Let's get down to business. How do we all come out, financially? Is it to be spot cash, or hope deferred?

LADY MIDDLEWICK: Freddie, I have a sick headache, produced by the motion of the train. I shall not be able to endure your conversation with any degree of resignation until after luncheon at the earliest. Eustace!

LORD MIDDLEWICK: Yes, dear.

LADY MIDDLEWICK: What time is luncheon?

LORD MIDDLEWICK: I ordered it for one o'clock. I have to catch the one-fifty.

LADY MIDDLEWICK: You are going to London?

LORD MIDDLEWICK: So Baxter says.

LADY MIDDLEWICK: Didn't you know?

LORD MIDDLEWICK: Not till this morning.

LADY MIDDLEWICK: Mr Baxter is becoming impossible.

LORD MIDDLEWICK: My dear, he's indispensable.

LADY MIDDLEWICK: Don't argue; I can't bear it today. When do you come back?

LORD MIDDLEWICK: Tomorrow afternoon.

LADY MIDDLEWICK: Good! You can bring Mr McTodd with you.

LORD MIDDLEWICK: Mr Mc Who?

LADY MIDDLEWICK: McTodd. Don't be silly, dear. Ralston McTodd, the Sweet Singer from Wisconsin.

LORD MIDDLEWICK: The street singer from where?

LADY MIDDLEWICK: *Sweet* singer! A poet!

LORD MIDDLEWICK: Oh – another! What sort this time?

LADY MIDDLEWICK: I haven't met him yet, but I believe he's very original and daring. He hates civilization and its hollowness, and all that sort of thing.

FREDDIE: Cheerful sort of bird.

LORD MIDDLEWICK: I have never heard of him. In fact, I don't think I have ever heard of any writer later than the early fifteenth century. Name some of his works.

LADY MIDDLEWICK: Well, they're all bound in limp mauve morocco, and you get them at a rather advanced place in the Charing Cross Road. His best known book is – let me think – 'Songs of Squalor.'

LADY MIDDLEWICK: 'Songs of what'?

LADY MIDDLEWICK: Squalor! But he has just published a tragedy in blank verse which quite surpasses anything else.

LORD MIDDLEWICK: What's it called?

LADY MIDDLEWICK [*rapturously*]: 'Mud.'

LORD MIDDLEWICK: } Mud?
FREDDIE:

LADY MIDDLEWICK: Yes. Such a vivid title! It sums up modern society in one word. I wonder no one has ever thought of it before. Anyhow, you can bring him down tomorrow afternoon. He'll be nice company for Miss Peavey.

LORD MIDDLEWICK: And who precisely is Miss Peavey?

LADY MIDDLEWICK: Eustace, you are very trying today. Aileen Peavey! Her name is known everywhere where streamlets run and fairies play.

LORD MIDDLEWICK: Oh, my lord!

FREDDIE: And what has she written, Mother?

LADY MIDDLEWICK: Oh, lots of things. Exquisite stuff, like gossamer – poems about flowers, and gnomes, and goblins, and things like that. She lives in quite a world of her own.

LORD MIDDLEWICK: Thank God for that!
[BELLOWS *enters with a jewel-case.*]

LADY MIDDLEWICK: What is it, Bellows?

BELLOWS: Your jewel-case, my lady. Your maid would welcome instructions as to its disposal.

LORD MIDDLEWICK: Are those the Dulworthy diamonds?

BELLOWS: Yes, my lord.

LORD MIDDLEWICK: Anastasia, those things *must* go to the bank. We shall all be murdered in our beds if we keep them here. The news is in the local paper already. I will take them with me this afternoon.

LADY MIDDLEWICK: Nonsense! I am going to wear them at the party I am giving for Miss Peavey and Mr McTodd tomorrow night. Tell Simms to lock them in my dressing-table drawer for the present, Bellows.

BELLOWS: Very good, my lady. [*Exit* BELLOWS.]

LORD MIDDLEWICK: Well, don't blame me if you wake up with your skull cracked. [*Exit* LORD MIDDLEWICK.]

FREDDIE: We will now take a nose-dive from fairyland to Lincoln's Inn Fields. How did Freddie come out? Any little keepsake for him?

LADY MIDDLEWICK: You have been left five thousand pounds.

FREDDIE: Oh, this is the hand of Providence! Phyllis darling, do you hear that? The banns can go right up. [*To* LADY MIDDLEWICK:] Mother, when do I touch?

LADY MIDDLEWICK: Touch?

FREDDIE: When do I handle the fruit?

LADY MIDDLEWICK: The money is in the bank now.

FREDDIE: Ah! Can any lady or gentleman oblige me with a fountain-pen?

LADY MIDDLEWICK: What for?

FREDDIE: I am about to write a cheque.

LADY MIDDLEWICK: Indeed? For whom?

FREDDIE: Mr Jackson.

LADY MIDDLEWICK: What?

PHYLLIS [*taking* FREDDIE'S *arm*]: My father has offered to take Freddie into partnership, Lady Middlewick.

LADY MIDDLEWICK: For how much?

FREDDIE: Five thousand pounds. That was where Providence came in.

LADY MIDDLEWICK: And why do you want to go into Mr Jackson's business?

FREDDIE: Well – it'll take me off the dole.

LADY MIDDLEWICK: Freddie, I may as well tell you something you don't know. There is a codicil in Aunt Calpurnia's Will.

FREDDIE [*resignedly*]: The south cone has been hoisted on the North Foreland. All right, spill it!

LADY MIDDLEWICK: To save you from yourself, Freddie, this eodicil to the Will provides that all cheques drawn by you against this legacy must be signed by me as well.

FREDDIE: *What?*

LADY MIDDLEWICK [*sweetly*]: By me as well, darling.

FREDDIE: For ever and ever?

LADY MIDDLEWICK: Until you are thirty-five.

FREDDIE: Same thing!

LADY MIDDLEWICK: Till then, both our signatures will be necessary.

FREDDIE: And Aunt Calpurnia bunged in this codicil herself?

LADY MIDDLEWICK: Yes. It was about the last thing she did.

FREDDIE: Obviously her mind had ceased to function, poor old girl. Forget her! [*Hoping against hope.*] I'll write the cheque at once, and bring it along to you.

LADY MIDDLEWICK: No, Freddie

FREDDIE: You won't sign it?

LADY MIDDLEWICK: Certainly not.

PHYLLIS: You mean you won't let Freddie come into my father's business?

LADY MIDDLEWICK [*sweetly*]: I am afraid I have other plans for him, my dear. I know it's a disappointment to you, but I must do what I consider my duty. Good morning! [*Exit* LADY MIDDLEWICK.]

[FREDDIE *and* PHYLLIS *sink side by side on the settee.*]

FREDDIE: Torpedoed! Torpedoed right in the engine-room!

PHYLLIS: What do we do now?

FREDDIE: Give me a kiss.

PHYLLIS: There! [*Kissing him.*]And now?

FREDDIE: Let's run over to Great Waffleden, as per original programme, and wallow in 'Blood on the Bathroom Floor.' It's the only thing left to do.

PHYLLIS: All right, dear. What have you got? [*Picking up a newspaper which is lying on the settee, and putting it under her arm.*]

FREDDIE [*going through his pockets*]: Piece of string – fourpence – an automatic lighter which sometimes lights – and a cigarette photograph of Amy Johnson. Oh, why is wealth so unevenly distributed in this world! My stepmother covered in diamonds, and you and I without the price of a meal! A single small diamond would keep us for weeks. [*Suddenly.*] Shall I run upstairs and twist one off the bunch? It wouldn't be robbery.

PHYLLIS: Why wouldn't it?

FREDDIE: Because it's not illegal to steal the property of your own relations. Only other people's.

PHYLLIS: Where did you learn that?

FREDDIE: From a film I once saw, called 'For Baby's Sake.' People sneer at the movies, but they have a great educational value. They taught me all I know, practically.

PHYLLIS: I don't think you're clever enough to steal anything, dear. Baxter would catch you for a certainty.

FREDDIE: I believe he would. I hadn't thought of that.

PHYLLIS: But what else can we do to get that five thousand pounds for Dad?

FREDDIE: Give me that paper. [*Taking it from* PHYLLIS *and turning over a page.*] There is a Scotchman called McGregor Samuelson who lives up a narrow staircase in Bond Street who might accommodate us at a reasonable rate of interest. [*With a laugh.*] I say, here's a funny advertisement.

PHYLLIS: What, dear?

FREDDIE [*showing it*]. There. In big print. 'Leave it to Psmith.'

PHYLLIS: Pea Smith?

FREDDIE: Persmith, I fancy. [*Reading.*] 'Persmith will help you.'

PHYLLIS [*reading*]: 'Do you want some one to manage your affairs?'

FREDDIE: Some one to handle your business –

PHYLLIS: Some one to take the dog for a run –

FREDDIE: Some one to assassinate your Aunt? Psmith will do it. Psmith will do anything – provided it has nothing to do with fish.

PHYLLIS: Fish? I mean – why fish?

FREDDIE [*reading again*]: 'Crime not objected to.' Crime? Crime! Phyllis, I've got it. We're saved!

PHYLLIS: What do you mean?

FREDDIE: We'll ring this fellow up. We'll ask him his terms for coming down here and swiping the Dulworthy diamonds.

PHYLLIS: Oh, Freddie! Darling! All of them?

FREDDIE: Well, five thousand pounds' worth, at any rate.

PHYLLIS: Do you think he will?

FREDDIE: There's no harm in asking. [*Suddenly sees* BELLOWS, *who is crossing the terrace, and calls.*] Bellows, old soul, will you ring up Trunks for me and get Gerrard five-two-four-one?

BELLOWS: With pleasure, sir. [*Enters and takes up the telephone, with his back turned, and begins to get the number.*]

PHYLLIS [*in a low voice*]: My poor boy. You *can't* arrange a burglary over the telephone!

FREDDIE: I am not going to. I am going to make an appointment with this man Psmith for tomorrow morning. Did you ever see a film called 'Strangled at Dawn'? It has a situation just like this in it. Two total strangers agree to meet at a given rendezvous. They are to recognize each other by signs, and all that. Let me think of a *rendezvous* and a sign.

BELLOWS [*hanging up the receiver of the telephone and turning*]: They will call you, sir.

FREDDIE: Thank you, Bellows.

[BELLOWS *disappears.*]

PHYLLIS: You're quite sure it isn't illegal, darling?

FREDDIE: I tell you I saw it in a film. Hollywood cannot lie.

PHYLLIS: But how are you going to get to town? You've only got fourpence.

[FREDDIE *stops.*]

FREDDIE: I'll get my noble father to take me up this afternoon. I'll make an appointment with the dentist, and then he'll have to. I've been meaning to have the old grotto attended to for some time.

[*The telephone rings.*]

PHYLLIS: There's the telephone.

FREDDIE [*excitedly*]: Psmith! [*Running and taking up the telephone.*]

Hallo! Is that Persmith? Oh, the 'P' is silent? Right! Good morning! H'm! I want to engage you professionally. The general idea is that you commit a crime for me. I understand you don't object to crime? Right! Then meet me at the Green Park Tube Station, at noon precisely, tomorrow. The lift exit. Got that? Let me see. Now listen, when you see me – say 'There will be rain in London and the home counties tonight.' I shall reply, 'Good for the crops.' And finally, wear a pink rhododendron in your buttonhole. So long! God bless! [*To* PHYLLIS, *triumphantly.*] Ta-taah!

BLACK OUT *and* CURTAIN.

SCENE TWO

The exterior of a tube station. Right, a recessed doorway. Left is the way out from the lift, an archway or doorway, of glazed tiles, such as are used in tube stations, with the usual Underground sign of red and blue circles. Also Underground Railway Map. This opening faces across the stage, so that all characters entering through it appear to be emerging from a tube station off left. These simple devices should be sufficient to indicate the scene, which can be set very quickly. The sound of the lift ascending and descending can be reproduced by means of an electric motor, run fast or slow, off left. There should also be some device to indicate the clashing of gates.

CYNTHIA MCTODD, *the young wife of* RALSTON MCTODD, *appears from the tube station. She looks up and down the street anxiously, then turns to the* LIFT MAN, *a gloomy person, who has followed her out.*

CYNTHIA: Could you tell me where the Morpheus Club is, please?

LIFT MAN: The Morphewce? Yes lady. That's it, three doors along – [*pointing off.*] – with the dead man in brass buttons leaning against the railings outside.

CYNTHIA: Is he really dead?

LIFT MAN: Well, they nearly all are about here. It's what's called a select neighbourhood.

CYNTHIA: It does seem quiet.

LIFT MAN: Quiet? It's unconscious. Why, you can hear Big Ben right across the Green Park!

CYNTHIA: Striking?

LIFT MAN: Ticking. Look at this station! Only about one train in six ever troubles to stop here, and if it does nobody gets out. [*Lift bell rings.*] 'Ullo! Another passenger! What is this – Cup Tie day? [*He goes off. The lift is heard descending.*]

[CYNTHIA *looks up and down the street, evidently in great indecision: then sets off to go out. Her courage fails, and she turns back.* EVE HALLIDAY *enters, a pretty and self-possessed girl of 20. The two recognise each other.*]

CYNTHIA: Eve Halliday?

EVE: Cynthia! [*They rush into each other's arms.*] My dear, how wonderful!

CYNTHIA: It's marvellous to see you. How long is it?

EVE: Years and years and years and years. One, anyhow.

CYNTHIA: Oh, it does so comfort me to see you!

EVE: What's the matter, darling?

CYNTHIA: My husband!

EVE: You've got a husband?

CYNTHIA: Yes. Ralston McTodd, the famous Scottish-American poet.

EVE: Oh, darling! [*They embrace.*] But he can't be Scottish *and* American.

CYNTHIA: Yes, he can, dear. His parents emigrated from Aberdeen thirty years ago.

EVE: Why?

CYNTHIA: Something called Local Option, dear. He was born in Wisconsin. And he's just left me, for ever!

EVE: Oh, darling! [*Embrace.*]

CYNTHIA: And it's the third time in six months!

EVE: Oh, darling! [*Embrace.*] But why?

CYNTHIA: He's temperamental, poor angel. And he doesn't like England. His habits are all American.

EVE: What doesn't he like about England?

CYNTHIA: Brussels sprouts. He says they're the only vegetable the English have ever heard of. And ice. He can't get any. Americans eat ice all day, in lumps; and he says the only ice he ever sees in England is hanging from the ceilings of English bedrooms, in icicles.

EVE: And he's left you?

CYNTHIA: Yes. He's gone to have a brainstorm somewhere.

EVE: Where, dear?

CYNTHIA: He never knows till he gets there. Then he comes to, and they tell him where he is.

EVE: Then you don't know where he is?

CYNTHIA: Well, I do know where he ought to be for lunch. At the Morpheus club, just there. [*Pointing.*] That's why I came here.

EVE: The Morpheus Club? That's where I'm bound for.

CYNTHIA: You? Are you going to lunch there?

EVE: No. I'm going there to see somebody about a job.

CYNTHIA: A job – you?

EVE: Yes; I'm just a poor working girl.

CYNTHIA: But you're so smart!

EVE: I should hope so; I've got to make an impression today, dear. I'm wearing every rag of chiffon I possess.

CYNTHIA: Oh – a gentleman?

EVE: An old gentleman! Lord Middlewick.

CYNTHIA: But Ralston is lunching with Lord Middlewick! He's been invited to stay the weekend with him at Blandings Castle.

EVE: Not you, too?

CYNTHIA: Oh, no. I'm never asked anywhere. I don't think Ralston always tells people he's married.

[*Sound of the lift is heard coming up, then the* LIFT MAN *enters.*]

LIFT MAN: False alarm! An old gent who thought it was the British Museum.

EVE: Now, Cynthia dear, don't hang about here waiting for your husband. Show your independence! Go home, and in a day or two I'll send him back to you, complete with collar and chain.

CYNTHIA: Oh, bless you, darling! [*They kiss.*] Goodbye. Are you going to the club now?

EVE: No. I'm going to a bun-shop first, for a bite of lunch. [*She puts her hand out.*] Oh, bother, it's raining! No umbrella, and my one Paris frock!

LIFT MAN: Lift going down!

CYNTHIA: Goodbye, dear! [*Embracing each other again.*]

EVE: Goodbye. Write to me at Blandings.

CYNTHIA [*from off*]: Yes, dear. Goodbye.

EVE: Goodbye, darling!

LIFT MAN [*off*]: Goodbye, miss! [*Clash. Sound of lift descending.*]
[EVE *goes off. The sound of rain increases. She hurries back, huddling herself up, and shelters in the house doorway* R.C. *She looks at her watch, examines herself in the mirror, powders her nose, etc., then looks up impatiently.*

Sound of lift ascending, and clash of gates. PSMITH *emerges. He is a man of about 30, with a rather serious expression, which he maintains habitually, even when talking the wildest nonsense. He is dressed in his best, with white spats, etc, and is wearing a large pink rhododendron in his buttonhole. He appears quite unconscious of this. He pauses in the entrance to the lift, and looks up and down the street.*]

LIFT MAN [*having followed him*]: Going to a wedding, sir?

PSMITH [*seriously*]: No, oh, no! A business appointment.

LIFT MAN: I see. [*Looking at the rhododendron.*] But this isn't the station for Covent Garden Market, you know.

PSMITH: I don't want to go to any more markets. I've just escaped from Billingsgate.

LIFT MAN: From where?

PSMITH: Billingsgate – the Hall of flapping fish. They kept me there for four long years.

[*The* LIFT MAN *stares at him.*]

I can imitate any fish that swims? What sort of fish would you like me to imitate? Just name it . . .

LIFTMAN: A skate

PSMITH: Ah, you would! Well, I'm not going to do it, so there!

LIFTMAN: Why not?

PSMITH [*indicating his waistcoat*]: Well, a skate keeps its face down here, and I'm all dressed for the day.

[*Exit* LIFTMAN *hurriedly, into lift.*]

[*Enter* RALSTON MCTODD *from lift, rather fancifully dressed. He sees* PSMITH'S *flower and stares at it.*]

PSMITH: Oy! [MCTODD *looks at him fiercely.*] There will be rain in London and the home counties tonight.

MCTODD: Don't be a dam' fool. It's raining now.

PSMITH: The wrong answer, old friend. But perhaps you're the wrong man.

MCTODD: Listen. No one ever called me a wrong man and got away with it.

PSMITH: All right. Pax! But haven't you an appointment with anyone here – by any chance?

MCTODD: I should say I had. At the Morpheus Club just there. [*Pointing.*] The swellest eats in London – and I haven't had a man's meal in weeks. Oh, boy! [*Exit* MCTODD.]

[*Enter from lift,* GLADYS RUMBELOW, *putting up umbrella.*]

PSMITH: There will be rain – No, it couldn't be you!

[GLADYS *glares at him, and goes off.*]

LIFT MAN [*who has followed* GLADYS RUMBELOW *on*]: Are you sure it was Billingsgate you escaped from?

PSMITH: Positive, comrade. The name of the place is grilled into my soul. Four long years each dawn beheld me there, up to my hips in halibut.

LIFT MAN [*pushing him gently*]: Stand clear of the gates, please! [*Sound of lift descending.*]

[PSMITH *steps into the street. He sees* EVE *sheltering in the doorway.*]

PSMITH: Oh!

EVE [*a little startled*]: Oh!

PSMITH [*taking off his hat to her*]: H'm! There will be –

EVE: Thank you; I know.

PSMITH: Can I get you a taxi?

EVE: No, thank you.

PSMITH: But you'll get all wet. People do, you know.

EVE: I can't help that.

PSMITH: I have it; I'll get you an umbrella. There's a Club just along here, full of umbrellas. I'll be back in a moment. You stick tight to that doorway. [*He hurries off.*]

[*Lift motor is heard off and crash of lift gates opening.* LORD MIDDLEWICK *emerges, and peers about,* LIFT MAN *following him.*]

LORD MIDDLEWICK: This is Green Park Station, isn't it?

LIFT MAN: Yes, sir.

LORD MIDDLEWICK: They're so much alike, and I have mislaid my glasses. [*Stepping into street.*] Thank you.

LIFT MAN: Thank you, sir, for getting out here.

[LORD MIDDLEWICK *puts up his umbrella and goes off.*]

[*To* EVE.] Still waiting, miss?

EVE: Yes. [*Smiling.*] I can't afford taxi-cabs.

LIFT MAN: Your misfortune is my benefit, miss. I like a bit of company; this station gives me the willies.

EVE: It seems a very nice station.

LIFT MAN: But who uses it? Nobody – except a few of them aristocratic pinchers belonging to Clubs round here, who are too mean to pay for a cab. I was at Piccadilly Circus once. Those were the days! People jammed so tight they was 'alf dead. That was life, that was!

[PSMITH *returns with an umbrella.*]

'Ullo!' 'Ere's Potty Percy again. Back to the dug-out for yours truly! [*Exit. The lift is heard descending.*]

PSMITH: Here we are. [*Opening the umbrella and handing it to* EVE.] There!

EVE: Oh, thank you! I really am grateful. I am on my way to an appointment – for a job – and I don't want to look like a drowned hen.

PSMITH: A job? – you? But no one like you ought to work, and get all over oil, and grease, and grit –

EVE: I'm not going to drive a traction-engine. It's a job to catalogue a library – in a big country house in Shropshire – a place called Blandings Castle. Do you think it will be a nice place?

PSMITH: It will be – if you go there.

EVE [*a little taken aback*]: Oh! Well, I think I'll go now. [*Going.*] Where shall I return the umbrella?

PSMITH [*glancing at the handle*]: The Honourable Christopher Walderwick, Morpheus Club.

EVE [*offering her hand*]: Thank you very much, Mr Walderwick.

PSMITH: Oh, I'm not Mr Walderwick. He's only the man who owns the umbrella.

EVE: Then will you thank him for me?

PSMITH: I'm afraid I don't know him.

EVE [*suddenly, pointing*]: Are you a member of that Club at all?

PSMITH: Oh, bless you, no! I can't afford to belong to a place like that. I'm looking for a job myself, like you. I'm here to keep an appointment. By the way, I suppose you aren't interested in the weather in London and the home counties?

EVE: No.

PSMITH: Well, I had to ask. Good morning.

EVE: Good morning!

> [*Sound of lift ascending.* EVE *goes out, looking back at him curiously.* PSMITH *stands gazing after her, fascinated.*
>
> EDDIE COOTES *emerges from lift. He is a flashily dressed, sharp-featured man, with a furtive manner. He stands looking up at the weather, and evidently in no particular hurry.* PSMITH *turns towards him.* COOTES *looks with some surprise at* PSMITH'S *rhododendron.*]

COOTES [*advancing upon him effusively*]: My dear fellow! [*Shaking hands violently.*] My dear old boy! For a moment I didn't recognize you. How are you? How are you?

PSMITH [*pulling himself together*]: There will be rain in London and the home counties tonight.

COOTES: I'm sure there will. I've never known you wrong. Well, well, well! And how are they?

PSMITH [*woodenly*]: Who?

COOTES [*boisterously*]: Why, the boys, my dear chap!

PSMITH: Oh, the boys?

COOTES: Yes – the dear old lads! [*Slapping* PSMITH *on the shoulder.*] What times those were!

PSMITH: Which?

COOTES: The times we used to have together.

PSMITH: Oh, those?

COOTES: I'd love you to come and have a drink with me. In fact, I'd insist on it – only my fool of a manservant has sent me out this morning without a penny in my pockets. Dam' careless of him! I shall sack him when I get home.

PSMITH: I would.

COOTES: All the same, I hate to give up a good idea. Don't you think we *might* wet our whistles together somewhere – and a mouthful of lunch, perhaps, and a pow-wow about old days?

PSMITH: Pass along, comrade.

COOTES: My dear old boy – surely you don't suggest – ?

PSMITH [*reciting solemnly*]: Look in my face; my name is Might Have Been.

I am also called No Hope – So Long – Farewell!

[PSMITH *regards* COOTES *steadily.* COOTES *immediately drops his boisterous manner.*]

COOTES: Nothing doing, guv'nor?

PSMITH: Nothing.

COOTES: No hope?

PSMITH: You have no more hope than a hen trying to lay a foundation-stone.

COOTES [*resignedly, going*]: Oh, very well. [*Turning.*] There was no harm in trying, was there?

PSMITH: None whatever.

COOTES: You see, you looked such a perfect mug. I had to have a shot for it.

PSMITH: I quite understand.

COOTES: No offence?

PSMITH: Absolutely none.

COOTES: So long!

PSMITH: Farewell!

[*Exit* COOTES. *Enter* FREDDIE BOSHAM, *with an umbrella up.* PSMITH *turns and sees him.* FREDDIE *walks towards* PSMITH, *then hesitates when he sees the rhododendron, then passes on.* PSMITH *looks after him dubiously.* FREDDIE *turns and looks at* PSMITH *again, then comes back. They stand face to face.*]

There will be rain in London and the home counties tonight – if not sooner.

FREDDIE: I've forgotten the answer, old man, but you're evidently Persmith.

PSMITH: Psmith. The 'P' is silent, as in psalmon.

FREDDIE: Of course; I forgot. [*Pointing to the rhododendron.*] About that thing. I'm sorry.

PSMITH: So am I.

FREDDIE: When I said rhododendron, I really meant carnation.

PSMITH [*taking it out of his buttonhole*]: I see. And when you said noon precisely, you meant about half-past twelve.

FREDDIE: I have been to the dentist. You know how they hang on to one. Now let us get down to business.

PSMITH: For a start, suppose you tell me your name.

FREDDIE: Oh, didn't I do that? I'm Freddie Bosham, youngest son of the Earl of Middlewick, the notorious bibliophile.

PSMITH: I see. And you want me to murder him.

FREDDIE: Murder? Good gracious, no! Nothing like that at all.

PSMITH: Still, you said a crime.

FREDDIE: But not a shady, disreputable crime like that. I want you to come down and stay with us as our guest, and swipe a diamond necklace belonging to my stepmother.

PSMITH: Oh, I see; that's different. Well, let's start!

FREDDIE: But we must have lunch first. We'll hop into the old Morpheus, just along the street, and have a stab at the steak and kidney pudding. Do you know the place?

PSMITH: I've been inside it – once.

FREDDIE: Stop! I forgot; we must be businesslike. What are your terms for pinching a diamond necklace?

[PSMITH *considers; then:*]

PSMITH: Is it a town or country job?

FREDDIE: Country – Shropshire.

[*Sound of the lift ascending.*]

PSMITH [*suddenly*]: Shropshire? What part of Shropshire?

FREDDIE: Blandings Castle.

PSMITH: Blandings Castle?

[*The* LIFT MAN *has reappeared at the entrance.*]

[*Throwing* LIFT MAN *the rhododendron.*] I'll do it for nothing!

[*Taking* FREDDIE'S *arm.*] Come on!

BLACK OUT *and* CURTAIN.

SCENE THREE

*The lounge of the Morpheus Club – a little hall just inside the front door.
Up right is an exit to the street, with umbrella-stand. Swing-doors opening
into the dining-room are in the L. wall, and above these swing-doors an
exit to the coat-room. A door down R. leads to a waiting-room. A table and
chairs.* MISS RUMBELOW, *a Club waitress, is discovered telephoning, at
the door of the coat-room. She is a prim, severe person, with spectacles. She
wears a black livery, with rather long skirt and an old-fashioned striped
waistcoat, and a white frilled cap with a black band round it.*

[EVE *enters, from the street, carrying* WALDERWICK'S *umbrella.*]

EVE: Is this the Morpheus Club, please?

RUMBELOW: Yes. [*Looking at* EVE *disapprovingly.*] And it's a Club
for gentlemen only. And noblemen, of course.

EVE: I know. That's why I'm here. I want to see Lord Middlewick.
Could you find him for me?

RUMBELOW: I might – but only as a favour, mind you. I'm
appointed here to look after hats and coats; it's no part of my
duty to be doing the page-boy's work. And he won't be back till
the day after tomorrow, little nuisance!

EVE: What's the matter with him?

RUMBELOW [*with a refined shudder*]. Green apples, I believe. [*Into
telephone.*] Hallo, is that Hatchard's? Lord Middlewick thinks he
left his glasses in your Antique Book Department this morning.
Will you inquire, please? You'll ring me up? The Morpheus
Club. Thanks. Bye-bye [*To* EVE.] I am afraid I can't permit you
to loiter about here; the ladies' annexe is through there.

EVE: But where is Lord Middlewick?

RUMBELOW: He's having his lunch, and a nice temper he's in. He
can't find his mouth.

[RUMBELOW *puts down the telephone and goes.* EVE'S *eye falls
on the umbrella, which she has laid down. She picks it up, and looks
round; then tiptoes to the umbrella-stand and puts it in with the other
umbrellas.* MISS RUMBELOW *re-appears.* EVE *hastily sits down.*]

EVE: Will he see me?

RUMBELOW: He can't see you. He can't see anybody until he gets his glasses back; but he'll talk to you. Oh, yes, he'll talk. Will you step right into the ladies' annexe. I'll pull up the blinds. We don't use it much. [*Exit* RUMBELOW *to the waiting-room.*]

[EVE *is about to follow her when* PSMITH *enters through the double doors.*]

PSMITH: Please don't go.

EVE: Have you got into this Club *again*?

PSMITH: Yes. But it's all right this time: I've been lunching with a member – Mr Bosham.

EVE: Are you sure? Where is this Mr Bosham?

PSMITH: We were coming out of the dining-room together, when he stopped to listen to another member who was reciting.

EVE: What was he reciting about?

PSMITH: His umbrella!

EVE: Mr Walderwick? [EVE *tries to maintain her gravity for a moment, then laughs, so does* PSMITH.] It's all right; I've put the umbrella back!

PSMITH: Good! And are you lunching here too?

EVE: No. I'm here for my appointment, about that job.

PSMITH: I hope you get it.

EVE: Thank you! You're nice.

PSMITH: In fact, you must get it.

EVE: Why are you so anxious?

PSMITH: Because I'm going to Blandings too.

EVE: Oh! What fun! As a guest?

PSMITH: Well, it's one of those semi-professional visits. Not quite congenial; but after all, one must live. It's not easy to live these days.

EVE [*with feeling*]: No, it is not.

PSMITH: Are you hard up?

EVE [*smiling*]: Yes.

PSMITH: So am I. Let's sit down.

EVE: All right. [EVE *sits in a chair,* PSMITH *on the hearthrug.*] What is your profession?

PSMITH: I have just given it up. It was fish.

EVE: Fish!

PSMITH: Yes. My only relative is an uncle who dotes on fish. Four years ago an opening occurred in his fish business, and he thrust me into it, head first. Three days ago I realized that fish and I had reached the limits of mutual forbearance. I resigned. For three days I've been a free man – and for three days the wolf has been moaning at my door. Now tell me the story of *your* life!

EVE: Oh, I'm not in your class at all. You seem to have been rich once: I've been hard up always. I'm a free-lance journalist. I write rapturous descriptions of other people's clothes at smart parties, and try to get them published in the papers.

PSMITH: I see. And whose clothes are you going to be rapturous about at Blandings? Lord Middlewick's?

EVE: No. I'm going there to catalogue the library. But you haven't told me yet why you're going.

PSMITH: Well, it's this way –

[MISS RUMBELOW *re-enters.*]

RUMBELOW [*to* EVE]: I think I informed you this was for gentlemen only.

EVE [*rising*]: I'm so sorry!

RUMBELOW: Will you be so kind as to step right into the ladies' annexe.

EVE: Very well. [*To* PSMITH.] *Au revoir!*

[PSMITH *rises. Exit* EVE. *Enter from the dining-room* FREDDIE *and* WALDERWICK, *a vacant youth.*]

WALDERWICK: And what I say is, if a Club can't protect the property of its members – well, who's property can it protect? I say, Gladys, hasn't anything been heard of my umbrella? –

RUMBELOW: Miss Rumbelow to you, Mr Walderwick!

WALDERWICK: Well, I'm going to write to the Committee about it. They ought to call a general meeting, and consider the whole question. Will you come, Freddie?

FREDDIE: Like a bird, old man!

WALDERWICK [*seeing* PSMITH]: If they call a general meeting to consider the whole question, will you come, sir?

PSMITH: I'll take the chair. But what was your umbrella like?

WALDERWICK: It had a white ivory handle, with my name on. I am very particular about my umbrellas.

PSMITH [*going to the umbrella-stand and taking out the umbrella*]: Is this it?

WALDERWICK: Yes! Give it to me! I say, what a wonderful fellow you are! We've turned the Club upside down, and you go and put your hand right on it! Thank you so much. [MISS RUMBELOW *gives him his hat.*]So long, Freddie! [*Under his breath to* FREDDIE.] Who is this fellow? Has he something to do with Scotland Yard?

FREDDIE: Not yet, old soul! Goodbye! See you at Blandings tomorrow.

WALDERWICK: He's a wizard – that's the word, wizard! [*Exit to street.*]

FREDDIE: Is our coffee coming?

RUMBELOW: I'll inquire – to oblige! [*She goes into the dining-room.*]

FREDDIE: Now, why don't you like my scheme?

PSMITH: It is both crude and inartistic.

FREDDIE: Crude and – ?

PSMITH: Yes. But we'd better not be seen together by your father. Isn't he in the dining-room?

FREDDIE: Yes – standing lunch to Ralston McTodd, the Sweet Singer from Wisconsin. But he's lost his glasses; we're all right. Now, what's the matter with my scheme?

PSMITH: In the first place, I don't think we are being very kind to stepmother. When a piece of property changes hands, as this diamond necklace is going to do, I say that everybody concerned in the transaction ought to be left happy and satisfied.

FREDDIE: That sounds great. How's it going to be done? [*Enter* MISS RUMBELOW, *and puts down coffee and liqueurs.*]

PSMITH: } Thank you, Miss Rumbelow.
FREDDIE: }

    [*Exit* MISS RUMBELOW, *angrily.*]

FREDDIE [*looking round and seeing that the coast is clear*]: Now, how do we start?

PSMITH: Well, first of all, stepmother loses her diamonds. There's a fuss – tears – lamentations. You offer to buy her a new necklace. Haven't you five thousand pounds to do it with – your legacy?

FREDDIE: Yes. But I want that to buy my partnership with.

PSMITH: Wait! You write a cheque for the five thousand pounds. You sign it, and ask her to sign it as well. She thinks it's to buy the new necklace with. Does she sign?

FREDDIE: You bet she does! She daren't face second cousin Ethelberta without it.

PSMITH: Very well, then. We hand the cheque to old man Jackson, and he takes you into partnership. You can then marry Flossie –

FREDDIE: Phyllis!

PSMITH: Phyllis – and that's the end of you.

FREDDIE: Yes; but what about stepmother's new necklace? Where's that coming from now?

PSMITH: Nowhere. You simply take the old one out of your left sleeve, or wherever it is, carry it round to the nearest jeweller's, and have the stones re-set, or whatever they do to make necklaces look new – and present the result to dear stepmother with a loving kiss. And there we are! She gets her necklace – you get your girl – and no crime is committed – everybody's happy, and nobody's a bit the wiser.

FREDDIE [*rising*]: Psmith, this is genius!

PSMITH: No – just a happy knack!

FREDDIE: But what do you get out of it?

PSMITH: Never mind that. I'm satisfied.

FREDDIE: You're satisfied?

PSMITH: Quite satisfied!

FREDDIE: Well, I'm not – about one thing.

PSMITH: What's that?

FREDDIE: It's just a detail, but how are we going to disconnect stepmother from her necklace in the first instance?

PSMITH: We'll settle that in the train. What times does is start?

FREDDIE: Three-forty-five. We've still got an hour. I'll tell you what. Where's my hat?

PSMITH: Where are you going?

FREDDIE: There's a super film running at the Mayfair Picture Palace, just round the corner, which covers the whole situation.

PSMITH: What's it called?

FREDDIE: 'The Man with One Ear.' I'll run round and have another look at it. There's a scene where Desmond Vansittart – that's the hero – finds the pearls which One-eared Jake has pinched –

PSMITH: Righto! Go ahead! But remember one thing.

FREDDIE: What?

PSMITH: You're not going to be the hero of our show: you're going to be the villain. Don't worry about Desmond's technique. Watch Jake!

FREDDIE: I will! [*Exit* FREDDIE *to street.*]

[PSMITH *strolls down towards the door leading to the ladies' annexe. He is just edging through when* MISS RUMBELOW *appears from the dining-room.*]

RUMBELOW: Were you looking for your hat?

PSMITH: Er–yes.

RUMBELOW: I expect it's in here. Have you got a ticket for it?

PSMITH: No.

RUMBELOW: You'd better come in and find it yourself.

PSMITH: Presently. [*Going off into the coat-room.*]

[*Enter from the dining-room* LORD MIDDLEWICK *and* MCTODD, *who looks as black as thunder.* LORD MIDDLEWICK *bumps into a chair.*]

LORD MIDDLEWICK: I beg your pardon, sir! [*Peering about as usual – speaking to nobody in particular.*] Have my glasses arrived yet?

RUMBELOW [*at his elbow*]: They're on their way by special messenger.

LORD MIDDLEWICK: Well, be as quick as possible. It's most inconvenient. I haven't seen a dam' thing for the last two hours. [*Looking round.*] Oh dear, where has Mr McTodd gone? Ah, there you are! Won't you sit down? We won't go into the smoking-room: it's always full of people smoking.

MCTODD [*rather emphatically*]: I always smoke myself after lunch.

[LORD MIDDLEWICK *nearly knocks over* FREDDIE'S *coffee cup and liqueur glass.*]

LORD MIDDLEWICK [*peering*]: Bless my soul, what are these?

MCTODD: Coffee cups and brandy glasses. [LORD MIDDLEWICK *and* MCTODD *sit at the table.*] They're empty.

LORD MIDDLEWICK: Waitress. [RUMBELOW *approaches.*] Take away these things, at once!

RUMBELOW: Yes, my lord. [*Taking them and going out to the dining-room.*]

　　[MCTODD *groans.*]

LORD MIDDLEWICK: Now, what do you think I do every Thursday? I take a simple vegetable luncheon – a savoury dish of carrots, turnips, spinach, and, of course, brussels sprouts [MCTOOD *gets up, and walks about.*] Weren't they delicious? Did you ever taste anything like them in your own country?

MCTODD: Never, in any country! [*Making a fresh effort.*] Some people say that cigar-smoking affects the digestion. I don't believe it.

LORD MIDDLEWICK [*taking no notice*]: That dish which you had at lunch contained more protein, more vitamins, more calories, than its equivalent weight in beefsteak.

　　[*Enter* MISS RUMBELOW *with a large glass-topped cigar-case. She approaches.* MCTODD *puts out his hand.*]

RUMBELOW [*to* LORD MIDDLEWICK]: There is a Miss Halliday waiting to see you, my lord. [*She goes to the coat-room.*]

LORD MIDDLEWICK [*starting up*]: Oh dear me, so there is. I will come at once. Make yourself at home, Mr McTodd. Relax and rest; you sound a little tired to me. No one will disturb you: this is Liberty Hall. [*Exit* LORD MIDDLEWICK *to the waiting-room.*]

　　[PSMITH *enters, and strolls down to where* MCTODD *is sitting, looking more furious than ever.*]

PSMITH: Have you enjoyed your man's meal, sir?

MCTODD: Like hell I have.

PSMITH: But I thought I saw you lunching with Lord Middlewick?

MCTODD [*rising and flaring up*]: Lord Middlewick? Curse Lord Middlewick! And your House of Lords! And the British Constitution! And the Star Chamber! And all swell pikers and brussels-sprout hounds!

PSMITH: Correct me if I am wrong, but I seem to detect in your manner a certain half-veiled annoyance. Is there anything the matter?

MCTODD [*shouting*]: The matter? Oh, nothing! Nothing whatever

– except that I came here for a square meal and a man's drink and an imported cigar, and that wall-eyed old penguin fed me a pile of garden garbage, and a glass of warm soda-water, and never a thing to smoke at all! And, what's more, he never let me get a word in edgeways the whole darn time. Was I born dumb?

PSMITH: I have no idea. Can't you remember?

MCTODD: Well, I wasn't! I like talking! I like eating! I like smoking! And now he's gone off to keep a date with some Jane in the back porch, and left me flat! [*Tries to open cigar-box and finds it is locked.*] Hell!

PSMITH: Scarcely the perfect host.

MCTODD: You said it! And if that cheap skate thinks I'm going to take any more chances on his hospitality, the sooner he comes out of the ether the better. [*Up to coat-room.*] Me go to Blandings Castle? Not on your life! I'd probably find brussels sprouts clinging to the walls, like poison ivy! [*To* RUMBELOW, *who is gazing at him from the coat-room.*] Hey you, check girl! Gimme my hat! [RUMBELOW *coldly hands him his hat and goes.*] And if that old total loss ever comes back, you can tell him from me that if he wants me he'll fine me at Simpson's, with a steak in my inside and a gun in my hand, waiting for him. Good-bye! [*Exit* MCTODD, *stamping, to the street.*]

[PSMITH *sinks down on to chair, in the place recently occupied by* MCTODD. LORD MIDDLEWICK'S *voice is heard off.*]

LORD MIDDLEWICK: We start immediately, Miss Halliday. [*Seeing* PSMITH:] Now, Mr McTodd! [PSMITH, *taken aback, rises. Picture.*] Pray sit down again. I am waiting for a Miss Halliday, who is going to accompany us to Blandings.

PSMITH [*enthusiastically*]: Miss Halliday? We are going to Blandings together. Ooh!

LORD MIDDLEWICK: Precisely, Mr McTodd. I am glad to observe a new and welcome note of animation in your voice.

PSMITH [*half to himself*]: I should think so!

LORD MIDDLEWICK: At luncheon you seemed to me a little distrait – a trifle depressed. You were not yourself, were you?

PSMITH: No.

LORD MIDDLEWICK: Now, you sound like a different man
altogether.

PSMITH: I am a different man altogether.

LORD MIDDLEWICK: Come, that's better! Do you mind if I tell
you something personal?

PSMITH: Go ahead, sir.

LORD MIDDLEWICK: I don't believe you're a poet at all –
[PSMITH *is alarmed.*]

– you're quite a human being. [*Taking his arm.*] How on earth
you came to write all that –

PSMITH: Bilge?

LORD MIDDLEWICK: Yes – damme! – bilge!

PSMITH [*nodding*]: Bilge is the word.

LORD MIDDLEWICK: I can't imagine. You don't sound like that
sort of creature, and when I get my glasses I don't suppose you'll
look like one, either. You are at present floating dimly before
my eyes – like –

PSMITH [*helpfully*]: Like a rusty goldfish in a muddy aquarium?

LORD MIDDLEWICK: Precisely. How do you *think* of these things?

PSMITH: My life is closely bound up with fish.

LORD MIDDLEWICK: Eh?

PSMITH: Only this morning I received a most pressing letter from
the editor of the Fishmongers' 'Gazette,' asking me to write him
a serial – in verse, of course – about a fish.

LORD MIDDLEWICK: About a *fish*?

PSMITH: Yes.

LORD MIDDLEWICK: But what was it to be called?

PSMITH: Herbert the Turbot.

[*Enter* MISS RUMBELOW *with a package.*]

RUMBELOW: Your glasses, my lord.

LORD MIDDLEWICK [*taking the package*]. Thank you. Now, Mr
McTodd, I shall see you in your true colours! [*Beginning to fumble
with the package.*]

[*Enter* FREDDIE.]

FREDDIE: Hallo, Psmith!

LORD MIDDLEWICK: Psmith! Don't be an idiot, my boy. There is
no one called Smith here.

FREDDIE: But, Dad –

PSMITH [*readily*]: Shut up! Are you looking for Mr Smith, Mr Bosham? Here he is, coming out of the dining-room. [*Pointing at nothing at all.*] He wants to say good-bye to you. [*He pushes the bewildered* FREDDIE *towards the dining-room door, explaining in dumb show.*]

> [LORD MIDDLEWICK *and* MISS RUMBELOW, *absorbed in opening the package, do not notice, as each is hindering the other.* PSMITH *whispering:*]

I'm McTodd!

FREDDIE [*grasping the idea, and going over to dining-room door*] My dear Psmith, how glad I am not to have missed you! You elusive fellow! Ha, ha, ha!

> [*He takes the invisible* PSMITH'S *arm and goes up to the street entrance. Shaking hands vigorously.*]

Well, good-bye, old fish, and heaven preserve! Say goodbye to McTodd. There he is! [*Points to* PSMITH. *Ventriloquially:*] Goodbye, Mr McTodd, sir.

PSMITH: Goodbye, Psmith, I'm delighted to have had the opportunity of seeing the last of you.

FREDDIE: Goodbye, Lord Middlewick.

LORD MIDDLEWICK.: Goodbye, Mr Psmith

> [*Exit* FREDDIE, *still arm in arm with nobody.* EVE *enters, and stands gazing in astonishment after him.*]

LORD MIDDLEWICK [*getting his glasses out at last, and turning suddenly on* PSMITH, *taking him by the shoulders and turning him round.*]: A-a-ah! I was right! I knew you wouldn't look like a poet. I'm going to like you, Mr McTodd!

EVE [*astonished*]: Mr McTodd! Is that Mr McTodd?

LORD MIDDLEWICK [*jovially*]: Yes; allow me to introduce you. Miss Eve Halliday, Mr Ralston McTodd.

EVE: How do you do, Mr McTodd? I know your wife.

BLACK OUT *and* CURTAIN.

ACT TWO

Scene: The Oak Gallery at Blandings, as before.
Time: It is nine o'clock, on the following evening.
The sun is just beginning to set: by the end of the act it is moonlight.
A gramophone on the table is playing, with EVE *in charge.*
The double doors are wide open, and chairs are seen set in rows in the library, overflowing into the Gallery. The circular settee is gone.
FREDDIE *and* PHYLLIS *are dancing together, so are* AGATHA *and* WALDERWICK. BELLOWS *appears on terrace, puts down coffee tray on the table and goes.*

The music stops. FREDDIE *and* PHYLLIS *applaud.*

FREDDIE: Go on, Miss Halliday; there's time for one more record before the gang arrives.

AGATHA: We shall get into a row for slipping away, anyhow.

FREDDIE: Let her go, Miss Halliday!

PHYLLIS: You dance with Miss Halliday this time, Freddie.

FREDDIE: All right. Come on, Miss Halliday!

EVE: Me? No, thank you; I know my place! I'm Baxter's Wage Slave! I'll work this. [*Putting on a record.*]

FREDDIE: Come along! Don't be silly.

PHYLLIS: Go on, Miss Halliday!

[*The gramophone starts,* FREDDIE *dances with* EVE, WALDERWICK *with* PHYLLIS. AGATHA *and another girl are about to dance together, when* LORD MIDDLEWICK *wanders in from library. He takes* AGATHA *and begins to dance with her, very solemnly.*]

LADY MIDDLEWICK, ETHELBERTA FITZWIGGIN, BAXTER *and* PSMITH *appear on the terrace.*]

LADY MIDDLEWICK: Eustace!

[LORD MIDDLEWICK *hastily stops dancing.* AGATHA *and the other girl run off, followed by* WALDERWICK.]

FREDDIE: Hallo, Mother!

LADY MIDDLEWICK: Stop that dreadful noise at once.

FREDDIE: Yes, Mother.

[EVE *runs and stops gramophone.*]

LADY MIDDLEWICK: And come out here. We want five minutes' absolute peace before all these people arrive.

FREDDIE: Righto!

[*The party settle down.* EVE *is arranging chairs,* LORD MIDDLEWICK *is conning a speech.* BAXTER *hands round coffee.* PSMITH *stands with his back turned.* LORD MIDDLEWICK *is stealing off.*]

LADY MIDDLEWICK: Eustace, where are you going to?

LORD MIDDLEWICK: I have to learn up my speech for tomorrow, dear – the Diddlecombe Institute, you know.

LADY MIDDLEWICK: It must wait; you have other duties tonight. Come and drink your coffee.

[LORD MIDDLEWICK *goes on to terrace.*]

LORD MIDDLEWICK [*looking round furtively*]: Where is Miss Peavey?

LADY MIDDLEWICK: She went upstairs to finish unpacking. She hadn't time before dinner.

LORD MIDDLEWICK: Then I'll stay.

LADY MIDDLEWICK: Of course you'll stay. Here's your coffee. Mr Baxter, give Lord Middlewick some sugar.

BAXTER [*taking the sugar*]: Yes, Lady Biddlewick. [*Sneezing violently.*]

LADY MIDDLEWICK: Where did you get that dreadful cold?

BAXTER: I ibagine it bust be through spendig sub tide id the garded late last dight.

FREDDIE: Id the garded – at dight? Baxter, I'm surprised at you! [BAXTER *is about to give him a reproving look, when he sneezes again, this time over* LORD MIDDLEWICK, *who is much annoyed.* FREDDIE *takes two cups of coffee, then leans over balustrade and calls – 'Agatha! – Walderwick! Coffee!' He hands down cups to the pair, who are below out of sight.* BAXTER *comes into the gallery, and sits at the table.*]

LADY MIDDLEWICK: Now, everybody, please listen to the arrangements for tonight.

ETHELBERTA: Will there be a crowd, Anastasia?

LADY MIDDLEWICK: No, Ethelberta. Just a few old friends. Everything will be quite informal. Freddie!

[FREDDIE *comes to the table for coffee. He takes coffee to* PHYLLIS.]

ETHELBERTA [*to* PSMITH]: What a nice useful word 'informal' is, Mr McTodd.

[PSMITH *takes no notice.*]

[*Louder.*] Mr McTodd!

FREDDIE [*seeing that* PSMITH *does not recognize his own name*]: McTodd, old man – you!

PSMITH: I beg your pardon! Day dreams – day dreams. [*To* ETHELBERTA.] I am sure you were saying something.

ETHELBERTA: When my cousin Anastasia says that a party is informal, she means that guests are expected to arrive after dinner and leave without any supper. [*She laughs acidly.*]

[PSMITH *smiles faintly, comes forward into gallery, and stands gazing at* EVE, *in library.*]

LADY MIDDLEWICK [*turning to* ETHELBERTA]: By the way, darling, I haven't asked you what you think of the Dulworthy diamonds. [*She is wearing the necklace.*] Don't they look rather lovely? Now, everybody, I have a delightful surprise for you. Miss Peavey and Mr McTodd have promised to read for us from their works tonight.

FREDDIE: Both at once?

LADY MIDDLEWICK: Don't be silly, dear.

FREDDIE: Well, Layton and Johnstone do. Where is it going to happen?

LADY MIDDLEWICK: In the library, at half-past nine. [*Indicating chairs.*] Everything is ready.

ETHELBERTA: What are you going to read to us, Mr McTodd?

PSMITH: H'm! I must think. Lady Middlewick, have you by any chance a copy of my poor poems in your house?

LADY MIDDLEWICK: Of course we have.

PSMITH: Are they in the library?

LADY MIDDLEWICK: Yes – in the place of honour.

PSMITH: Then I'll run in and give them the works – a preliminary perusal.

LADY MIDDLEWICK: Oh, Mr Baxter will get them for you. Famous poets must not run their own errands.

PSMITH: Ah, but I'm not a famous poet. Sometimes I wonder to myself whether I am a poet at all.

LADY MIDDLEWICK: Isn't his modestly delightful? Of course you are a poet.

PSMITH: I don't really feel like one.

LORD MIDDLEWICK [*cordially*]: And he doesn't look like one! I noticed that when I met him. His hair's short, for one thing.

PSMITH [*solemnly*]: Yes. And it's quite possible that within a few weeks' time it will be much shorter. [*He joins* EVE *in the library. They disappear off.*]

FREDDIE [*looking after him*]: Ha, ha, ha! Very droll! Very droll! [*To* PHYLLIS.] The fathead!

[LORD MIDDLEWICK *begins to walk up and down, muttering to himself.*]

LADY MIDDLEWICK: Eustace, don't walk about like a hyena. This is not Whipsnade. Sit down and concentrate.

LORD MIDDLEWICK: I am concentrating.

LADY MIDDLEWICK: Yes – on foundation-stones. I want you to think of a few words of introduction for tonight, about Miss Peavey and Mr McTodd.

LORD MIDDLEWICK: I won't. I don't know what to say.

LADY MIDDLEWICK: Mr Baxter will help you to prepare something.

BAXTER [*rising from his table*]: Subthig is prepared, Lord Biddlewick. [*Handing him a paper.*]

LORD MIDDLEWICK [*taking it*]: Thank you, Baxter. What a curse you are.

[BAXTER *goes out.*]

ETHELBERTA: What did you and Miss Peavey talk about at dinner, Eustace?

LORD MIDDLEWICK: Fairies! *Fairies!* I don't think she's quite right in her head.

LADY MIDDLEWICK: Nonsense! Hush! Here she is.

[MISS PEAVEY *enters on the terrace. She is young and attractive-looking, with an intense and ethereal expression. She stands with clasped hands gazing towards the garden, taking no notice of anybody.*]

Ah, dear Miss Peavey! Come and enjoy the sunset!

[MISS PEAVEY *takes no notice. She continues to gaze, then comes slowly right down stage, as in a trance.* FREDDIE *and* PHYLLIS *follow her. She gazes at audience, then goes back to balustrade. All watch her, breathlessly. Presently she speaks, in a strained and exalted voice.*]

MISS PEAVEY: Listen, folks. Is this real, or am I in some place in fairyland? [*Gazing out on the garden.*] Oh!

LORD MIDDLEWICK: There you are!

LADY MIDDLEWICK [*to* FREDDIE]: I told you she lived in a world of her own.

FREDDIE: But she can't have this one. It's ours.

MISS PEAVEY [*to* LADY MIDDLEWICK]: Can you see them? Do you observe them?

[*All rise to look.*]

LADY MIDDLEWICK: See what, Miss Peavey?

MISS PEAVEY: Fairies!

[*All sit again.*]

The cutest little real fairies, running around among those elegant flower-beds!

LADY MIDDLEWICK: What a charming thought!

FREDDIE [*to* PHYLLIS]: Potty!

MISS PEAVEY [*leaning over balustrade, and looking into the garden*]: And what are those white things glittering in the heart of the sunset? Fairy palaces?

LORD MIDDLEWICK: [*going to balustrade, and looking over*]. They are cucumber frames!

[ETHELBERTA *rises and takes her coffee to balustrade.*]

LADY MIDDLEWICK: Tomorrow my husband will take you round everywhere, and show you the rest of our sights. By the way, this is my stepson, Frederick.

MISS PEAVEY: [*gazing at him*]. Oh! A big man!

FREDDIE: One of our outsize local goblins.

MISS PEAVEY: Lord Middlewick, may I ask a favour of you right now?

LORD MIDDLEWICK [*cautiously*]: Oh, certainly, certainly!

MISS PEAVEY: May I come out here at nights, all alone, after sundown, and watch my elves and fairies dance around by the light of the glow-worms and the lightning-bugs –

LORD MIDDLEWICK: Bugs?

MISS PEAVEY: And may I come out here mornings, too, before sun-up, and watch the early dew fading off of the grass?

LADY MIDDLEWICK: Of course you shall, dear Miss Peavey. But you must be careful of the damp, you know. We can't have you catching a chill. Now sit down and have a cup of coffee. I know you Americans like that. Have you had a chat with your fellow-countryman yet – Mr McTodd?

MISS PEAVEY [*dramatically*]: No. He scares me. I guess he's a bad man. He don't love fairies. I can't tune in on his ego. Just what is his line?

LADY MIDDLEWICK: He writes wonderfully modern poetry.

FREDDIE: About mud. You must let him have the garden on wet nights.

[LADY MIDDLEWICK *is handing coffee.*]

MISS PEAVEY [*suddenly noticing* LADY MIDDLEWICK'S *diamonds*]: Oh, oh, oh!

LADY MIDDLEWICK: [*putting the coffee down again*]. What's the matter, Miss Peavey?

MISS PEAVEY [*pointing*]: Those lovely beads! Oh!

LADY MIDDLEWICK: My diamonds! Yes, they are rather sweet, aren't they?

MISS PEAVEY: Diamonds! Are those really diamonds? Oh! [*Beginning to weep into her handkerchief.*]

LADY MIDDLEWICK: What are you crying for, dear Miss Peavey?

MISS PEAVEY: I can't help it! I always think that diamonds are fairies' tears, turned to ice by the cold world around them.

[FREDDIE *and* LORD MIDDLEWICK *each make desperate noises.*]

LADY MIDDLEWICK: Dear Miss Peavey, I'll put them away! I won't wear them.

MISS PEAVEY: [*recovering herself*]. No. Pain is often an inspiration. Leave them lay – keep right on wearing them.

[*Enter* BELLOWS.]

BELLOWS: Lord Chipstead and party are in the drawing-room, my lady.

LADY MIDDLEWICK: Very well. [*Exit* BELLOWS.] Come along, everybody! People have begun to arrive. [*Going to balustrade, and in an undertone to* LORD MIDDLEWICK.] Eustace, give Miss Peavey your arm. She is a little upset. [*Goes out with* ETHELBERTA.]

[LORD MIDDLEWICK *reluctantly gives his arm to* MISS PEAVEY, *who rises and looks back at the garden*.]

MISS PEAVEY: Listen, lord! Do you have any nightingales located around here?

LORD MIDDLEWICK: A few.

MISS PEAVEY: I guess the nightingales are the angel voices of the Great Outdoors.

LORD MIDDLEWICK: Mind the step.

[*Exit* MISS PEAVEY *and* LORD MIDDLEWICK. FREDDIE *and* PHYLLIS *gaze after them*.]

FREDDIE [*quoting*]: 'We must all be very kaind to Auntie Jessie.' She's cuckoo!

PHYLLIS: Never mind her: we've got troubles of our own. Freddie, this man Psmith of yours is perfectly useless.

FREDDIE: He's worse – he's dangerous. Half the time he doesn't even remember his name's McTodd. What's the matter with him?

PHYLLIS: Can't you see? He's in love.

FREDDIE: With Miss Peavey, or Cousin Ethelberta?

PHYLLIS: Idiot! Miss Halliday!

FREDDIE: Oh, well, he mustn't. He's under contract to us. I'll fix him. Oy – Psmith!

PSMITH [*calling from the library*]: Hallo!

FREDDIE: Wanted!

PSMITH: Right away, sir!

PHYLLIS: We've got to get a move on, Freddie. Dad says he must have the cheque tomorrow.

FREDDIE: If Psmith goes on at his present rate there won't be any tomorrow. Another gag like that one about wearing his hair shorter, and so far as we are concerned life in this planet will cease.

[PSMITH *enters unnoticed, and sits in one of the chairs. He begins to clap and stamp solemnly.*]

Ah, here you are! Now, listen to me!

PSMITH [*producing a mauve book*]: 'Across the pale parabola of joy.'

PHYLLIS: } Across the what?
FREDDIE:

PSMITH: 'Across the pale parabola of joy.' Can you throw out any kind of suggestion as to what that is likely to mean?

FREDDIE: Why?

PSMITH: Because I wrote it – at least, McTodd did. I've got to recite it tonight.

FREDDIE: Never mind that. What about fulfilling your contract, old man?

PSMITH: Contract?

PHYLLIS: Yes. Diamonds!

[FREDDIE *and* PHYLLIS *are now kneeling on the chairs, talking to* PSMITH *over the backs.*]

FREDDIE: And not hearts! Why don't you start something? What's the matter with you?

PHYLLIS: Don't ask him, Freddie. He knows. [*To* PSMITH:] You're in love.

PSMITH: Ah! Then you've noticed it too? Already the whisper runs round the fair country of Salop: 'Psmith has been wrecked on a permanent wave.'

FREDDIE: Well, we're the lifeboat crew, and we're in a hurry. Phyllis's old pop won't keep my job open after tomorrow. Get down to it, laddie! Be executive! Action!

PSMITH [*rising, and going to terrace*]: Don't rush me. All in good time! I've got this job to attend to first. [*Indicating book.*] Let me get this Pale Parabola of Joy off my chest, and the diamonds are yours.

FREDDIE: Well, go carefully. No more funny stuff about short hair, or anything of that kind. You should have seen Baxter's ears stand up when you said it. He's convinced there's something fishy about you.

PSMITH: Fishy? Not that word, I beg! But Baxter has been on my track from the start. The human bloodhound! [*Proudly.*] I'm responsible for his cold.

FREDDIE: } You?
PHYLLIS: }

PSMITH: Yes – me. I'm sleeping out – in the keeper's cottage at the end of the Yew Walk. There it is. [*Going to the balustrade and pointing down.*]

PHYLLIS: Why?

PSMITH: Well, I suppose if you write 'Songs of Squalor' you rather ask for that sort of accommodation. Anyhow, Baxter was hanging about outside my rural nest at two o'clock this morning – in pink pyjamas and a heavy shower of rain. That's why he badaged to get that bad cold in his dose.

[WALDERWICK'S *voice off.*]

PHYLLIS: Look out! They're coming back!

PSMITH: We mustn't be seen together. Give me ten minutes to mug up this stuff, and then I'll join you.

FREDDIE: Where?

PSMITH: In the middle of the fourth rhododendron bush in the West Shrubbery.

FREDDIE: Righto! Don't be long. [*They go out through the terrace.*]
[PSMITH *takes up his book again, and sits at the table on the terrace.*]

PSMITH [*calling after* FREDDIE]: And when I say rhododendron I don't mean carnation. 'Across the pale parabola of joy – '
[*Enter* LADY MIDDLEWICK, MISS PEAVEY *and* LORD CHIPSTEAD, *Christopher Walderwick's father, a deaf old gentleman,* BAXTER *follows with* ETHELBERTA.]

LADY MIDDLEWICK: Now, Miss Peavey, I'm going to show you our sunset. The Blandings sunsets are quite famous, you know.

MISS PEAVEY: That'll be too lovely.

LORD CHIPSTEAD: What's that you're saying, Anastasia?

LADY MIDDLEWICK [*shouting*]: Our sunsets are famous, Cousin Henry.

ETHELBERTA [*to* BAXTER]: As a substitute for other forms of
hospitality.

BAXTER: Oh, Miss Fitzwiggin! [*He sniggers.*]

   [LORD CHIPSTEAD goes to the terrace. ETHELBERTA *follows
him.* BAXTER *detains* MISS PEAVEY *at the table, where she writes
in his autograph book.*]

LADY MIDDLEWICK: Why, here's Mr McTodd!

   [PSMITH *looks up from his book, talking to himself.*]
Everybody is coming out to the Yew Walk, to see the sunset.
Won't you?

PSMITH [*rising*]: Dear Lady Middlewick, may I stay here? I have an
appointment.

LADY MIDDLEWICK: An appointment? With whom?

PSMITH: With my muse.

LADY MIDDLEWICK: Muse?

PSMITH: Yes, with my muse – not at my mews. You know – one
of the well-known family of nine. I wish to steep myself in one
of my own poor efforts, for the recital. All I ask is a moment's
solitude.

LADY MIDDLEWICK: Of course. You shan't be disturbed.

   [CHRISTOPHER WALDERWICK *and* AGATHA CROFTON
enter, chattering and pushing each other about.]
Hush, hush! Christopher and Agatha, run and tell all the other
people to go out by the drawing-room window. Mr McTodd
must not be disturbed here.

WALDERWICK: Righto, Auntie!

   [*They rush out together.*]

LADY MIDDLEWICK: Come along, everybody! Au revoir, Mr
McTodd.

   [LADY MIDDLEWICK, LORD CHIPSTEAD, *and* ETHELBER-
TA *go out through the terrace.* BAXTER *lingers, with* MISS
PEAVEY.]

PSMITH: Au revoir, Auntie. [*Sitting again at table on terrace.*]

BAXTER: Mr McTodd, Miss Peavey has just dud be a great [*sneeze*]
favour. She has written her dame in by autograph book. Will
you do the sabe, od the sabe page?

PSMITH: May I have that honour, Miss Peavey?

MISS PEAVEY: Why, sure!

PSMITH [*to* BAXTER]: Avez vous a fountain plume?

    [BAXTER *offers a fountain-pen and the book, open at the right page.*]

PSMITH [*reading*]: 'Aileen Peavey'. [*Writing.*] 'Ralston McTodd'. There! Where are your Sitwells the noo? [*Handing back the book.*]

    [BAXTER *looks at the signature, then closes the book with a little nod.*]

    BAXTER [*going*]. Thank you, Bister McTodd [*Exit.*]

MISS PEAVEY: Oh, Mr McTodd, won't you be lonesome?

PSMITH: Oh, no. I've lots of funny little thoughts to keep me company.

MISS PEAVEY: But don't you want to come along and see the sunset? [*Raptly.*] Whenever I see a sunset, it seems like I am looking at a great ball of gold sinking right down into an ocean of silver.

PSMITH: And whenever I see a sunset, I always think of a great big poached egg bursting on a Turkey carpet. Don't pinch that – it's copyright. So long!

    [MISS PEAVEY, *looking thoroughly annoyed, goes off through the terrace.* PSMITH *resumes his seat, and begins to memorize the poem again.* EVE *appears from the library.*]

EVE: Mr McTodd!

PSMITH [*rising*]: Hallo!

EVE: Have all those people gone at last?

PSMITH: Every one.

EVE [*shyly*]: Have you anything to do for the next five minutes?

PSMITH: Nothing in the world. [*Throwing his book on the floor of the terrace.*] Come along! [*They sit.*]

EVE: I've given Mr Baxter the slip. I felt I must have a chat with you.

PSMITH: And I'm aching for a chat with you! We haven't really met since we were introduced in the Morpheus Club yesterday.

EVE: No, I *was* surprised when I heard that you were Mr McTodd.

PSMITH: So was I.

EVE: Why?

PSMITH: I mean, I was surprised when you said you knew my wife.

EVE: But hasn't she ever mentioned my name to you?

PSMITH: Never to me. Wait a minute – what does she call you?

EVE: Just Eve.

PSMITH: Just Eve! And – what do you call her?

EVE: Just Cynthia.

PSMITH: Cynthia. [*With satisfaction.*] Cynthia! Thank you!

EVE: You can call me Eve, if you like.

PSMITH [*ecstatically*]: May I? Wonderful! Eve!

EVE: May I call you Ralston?

PSMITH: Why? [*Hastily.*] I mean, yes!

EVE [*smiling*]: Thank you. I'm asking this because – well – why should two good friends like you and me be so formal?

PSMITH: Why indeed? [*Taking another chair, and sitting closer.*]

EVE: Now, Ralston, I want to ask you a question. Aren't you treating Cynthia rather badly?

PSMITH: Cynthia? Have we got back to Cynthia again?

EVE: I think you sometimes forget that you are married to her. Now, don't you?

PSMITH [*turning to her solemnly*]: Sometimes I find it hard to remember that I know her at all.

EVE [*appealingly*]: Ralston, won't you tell me what the trouble was? Perhaps I could put it right.

PSMITH [*shaking his head solemnly*]: I doubt it.

EVE: Won't you confide in me? You've been so sweet to me that I can't believe you are the sort of man that Cynthia says you are.

PSMITH: You're right. I'm not.

EVE: I thought not. It's Cynthia's fault after all. [*Rising.*] I always suspected it. Let me talk to her, and bring you together again.

PSMITH [*rising*]: I thank you. [*Taking her hand. She gives it quite willingly.*] I thank you a thousand times. But love, dear Eve – may I say dearest Eve? – is a delicate and tender plant. There are certain things which it can never survive. Rashers of bacon, for instance.

EVE: Rashers of bacon?

PSMITH: Yes – rashers of bacon, slung at a husband across a breakfast-table.

EVE: Slung?

PSMITH [*nodding*]: Complete with dish.

EVE: Cynthia did that?

PSMITH: You ask her. [*Suddenly.*] No – don't!

EVE [*moving away*]: But I shall! I can't understand it. She used to be such a gentle creature. She can't have meant it. Did she miss you?

PSMITH: Not the third time.

EVE: Oh, I *must* bring you closer. [*Offering her hand again impetuously.*] Ralston!

PSMITH: [*taking it*]. Eve!
   [*There is a silent pause, then a loud sneeze, and* BAXTER *appears on the terrace.*]

BAXTER: Miss Halliday, I have beed searching for you everywhere. I shall be obliged if you will come and tidy up the library for the recital.

EVE: Certainly, Mr Baxter.

BAXTER: As for you, sir – [*Sneezes violently and disappears from terrace.*]

EVE: I must run, Ralston. [*At door of library.*] I'll see you again. Tomorrow?

PSMITH: Rather! Come and inspect my cottage in the wood. The furniture is wrong: I'm sure it needs a few deft feminine touches.

EVE: All right.

PSMITH: But I'll see you before then, I hope.

EVE: If I can get away from Mr Baxter, we'll take a stroll by the lake before the recital. [*Coming back to him for a moment.*] You poor, poor thing! [*She runs out through the double doors*]
   [PSMITH *stands gazing after her, obviously divided between joy and perplexity.*]
   [FREDDIE *and* PHYLLIS *reappear on the terrace.*]

FREDDIE: Oy – Psmith! When are you coming? We're getting tired of the middle of that rhododendron bush, old man.

PSMITH: Then go and try the middle of the lake. You poor, poor thing! [*Exit through terrace.*]

FREDDIE: Goofy!

    [BAXTER *appears on terrace. Looks back after* PSMITH.]

BAXTER [*to* FREDDIE]: Hush!

FREDDIE: Hallo, Baxter!

BAXTER: Mr Frederick, this is bost fortunate. I bust see you alone for a bobent.

PHYLLIS: Don't I come in on this?

FREDDIE: If she doesn't, Baxter, count me out.

BAXTER: Certainly, Biss Jackson! You may be able to help. [*He has the autograph book in his hand.*] Mr Frederick, bay I ask you to exabine these two sigdatures? Do you see any resemblance between theb? [*Producing the autograph book and a letter.*]

FREDDIE [*reading*]: 'Ralston McTodd. Ralston McTodd.' They don't sound any different to me.

BAXTER: This is Mr McTodd's letter accepting Lady Biddlewick's invitation to stay here. This is the sigdature of Ralston McTodd, written id this book a quarter of ad hour ago by the bad who calls hibself Ralston McTodd. Ad impostor!

FREDDIE: Impostor!

BAXTER: Yes. He is not Ralston McTodd at all.

FREDDIE [*showing signs of great alarm*]: Oo – er! Then what's he doing here?

BAXTER: He has cub to steal the Dulworthy diabonds.

FREDDIE [*really frightened this time*]: Er – hur – hur – hur!

BAXTER: No wonder you look alarbed. The castle is at his bercy. You and I, Mr Frederick, as the only two able-bodied bed who know the secret, bust udite – udite to frustrate [*sneeze*] hib! [*Going.*] And, Biss Jackson, will you very kindly keep an eye on his confederate – Miss Halliday.

PHYLLIS: Miss Halliday? Is she one?

BAXTER: I am albost sure of it. They were in close codference dot five binutes ago, out here. Udfortunately I was udable to overhear what they were saying.

    [LORD MIDDLEWICK *appears with a manuscript in his hand.*]

LORD MIDDLEWICK: Baxter, will you kindly come here and explain what this first paragraph means. Something about 'a pair of gin-slingers with wide-open faces.'

BAXTER: 'A pair of twid siggers from the wide-open spaces,' Lord Biddlewick.

LORD MIDDLEWICK: Well, why the devil can't you write clearer? Come and read it to me.

BAXTER: Yes, Lord Biddlewick. [*Sneezes again and goes.*]

    [FREDDIE *and* PHYLLIS *sink on to chairs*]

FREDDIE [*resignedly*]: Goodbye, darling! I should have loved to marry you.

PHYLLIS: You are going to marry me, my lamb. Where *is* PSMITH?

    [PSMITH *enters from terrace.*]

PSMITH: Psmith is here!

FREDDIE: You heard what Baxter said?

PSMITH: Every word. And I'm going to down him. [*Reassuringly.*] I'm all right now. The cry rings out from the battlements: 'Psmith is himself again.'

FREDDIE: You've got a plan, old man?

PSMITH: Psmith always has a plan. Listen! Tomorrow the whole family goes foundation-stone laying. What times does the excursion move off?

FREDDIE: Ten-thirty.

PSMITH: Right. Do you have to go?

FREDDIE: I'm warned for it, but I'll wriggle out.

PSMITH: The foundation-stone is well and truly laid. The party return home. What do they find?

FREDDIE: What?

PSMITH: You and me lying bound and gagged on the library floor! And the Dulworthy diamonds gone from stepmother's dressing-table drawer!

FREDDIE: Who is going to bind and gag me?

PSMITH: I am.

FREDDIE: Oh! Well – who's going to do it to you?

PSMITH: Miss Jackson. [*To* PHYLLIS.] Will you?

PHYLLIS: Charmed.

PSMITH: Thank you so much. [*Shaking hands.*]

FREDDIE: And where are the diamonds?

PSMITH: In your pocket, where nobody finds them.

FREDDIE: In my –

PSMITH: Yes. You swiped them during stepmother's maid's luncheon hour. After that, all proceeds according to plan. Cheque for five thousand for Pop – partnership for you – new necklace for stepmother – and wedding bells for young Jackson here. What about it?

PHYLLIS: What about Miss Halliday? Baxter suspects her as well.

PSMITH: I know. I am going to warn her. You had better go and practise tying up Freddie, Miss Jackson. Get a clothes-line. Can you do reef-knots and clove-hitches?

PHYLLIS: Rather.

FREDDIE: She was a Girl Guide once. [PHYLLIS *and* FREDDIE *salute one another.*] Be prepared! [*They go.*]

[PSMITH *goes to the terrace; picks up the book, consults it, then lays it on the table. He then goes to the balustrade, evidently memorizing. It is getting rather dark. The sunset is glowing red.* EDDIE COOTES *enters from terrace. He is carrying a suitcase, and moves furtively.*]

COOTES [*cautiously*]: Ahem! [PSMITH *swings round.*] I say – dear old boy – I wonder if you could help me.

PSMITH: By all means. What do you want – the back door?

COOTES: Very good! Capital! No, I rather thought of the front. The fact is, I forgot to wire, so I've had to walk up from the station.

PSMITH [*with his back to the light – coming closer*]: You're coming to stay here?

COOTES: Yes, old man, temporarily. Lady Middlewick was very keen on my running down for the week-end.

PSMITH: Oh! You're a friend of Lady Middlewick's?

COOTES: By a sort of correspondence course. She wrote and invited me. I suppose she had heard of my work.

PSMITH: Your work?

COOTES: Yes. I wrote – [*Going to the table; picking up book.*] Hallo! Now, isn't that curious? One of my little volumes, lying right here.

PSMITH: What is your name?

COOTES: Ralston McTodd. I expect you've heard of me. [PSMITH *puts a hand on his shoulder, and turns him to the light.*] Here, I say!

PSMITH: It's no use, comrade. Once more, there is nothing doing.

COOTES: What do you mean – once more?

PSMITH: We met yesterday, outside Green Park tube station.

COOTES: You were the guy behind the rhododendron? [PSMITH *nods.*] And you know Ralston McTodd?

PSMITH: I ought to, by this time.

COOTES [*sinking down on chair by table, and dropping his hearty manner*]: Well, of all the rotten luck! Gee, I'm right out these days! It's kinda tough on a guy, ain't it?

PSMITH: It is unfortunate. What's your name?

COOTES: Cootes.

PSMITH: Your nationality?

COOTES: English, to start with. I got my education in Camden Town and my final polish in Chicago. What are you going to do with me, brother?

PSMITH: I take it your object in coming here was to have a pop at Lady Middlewick's diamonds?

COOTES: Sure.

PSMITH: And what made you suppose that the real McTodd wouldn't be here when you arrived?

COOTES: He told me he wasn't coming here.

PSMITH: He told you?

COOTES: I got acquainted with him yesterday afternoon – outside the Morpheus Club. He was madder than a hornet. Said he'd been insulted by this Lord Middlewick. I couldn't figure what it was all about, but he wasn't coming here at any price. I decided to take a chance, and – and –

PSMITH: Impersonate him?

COOTES: What you said. And now I have to bump right into a special friend of his. Hell!

PSMITH: You express the situation exactly. The cry goes round the underworld: 'Poor old Cootes has made a bloomer.'

COOTES: You needn't rub it in. Send for the Bulls.

PSMITH: The what?

COOTES: The Bulls.

PSMITH: We haven't any.

COOTES: The Fly Cops.

PSMITH: Do they?

COOTES: The Police Officers.

PSMITH: My dear comrade Cootes, I shall do no such thing.

COOTES [*rising, incredulously*]: You're going to let me go?

PSMITH: I am.

COOTES: Oh, guv'nor!

PSMITH: Pass away, quietly, friend. And the sooner you do it, the better pleased I shall be.

COOTES: Thank you – thank you! I'll hit the trail right away. [*Going.*] There was no harm in trying, was there?

PSMITH: None whatever.

COOTES: Give us a drink, guv'nor, just for old times' sake.

PSMITH: Well, I think I owe you that much. I'll get you something that will bring back the roses to those cheeks.

COOTES: Oh, guv'nor!

PSMITH: By the way, have you enough money for your railway ticket?

COOTES: No.

PSMITH: Then you'll have to walk.

[*Exit* PSMITH. COOTES *is following him when* MISS PEAVEY *appears on terrace. She sees* COOTES *and gives a ladylike little cough.* COOTES *turns and faces her. There is a gasp of astonishment from each.*]

MISS PEAVEY: *Eddie Cootes! is it?*

COOTES: *Smooth Lizzie! it is!*

[*They rush into each other's arms.*]

MISS PEAVEY: ⎫

⎪ [*together*] ⎰ You old rascal! What are you doing here, anyway? Gee, but I'm glad to see you!

COOTES: ⎪ ⎱ Lizzie – for goodness' sake! Can you beat it? Oh, gosh jiminy, this is fine!

⎭

[*They embrace again, then separate.* MISS PEAVEY *rearranges herself – then embraces him once more.*]

COOTES: Lizzie, you're prettier than ever!

MISS PEAVEY: Eddie, lay off of that! I got a lot to say to you before we get back to the heart stuff. Tell me, what are you doing around this dump? So far inland? Are you taking a vacation, or don't you work the boats no more?

COOTES: I had a vacation kinda forced on me, dearie.

MISS PEAVEY: The Cops? [*Consolingly.*] Tell Mother!

COOTES: No, not the Cops. Three weeks ago a great rough feller in a ship's smoking saloon nearly chewed my right thumb off. Look! [*Showing her a bandaged thumb.*]

MISS PEAVEY: Ain't the ocean dangerous! But what had you done, Eddie?

COOTES: I dealt myself five aces.

MISS PEAVEY: Eddie, I'm ashamed of you. You poor yap, where was your mind?

COOTES: I guess I left it behind in New York – right where I left my heart, three months ago!

MISS PEAVEY: I told you you'd never get anywhere without me, Eddie – not with that concrete dome of yours. Look at it. You didn't ought to be allowed around loose.

COOTES: I guess you're right, sweetie. Anyway, he bit me to the bone, the big brute! After that I couldn't make the cards behave nohow, so I had to come ashore and lay off. I've been around in London for two weeks now – out. Liz, I ain't had a bit of luck since the day you gave me the gate.

MISS PEAVEY: I'm not surprised, dearie.

COOTES: But say, what are you doing in this high-grade joint, anyway, and in that swell scenery?

MISS PEAVEY [*carelessly*]: Just visiting here.

COOTES: You're not married?

MISS PEAVEY: No. [*Cootes embraces her.*] Now, don't get fresh, Eddie.

COOTES: O, Lizzie! [*They embrace again.*] But what are you doing in a refined English home?

MISS PEAVEY: I'm pulling highbrow stuff. Soulful. You know the racket.

COOTES: You ain't been and retired?

MISS PEAVEY: Retired? Not me! I'm sitting in at a game with real worthwhile stakes. Di'monds, Eddie! Some of the best ice I've seen in years. Worth every cent of fifty thousand berries.

COOTES: Di'monds? Those Dulworthy di'monds? But that's what I'm after, too.

MISS PEAVEY: You are?

COOTES: Sure.

MISS PEAVEY: Great! We'll work together. Fifty-fifty.

COOTES: I'll say we will! But, Liz, I'm just going to get fired out.

MISS PEAVEY: You? Here?

COOTES: The darndest luck. I came to impersonate a poetical gink called McTodd. They'd asked him to visit here – and he didn't come after all – so –

MISS PEAVEY: But, Eddie, he's here!

COOTES: Here?

MISS PEAVEY: Sure. Him and me's dated in ten minutes' time to do a sister act right in this parlour – spilling poetry all over the place.

COOTES: Shush!

[*Enter* PSMITH *with two glasses of whisky and soda.*]

MISS PEAVEY [*resuming her refined accent*]: Oh, I want to have you know an old friend of mine – Mr Cootes – Mr McTodd.

COOTES: Hey, hey, hey! That bimbo's no more McTodd than I am.

MISS PEAVEY: Is that so? [*Swiftly.*] Got your gun, Eddie?

COOTES: Sure. [*Bringing out an automatic.*] Put 'em up! [PSMITH, *quite cool, looks at the gun, then takes a sip of whisky and soda.*] Put 'em up!

[PSMITH *raises his hands resignedly, with a glass in each hand.*]

MISS PEAVEY [*going to* PSMITH]: You dirty crook! [*She reaches up, and takes one glass from* PSMITH, *then takes a sip and hands it to* COOTES.] I knew that guy wasn't on the level the first time I lamped him.

COOTES: And I thanked him – *thanked* him – for letting me go! [*To* PSMITH, *who is trying to put his hand in his pocket.*] Keep them hands up!

MISS PEAVEY: Eddie, are we going to let him get away with it?

COOTES: Get away with fifty thousand smackers' worth of ice? [*Taking the other glass.*] Are we crazy?

PSMITH: But, dear friends – may I ask a question?

COOTES: ⎫
MISS PEAVEY: ⎭ What?

PSMITH: Yes – what? What are you going to do about it?

COOTES [*going to him, truculently*]: What are we going to do about it? I'll tell you what we're going to do about it. We're going to – we're going to – [*Feebly, to* MISS PEAVEY.] Say, what the hell *are* we going to do about it?

MISS PEAVEY: It's no use, Ed, he's got us framed.

PSMITH: Exactly. If you two dear people run about telling the world that I am not McTodd, I shall be compelled to tell the world [*to* MISS PEAVEY] that you are not Miss Peavey.

MISS PEAVEY: But I am Miss Peavey.

COOTES [*reverently*]: Smooth Lizzie, the Baby Bard of the Underworld.

PSMITH: A genuine bard?

MISS PEAVEY [*indignantly*]: Did you say gen-u-wine?

PSMITH: I didn't, but I will. Gen-u-wine.

MISS PEAVEY: You bet I'm gen-u-wine. Eddie, tell this big ham about that poem I had the publishers print way back home last fall. Tell him what it was called.

COOTES [*more reverently still*]: 'Granny the Grafter, a Tale of Mother Love.' Half the crooks in Chicago cried themselves to sleep over it.

PSMITH: I apologize for not having heard of it.

MISS PEAVEY: Say, where have you been all your life? What's your name, anyway?

PSMITH: Psmith. The 'P' is silent, as in pterodactyl.

COOTES [*raising revolver again*]: Lizzie, can't I knock him for a goal?

MISS PEAVEY: Aw, cheese it! Leave me to fix him.

COOTES [*humbly*]: All right, honey.

MISS PEAVEY [*to* PSMITH]: Now listen. We got the goods on each other. Let's be friendly. Let's work together. Fifty-fifty?

PSMITH: No. I'm sorry. Psmith never works with amateurs.

MISS PEAVEY [*angrily*]: Amachooers? Us?

PSMITH: Both of you. And beginners, at that!

COOTES [*offering his gun*]: Go on! No jury would convict.

MISS PEAVEY: Will you keep quiet! [*To* PSMITH *suddenly, as if having made up her mind about something.*] You prefer to work alone?

PSMITH: Invariably.

MISS PEAVEY: All right. There'll be no hard feeling. We'll leave you be – and let the best man win!

PSMITH: You flatter me.

MISS PEAVEY: But you've got to do one thing. You've got to put Eddie on the map.

PSMITH: Map?

MISS PEAVEY: Yes. You gotta get him into this joint.

PSMITH: Secure his admission into these premises?

COOTES: That's what she said.

MISS PEAVEY: You can tell the folks he's a friend of yours, and you asked him down to stay.

PSMITH: But – leaving aside Mr Cootes's rather unfortunate personal appearance – may I point out that I am only a guest here myself? I can't go wishing my old chums on –

MISS PEAVEY: Ah g'wan! Fix it for him! Poor old Eddie won't cramp your style.

[COOTES *gets the bag.*]

He couldn't cramp anybody's. He's too dumb.

COOTES [*earnestly*]: Sure!

[*Enter* BELLOWS.]

Say, here's one of your guests of honour.

BELLOWS: Mr McTodd, sir, and Miss Peavey, her ladyship's compliments, and are you quite ready for the recital? If so, I am instructed, to sound the gong for the company to assemble.

PSMITH: I'm ready, Bellows. Are you, Miss Peavey?

MISS PEAVEY [*reverting to her former manner*]: Why, yes, Mr McTodd. Let's get it over with. I'm so nervous!

PSMITH: All right, Bellows.

BELLOWS: I thank you, sir. [*Going.*]

PSMITH [*suddenly*]: By the way, Bellows –

BELLOWS: Sir?

PSMITH: This is my – valet. He has just arrived. I suppose you can find accommodation for him?

BELLOWS: Certainly, sir. [*To* COOTES.] This way, please.

[COOTES *turns to* MISS PEAVEY *inquiringly.*]

MISS PEAVEY [*aside, to* COOTES]: Find out where the main electric switches are, back of the house.

COOTES: I getcher.

PSMITH: His name is Cootes. I know you will treat him kindly in the servants' hall. He is rather timid with strangers.

BELLOWS: Nothing shall be left undone to make him feel one of us, sir.

PSMITH: Thank you, Bellows. Oh, Cootes?

COOTES: Yes, Mr McTodd?

PSMITH: I don't think I need trouble you to carry my revolver any longer. I'll take it myself. [COOTES *reluctantly gives him the revolver.*] Thank you, Cootes.

[*Exit* COOTES *and* BELLOWS.]

Well, Miss Peavey, I must leave you. I have an appointment with the moon, down by the lake.

MISS PEAVEY: Say, cut out that professional stuff!

PSMITH: I'm sorry; I was forgetting. [*Taking the two glasses from the table and handing one to her.*] Before I go, here's success to our – recital!

MISS PEAVEY: Oh, that? Sure! [*Taking a sip.*]

PSMITH: What are you going to give them tonight? Something about fairies?

MISS PEAVEY: Listen, and let me tell you sumpun. I shouldn't know a fairy if I met one.

PSMITH: You wouldn't?

MISS PEAVEY: No – not if it was walking around Kensington Gardens with that guy Barrie himself.

PSMITH: Surely you're not going to give them 'Granny the Grafter'?

MISS PEAVEY: No. I'm going to give them a surprise item.

PSMITH [*quickly*]: What does that mean?

MISS PEAVEY [*recovering herself*]: Never you mind what it means. What are you going to recite, anyway?

PSMITH [*putting down his glass*]: Oh, I'll throw something off when the time comes. I have a natural gift for improvising.

[*He goes to the terrace and strikes an attitude.*]

> The stag at eve had drunk his fill
> Adoon the glen beyont the hill;
> And welcomed with a friendly nod
> Wisconsin's pride, the brave McTodd!

Au revoir! [*Exit.*]

[MISS PEAVEY *stands watching him, her lips moving silently. Enter* BELLOWS *with a gong. He goes to the terrace and beats it. Then he goes off and is heard beating it again in the garden. Enter* COOTES *furtively.*]

COOTES: Hey – Lizzie!

MISS PEAVEY: Did you find the switchboard?

COOTES: Sure. It's on the wall in the passage, back of the servants' hall.

MISS PEAVEY: Now, listen. Me and the boy friend are going to pull our sister act right away. The folks'll be parked on those chairs. [*Pointing.*] There'll be nobody out on that terrace. That's where you stay, and listen in.

COOTES: Won't they see me?

MISS PEAVEY: They will not. I'm gonna have these curtains drawn – as a kinda background for this frock. When they're drawn, you come and stand right on that spot there. Get me? [*Indicates spot.*]

COOTES: Sure.

MISS PEAVEY [*on terrace now*]: First of all, the old Earl will speak his little piece. Well, the minute he starts, you ankle out of here, round that corner [*pointing off*], in at the side door, and switch off all the lights – every light in the house, if you can. Then whirl around to this terrace again, and wait for what's coming to you out of these curtains.

COOTES: And what is coming, sweetheart?

MISS PEAVEY: Say, what do you think's coming – a grand pianner? The di'monds, boob!

COOTES: How are you going to get them, honey?

MISS PEAVEY: Don't let that weigh on *your* mind! Your part in this opera is to pick 'em up when I pass them out, and hide 'em some place, where we can find 'em again when the riot's over. But they mustn't be found on you – or me – because we're all liable to

205

be searched. [*Noises off.*] Here's the mob coming back. Have you got everything straight?

COOTES: Yes, honey. But where do I hide 'em?

MISS PEAVEY: Oh, any place! A flower-bed – a bird's nest – any place that's unlikely and safe. One of those pots, if you like. Now, slide around that corner. And don't go to sleep, or start playing yo-yo, or anything.

COOTES: No sweetness. [*Exit.*]

> [MISS PEAVEY *strikes an attitude, and gazes over the balustrade.*
> BELLOWS *enters from terrace, with final beat of gong, then comes
> and rearranges chairs. Brings them out from library into gallery, etc.*
> WALDERWICK *and* AGATHA *appear from library.*]

WALDERWICK: I say, let's get good seats.

AGATHA: Settee for us, my lad.

WALDERWICK: Right. Let's put it where we want it.

> [*The settee is just visible. They put it where they want it, then bring
> chairs out and help* BELLOWS *to arrange them well towards the
> window. Two footmen carry on from terrace a small wooden dais,
> about four feet square, covered with red baize, and place it as*
> BELLOWS *tells them. They remove the table and chairs from terrace.
> Enter from terrace* LADY MIDDLEWICK, LORD CHIPSTEAD
> *and* ETHELBERTA.]

LADY MIDDLEWICK: Ah, dear Miss Peavey! Here we are, all impatience. Where's Mr McTodd?

MISS PEAVEY: He's down by the lake, Lady Middlewick, speaking his piece to the moon.

LADY MIDDLEWICK [*to* ETHEL]: Isn't that quaint? Miss Peavey, this is Lord Chipstead.

MISS PEAVEY [*shaking hands with* LORD CHIPSTEAD]: Pleased to meet you.

LORD CHIPSTEAD: What do you say?

> [LADY MIDDLEWICK *leaves them and comes down to chairs.*]

LADY MIDDLEWICK [*calling*]: Eustace!

> [LORD MIDDLEWICK *appears and they begin to talk.* BAXTER
> *and* EVE *appear, and put people in seats.*]

LORD CHIPSTEAD: Dam' damp in that garden! Wet spiders' webs hangin' about all over the place.

MISS PEAVEY: Oh, Lord Chipstead! I always think spiders' webs are the fairies' bridal veils.

LORD CHIPSTEAD: I can't hear a word you say.

MISS PEAVEY: You big – [*Suddenly recollecting herself, softly:*] Go get yourself wired for sound!

LADY MIDDLEWICK: Now, shall we sit down?

MISS PEAVEY: Yes, Lady Middlewick.

LADY MIDDLEWICK: Come along, Cousin Harry.

[*Lights go up in library and gallery. There is a babble of voices.* LORD MIDDLEWICK *is seen in the library, shaking hands with guests who then settle in their seats, supervised by* BAXTER. PSMITH *appears on terrace. At the same moment* FREDDIE *and* PHYLLIS *appear.*]

FREDDIE [*cheerfully*]: Ha-ha! Enter three conspirators! Psmith, have you broken the news to Miss Halliday – about Baxter?

PSMITH: No, I can't find her. But there's some news I want to break to you.

PHYLLIS: To us? What's happened?

PSMITH: Oh, just one of those laughable trifles. We've had an unexpected addition to the house party. Meet me out here directly the show's over, and I'll tell you.

FREDDIE: Righto! Come on, Phyllis! We'll tip Baxter sixpence to put us on the sofa.

PHYLLIS: I bet you Chris Walderwick has got it.

[*They go to their seats.* EVE *goes to terrace from library.*]

PSMITH [*going to her, affectionately*]: Eve!

EVE [*coldly*]: Yes?

PSMITH: I've been waiting down by the lake for you. Where have you been?

EVE [*very distinctly*]: I have been answering a telephone call – a trunk call – from London – Mr McTodd! [*Exits.*]

PSMITH [*to himself*]. There was a nasty hollow clang about that!

[*Chorus from the library, headed by* FREDDIE *and* PHYLLIS.]

CHORUS: We want McTodd! We want McTodd!

PSMITH [*turning and calling*]: All right, I'm coming! Where shall I sit, Lady Middlewick?

LADY MIDDLEWICK: Take my husband's seat. Eustace, get up, and say a few words of introduction.

LORD MIDDLEWICK [*rising*]: Just a very few words, dear. [*He catches* BAXTER'S *eye.* BAXTER *signals to him anxiously. He produces a manuscript, and waves it reassuringly.*]

LADY MIDDLEWICK: Now, Eustace, we're all ready.

> [LORD MIDDLEWICK *takes his place on dais. There is applause. The younger people are rather boisterous. He takes off his prince-nez.* BAXTER *hands him his spectacles, and returns to his seat.* LORD MIDDLEWICK *begins to read from the manuscript. The moment he does so,* COOTES *steals on to the terrace, listens a moment, then hurries off.*]

LORD MIDDLEWICK: My dear friends, four score years ago, within a mile of this spot, a babe was born who was destined to achieve signal honour and affection amid all the denizens of his native county.

> [*There is loud applause.*]

FREDDIE [*to* BAXTER]: He's reading the wrong speech.

> [BAXTER *tries to attract* LORD MIDDLEWICK'S *attention without success.*]

LORD MIDDLEWICK: Thomas Diddlecome, whose memory we are here assembled to perpetuate –

> [BAXTER *crosses to him and plucks at his sleeve.*]

Eh, what?

BAXTER: You have got the wrong speech.

LORD MIDDLEWICK: Dam' it all, Baxter –

FREDDIE: False start, Papa! Back to the old chalk-line!

> [*Laughter and applause. After an argument with* BAXTER, LORD MIDDLEWICK *produces another manuscript and tries again.* BAXTER *returns.*]

LORD MIDDLEWICK: Ladies and gentlemen, it is my privilege tonight to introduce to you a pair of – [*reading very carefully here*] – twin singers from the wide-open spaces. [*To* BAXTER.] Is that right?

BAXTER: Perfectly.

> [*There is loud applause.*]

LORD MIDDLEWICK: The names of Aileen Peavey and Ralston McTodd need no introduction from me –

FREDDIE [*loudly*]: Hear! Hear! Cut it short, Dad!
[*Laughter from the young people.*]

LADY MIDDLEWICK: Freddie, be quiet!

FREDDIE: It was Walderwick.

WALDERWICK: No, it wasn't!
[*Cries of 'Hush! Shut up!' etc.*]

LORD MIDDLEWICK: Now, I am going to ask myself a question.

FREDDIE: He'll get a damned silly answer!

LORD MIDDLEWICK [*proceeding*]: What is the outstanding characteristic of modern poetical thought?

FREDDIE: Mud.

ALL: Hush! Hush! Hush!

LORD MIDDLEWICK [*taking no notice*]: It is – clearness of vision – merciless penetration of dark places –
[*Suddenly all the lights go out.*]
What the devil's happened?
[*There is a hubbub and a few screams – cat-calls from some of the young people.* PSMITH *goes on to dais.* LORD MIDDLEWICK *gets down.*]

PSMITH: Order, please! Order!
[*Cries of 'Hush!' and finally silence.*]
Ladies and gentlemen –

FREDDIE: Order for the Street Singer!

PSMITH: Ladies and gentlemen, I rather think the lights must have gone out.

FREDDIE: Hear, hear! Nothing escapes him! [*Laughter.*]

PSMITH: What are we going to do about it? [*Cries of 'Go home' from* FREDDIE, AGATHA *and* WALDERWICK.] Nothing of the kind! [*Groans.*] What does artificial light matter to Nature's favourite child? I suggest that Miss Peavey should stand here [*he reaches down and leads* MISS PEAVEY *on to dais*] in the moonlight, where we can all see her, and recite to us – and keep on reciting – until the lights go up again!
[*Applause. Cries of 'Miss Peavey!'*]

[MISS PEAVEY *totters, gives a little cry, and collapses on the dais. As she falls she throws the diamonds out on to the terrace.*]

LADY MIDDLEWICK: Good gracious! She's fainted! It's the shock of the sudden darkness.

[*There is a babble of sympathy.*]

[EVE *appears on the terrace. She approaches the diamonds, then, apparently seeing somebody off left, hurries off.*]

Oh, poor thing!

LORD MIDDLEWICK: Give her air.

[PSMITH *begins to draw the window curtains.*]

Don't draw those curtains! She wants air.

PSMITH: But not pneumonia, Sir. [*Completes drawing of curtains, watching terrace all the time.* BAXTER, *suspicious, stands up and watches* PSMITH.]

LADY MIDDLEWICK: Has anybody got any smelling-salts? Agatha dear, run up and see if you can find some in my room.

AGATHA: All right, Lady Middlewick. [*She goes.*]

LORD MIDDLEWICK: Hadn't we better slap her hands, or something? Or cut her staylaces?

FREDDIE: Or cut her staylaces?

FREDDIE: Girls don't wear stays nowadays.

LORD MIDDLEWICK: How do you know?

FREDDIE [*with his arm around a girl's waist*]: One keeps in touch with the situation.

LADY MIDDLEWICK: Be quiet, everybody! [*Bending over her.*] Her poor heart is beginning to beat again.

FREDDIE: She's coming round. Three hearty cheers –

LADY MIDDLEWICK: Freddie!

FREDDIE [*in a whisper*]: Hip – hip –

[AGATHA *enters with the smelling-salts, and gives them to* LADY MIDDLEWICK.]

LADY MIDDLEWICK: There, Miss Peavey! Look, her eyes are opening.

FREDDIE [*to* WALDERWICK]. Bet you half a crown I know what she says when she comes to.

WALDERWICK: I'll take you.

[MISS PEAVEY *sits up, aided by* PHYLLIS.]

MISS PEAVEY [*with a deep sigh*]: Oh, where am I?

FREDDIE: Half a crown, please.

[WALDERWICK *pays.*]

MISS PEAVEY: Some place in heaven?

FREDDIE: Our Aileen is herself again!

[*Lights go on. Cheers from everybody.*]

LADY MIDDLEWICK [*rising from her knees, beside* MISS PEAVEY]: Quiet, please, everybody. You'll be quite well in a moment now, Miss Peavey. [*Puts her hand to her neck and looks down. The necklace has gone.*] Oh, dear! I must have dropped my necklace when I knelt down just now. Can anybody see it? It's on the floor somewhere.

[*There is a general search by everybody.*]

FREDDIE: Are you sure it hasn't slipped down inside your little ready-to-wear dance frock, Mother?

LADY MIDDLEWICK: No, Freddie, it has not.

[PSMITH *is quietly peeping out, through opening of curtains.* BAXTER *watches.*]

ETHELBERTA: I wonder where it can be. It's a dreadful responsibility to own such things, isn't it, darling? Suppose they can't find it?

LADY MIDDLEWICK [*in an agitated voice*]: Don't talk like that, Ethelberta. We shall find it in a moment.

BAXTER [*clearing his throat importantly*]: No, Lady Biddlewick we shall *dot* fide it id a bobent.

LADY MIDDLEWICK: What do you mean?

BAXTER [*solemnly*]: The Dulworth diamonds have beed stolen.

[PSMITH *swings round, to face* BAXTER.]

EVERYBODY: Stolen?

LADY MIDDLEWICK: Who has stolen them?

BAXTER: I have by suspicions.

LORD MIDDLEWICK: Don't be a dam' fool, Baxter. My guests don't go about stealing diamonds.

PSMITH: Baxter is right, Lord Middlewick. Baxter is always right. Lock the library door, Mr Walderwick. We must all be searched.

[WALDERWICK *goes off and returns.*]

EVERYBODY: Searched?

PSMITH: Yes. Start with me, Baxter. Then I'll search you.

BAXTER [*indignantly*]: Search be?

PSMITH [*locking the door*]: Certainly. We must all go through it. It's nothing to be afraid of. We often search one another in Wisconsin.

FREDDIE: I know exactly how it's done, Baxter. I'll show you.

PSMITH: Watch Freddie Bosham. Freddie knows how!

[FREDDIE *and* BAXTER *go through the approved searching movements, patting* PSMITH *all over. Then* PSMITH *and* FREDDIE *search* BAXTER. *Meanwhile,* LORD MIDDLEWICK *is trying to search* LADY MIDDLEWICK.]

LADY MIDDLEWICK: Don't do that, Eustace! You're tickling me.

FREDDIE: No – nothing there.

PSMITH: That lets Baxter and me out, then. Now that you all know how it's done, let the treasure hunt begin. The gentlemen will adjourn to the dining-room [*unlocking the door*], the ladies will go into the library. Baxter and Freddie Bosham will search the gentlemen.

[FREDDIE *and* BAXTER *go.*]

Lady Middlewick and I will search –

LADIES [*in chorus*]: Oh!

PSMITH: Well, perhaps you're right. The ladies will search each other.

[*Ladies go to library through the double doors.* LADY MIDDLE-WICK *and* ETHELBERTA *last. Men go out.*]

LADY MIDDLEWICK: I will search you, Ethelberta dear.

ELTHELBERTA: Certainly, darling. But what are you going to do if you don't find the diamonds. After all, they don't really belong to you, do they?

LADY MIDDLEWICK [*agitated*]: What do you mean?

ETHELBERTA: They are heirlooms. How are you going to replace *them*?

LORD MIDDLEWICK [*going*]: I told you to send them to the bank, Anastasia.

LADY MIDDLEWICK: Eustace, go and be searched!

[*Exit* ETHELBERTA. *Exit* LORD MIDDLEWICK.]

MISS PEAVEY [*sitting up*]: Lady Middlewick, I should like to be searched, too.

LADY MIDDLEWICK: Nonsense, dear Miss Peavey! Nobody suspects you.

MISS PEAVEY [*weakly*]: Oh, but I insist.

PSMITH: You must stay where you are for the present, Miss Peavey. Miss Jackson will look after you. Now, ladies, are you quite ready?

LADIES: Yes – quite ready!

PSMITH: Very good. Now, carry on! [*Closing the library doors, then exit.*]

PHYLLIS: How are you feeling now, Miss Peavey?

MISS PEAVEY: Thirsty.

PHYLLIS: Shall I get you a glass of water?

MISS PEAVEY: Please.

[*Exit* PHYLLIS. MISS PEAVEY *promptly sits up, and parts curtains behind her.*]

Eddie, are you there?

[COOTES *appears through curtains, and draws them back, partially.* EVE *runs across terrace unseen by him, carrying the diamonds.*]

COOTES: Yeah.

MISS PEAVEY: Did you get them?

COOTES: Sure I got them.

MISS PEAVEY: Where are they?

COOTES: In that elegant ornamental vase [*Indicating the flower-pot on the terrace.*]

MISS PEAVEY: You big beautiful boy! I'm pleased with you, Eddie.

COOTES: I'm glad. Shall I beat it now?

MISS PEAVEY: Yep. But are you sure it's all right? You're such a bone-head, dearie. Flash them pretty things just a minute: I want to be sure they're there.

COOTES: All rightie! [*Going to the flower-pot and bringing it to dais.*] I'll show you! [*Digging his fingers in. Finally becoming very agitated.*]

MISS PEAVEY: Come on! Step on it! What's the matter?

COOTES: I shoved them in deeper than I thought.

MISS PEAVEY [*impatiently*]: Empty the whole shebang on the ground!

[COOTES *breaks the pot behind the dais, and gropes about in the earth. Meanwhile* EVE *is dimly visible on the terrace, doing something with another pot. She hurries off, and disappears.*]

COOTES [*finally*]: Liz–they ain't there no more!

MISS PEAVEY: They've gone?

COOTES: They've certainly gone somewheres.

MISS PEAVEY: Eddie Cootes, if you was a dog living on buried bones, you'd starve to death. Look in some more pots.

COOTES: But I didn't put nothing in no other pots.

MISS PEAVEY: You ain't got enough brains to remember where you put anything. Try them other pots. [*Pushing back the curtains further.*]

COOTES: But I ain't *put it* –

MISS PEAVEY: Go on! Find it!

COOTES: I tell you I can't, Lizzie!

MISS PEAVEY [*standing up*]: You poor Dumb Issac, you couldn't find a big drum in a telephone booth! Will you dig out them di'monds, or must I?

[PSMITH *strolls on to the terrace, carrying an umbrella. This he puts up, and having selected from the balustrade the pot with which* EVE *has been occupied, mounts on centre of balustrade, using the seat as a step.*

Come on, Eddie – hustle! The whole bunch will be back on us.

[MISS PEAVEY *and* COOTES *suddenly catch sight of* PSMITH *and stand transfixed. Then:*]

Who are you?

PSMITH: Me?

MISS PEAVEY: Psmith!

COOTES: Put down that flower-pot!

PSMITH: Don't be greedy, Cootes; you've got one of your own.

[*There is a babble of voices. Evidently the party are returning.* PSMITH *jumps off the balustrade, using the umbrella as a parachute, and disappears. There is a faint crash. At the same moment the doors are thrown open on each side, and the whole company reappear.* MISS PEAVEY *gives a wild shriek and falls flat. There are cries of sympathy, and* PHYLLIS *runs and kneels beside her with the glass.* COOTES *rushes off, unnoticed.* EVE *appears and looks anxiously over the balustrade into the garden below.*]

CURTAIN

ACT THREE

Scene: *The interior of the Keeper's Cottage at the end of the Yew Walk.*
Time: *Next morning.*
The hydrangea in its pot stands in the fireplace.
EVE *appears at the window and peeps in. Finding the room empty, she returns to the door and enters. She looks round cautiously, then tiptoes to the staircase door and opens it carefully. She listens, then leaves it open and opens the cellar door. She looks down into the cellar, then closes the door. She turns and catches sight of the hydrangea in the fireplace. With an exclamation of delight she runs to it and seizes it. She is about to empty the pot into the fender, when suddenly there is a tap on the outer door. She goes up, carrying the pot, and opens it.* FREDDIE *is standing outside, immaculate with top-hat, etc.*

EVE: Mr Bosham!
FREDDIE [*entering*]: Call me Freddie. Everybody calls me Freddie, as soon as they recover consciousness. [*Laying his hat and stick on the small table by staircase door.*] And may I ask what you are doing here, in a single gentleman's leafy bower at this hour of the morning? [*Indicating the hydrangea.*] Come to arrange the flowers?
EVE [*warningly*]: Sh! [*She runs and closes the staircase door.*] Why aren't you helping to lay the foundation-stone at Great Waffleden?
FREDDIE [*imitating her*]: Sh! I slipped away while the starter was getting the runners in line. I've come to call on our friend the poet. Is he in?
EVE: He may be upstairs, still in bed.
FREDDIE: I'll go and wake him.
EVE: Don't do that, whatever you do!
FREDDIE: Why not?
EVE: Go and see if he's there; then come down, and I'll tell you.

[FREDDIE *tiptoes upstairs.* EVE *puts hydrangea back into fireplace, then sits on the settee and waits anxiously.* FREDDIE *comes down again.*]

Did you see him?

FREDDIE: No, but I heard him! Now, why mayn't I wake him?

EVE: Because his name isn't McTodd at all.

FREDDIE: I know that.

EVE: You know it?

FREDDIE: Of course I know.

EVE: Then why haven't you shown him up?

FREDDIE: I couldn't very well. You see, I invited him down here.

EVE: Are you in – colloboration with him?

FREDDIE: The exact word.

EVE [*suddenly*]: With Miss Peavey too – and that fat man?

FREDDIE: Peavey? Our fairy child? You don't mean to suggest – ?

EVE: I *do*!

FREDDIE: How many people in this house-party *are* actually trying to snitch Stepmother's to-do-ments?

EVE: I'm not, for one.

FREDDIE: Oh, but I beg your pardon; you are.

EVE: I am?

FREDDIE: I should think so. Baxter the bloodhound has been on your track from the start. He thinks you are the one who's in league with our friend upstairs.

EVE: Oh, how dare he? Do you believe that too?

FREDDIE: Of course I don't. How could you be in the league without my knowing it? It's my league! I'm the secretary. [*Pointing upwards.*] I engaged *him*! It's a long story. I'll tell you later.

EVE: You mean you hired him to steal the necklace?

FREDDIE: Well, you couldn't quite say hired. He offered to do the whole job for nothing. I can't think why?

EVE [*dismayed*]: I can tell you – he's an imposter. Freddie, you've been Charing-crossed, or whatever they call it.

FREDDIE [*alarmed*]: You mean to say he isn't going to give me the necklace?

EVE [smiling]: I'm quite sure of *that*!

FREDIE: But he's got to! I'm sunk if he doesn't. I've promised to buy Stepmother a new one. We both signed the cheque for it this morning after breakfast.

EVE: Well, why not buy it?

FREDDIE: Because I gave the cheque to Phyllis, to buy my partnership, not half an hour ago! Her old pop has got it by this time. Is there no way of making this cad cough up?

EVE [*smiling*]: None whatever.

FREDDIE: Why are you so certain?

EVE: Because he hasn't got the necklace.

FREDDIE: Who has, then?

EVE: I have

FREDDIE: You? You marvellous girl! Where?

EVE [*picking up flower-pot*]: Here.

FREDDIE: My dear, what *are* you talking about?

EVE: It's a long story; I'll tell you later. Now watch [*She pulls the hydrangea out of the pot and empties the pot on the hearthrug. There is nothing there.*] Why – good gracious!

FREDDIE: What's the matter now?

EVE [*with her nose right down on the floor*]: It's gone!

FREDDIE [*putting his nose down too*]: Gone? [*Looking up again.*] Was it ever there?

EVE: Miss Peavey stole them from Lady Middlewick in the dark, last night, and then threw them out on the terrace. Cootes was waiting, and picked them up. He put them into a flower-pot –

FREDDIE: That one!

EVE: No – another. I was out there too –

FREDDIE: Why weren't you inside, sitting at our sweet singer's feet?

EVE: Never mind!

FREDDIE [*injured*]: All right. And when Cootes was talking to his lady friend you pulled the necklace out of one pot –

EVE: And put it into this one.

FREDDIE: And then that low person Psmith pinched the pot.

EVE: Yes. That's why I came here this morning – to get it back.

FREDDIE: Where did you find it?

EVE: In the fireplace.

FREDDIE: Well, naturally, he couldn't leave diamonds in a fireplace all night. He's taken them to bed with him. They're under his pillow.

EVE: I don't think so.

FREDDIE: Why?

EVE: If you stole something and expected someone to come and look for it, would you hide it under your pillow? No!

FREDDIE: Why not?

EVE: Because that's the first place where people would look. I believe it's hidden somewhere in this room. Let's hunt for it.

FREDDIE: Right! I'll try the chimney, you tease the furniture. Stand that grandfather's clock on its head; then tear the settee to pieces.

EVE: All right.

FREDDIE: Now then – action!

[EVE *goes to the clock, opens it, and peeps inside.* FREDDIE *goes to the mantelpiece and looks inside two vases.* EVE *puts her hand up inside the clock. The pendulum falls off with a crash.*]

EVE: I say – this thing has fallen off.

FREDDIE: Never mind. Just say it 'came away in me 'and.' [*Peering up the chimney.*] Hallo, this is fun! I can see right out of the top of this chimney.

EVE: You are supposed to be a detective, not an astronomer.

FREDDIE: Sorry! [*Putting his head up the chimney again.*]

[EVE *goes to the settee and feels down the back and sides, etc. She then turns the settee upside-down and finds a small hole in the bottom. She pulls out a handful of stuffing.*]

EVE: Hallo, here's a hole! [*Putting her hand in it.*] No – false alarm! Just a hole! [*Leaving the settee and going to the Welsh dresser: opening the drawers and looking in.*] Any luck up that chimney?

FREDDIE [*standing up inside the chimney now*]: There's a sort of shelf up here. I can't quite reach it.

EVE [*crossing and handing the poker*]: Take the poker.

FREDDIE: I thank you. [*He takes the poker.*]

[EVE *stands on a chair and tries to reach the top shelf of the dresser. The dresser tilts over: two or three plates fall on the floor with a crash. At the same moment a cascade of rubbish comes down the chimney with another crash.*]

FREDDIE: ⎫
EVE: ⎭   [*to each other indignantly*]. Sh!

> [EVE *runs to the staircase door and listens.* FREDDIE *has come out of the chimney. He stands by the fireplace, also listening. His face is covered with soot.*]

FREDDIE: The Silent Service – that's what we are!

EVE: Sh! [*By the staircase door.*]

FREDDIE: Can you hear anything?

EVE: Not a sound.

FREDDIE: The man must be dead.

EVE [*closing the door again*]: Well, he hasn't heard us, anyhow. Let's breathe again.

> [*They both breathe hard.*]

What have you got out of that chimney?

FREDDIE: Two bricks, half a hundredweight of soot, and a dead bat. This is the rottenest treasure hunt I ever got mixed up in.

EVE: There's nothing left to search here. What do we do next?

FREDDIE: I was right! It's under his pillow.

EVE: I don't believe it. Something tells me it's downstairs. There's a cellar there. [*She goes to the cellar door and opens it. They both peep in.*] You go down and look.

FREDDIE: No, Eve. I'm sorry – but no!

EVE: Why not?

FREDDIE: I'll climb the highest mountain for you – but I will not go down into that cellar.

EVE: But why?

FREDDIE [*pointing downward*]: Beetles! Since a child!

EVE: You *are* a coward!

FREDDIE: I know; but only about beetles. Put me up against a couple of mice, and I'd laugh in their faces.

EVE: I'll go myself.

FREDDIE: That is what I was about to suggest. Take this. [*He hands her his cigarette lighter, lighted.*] If you aren't back in five minutes, I promise to send for Mr Keating. [EVE *goes down into the cellar.*]

> [*The staircase door opens softly and* PSMITH *appears, with* COOTES, *revolver in his hand.*]

PSMITH: Freddie! [FREDDIE *stiffens.*] Is this worthy? Is this the true

spirit of cooperative crime? Hands up, you low profiteer!
[FREDDIE *puts his hands up.*] Turn round! [FREDDIE *turns and
faces him.* PSMITH *shakes his head at him.*] Freddie, I'm shocked –
shocked and disappointed. [*Indicating the disordered room.*] Why
did you do it?

FREDDIE [*dramatically*]: I did it to help a woman. A little pal – that's
all. Pals till Hell freezes – and I'll see her through, Sonny boy!
[*Drops dramatically on one knee.*]

PSMITH: Have you gone potty?

FREDDIE [*apologetically*]: It's a sub-title – out of a film I once saw,
called 'Mammie's Coal Black Rose.' It seemed to fit in: I thought
I might as well use it.

PSMITH: Now, my poor misguided fellow. Step off briskly with
the left foot and advance to that staircase. [FREDDIE *obeys.*] Up!
One, two, three, four! Halt! About turn! Sit down! *Freddie
obeys.*] Stay there until I've dealt with your fair but misguided
accomplice.

FREDDIE: But I say – I'm your employer!

PSMITH: This is a General Strike. [PSMITH *shuts the door, locks it,
and crosses to the fireplace, where he examines the debris in the fender.
He picks up the dead bat delicately, and drops it on to the chair by the
fire.*] Somebody's Mother! [*Covering it with a bit of sacking.*]
  [*The door of the cellar opens, and* EVE *reappears. She closes the
  cellar door and turns round, to find herself face to face with* PSMITH,
  with a revolver in his hand.]

EVE [*startled*]: Hoo! [*She puts her hands up.*]

PSMITH: Good morning! Don't trouble to do your Swedish
exercises just now. [*Indicating the settee, which is still upside-down.*]
Will you be seated?
  [EVE *sits, staring at him defiantly. He puts the revolver on the
  mantelpiece, and strolls about the room examining the mess which
  has been made, and shaking his head solmenly.*]

EVE [*sitting bolt upright – boldly*]: I'm not afraid of you. [PSMITH
takes no notice, but puts the pendulum back into the clock.] Your name
isn't McTodd.

PSMITH [*coming down to the fireplace*]: Thank you for telling me, but
I know.

EVE: What *is* your name?

PSMITH: Ronald. Ronald Eustace.

EVE: Ronald Useless what?

PSMITH: Psmith. The 'P' is silent, as in 'psoup'.

EVE: Thank you. I suppose you know why I came here?

PSMITH: To rearrange my furniture for me, as you promised. It was a gracious thought, but, thank you very much, I think you've overdone it.

EVE: I've come for that necklace. Tell me where it is. You shan't do poor Freddie out of it.

PSMITH: What makes you think I want to do poor Freddie out of it?

EVE [*rising*]: Because you promised to steal it for nothing! If you'd been a gentleman you'd have charged 10 per cent or something.

PSMITH: Shall I tell you the real reason why I offered to steal it for nothing?

EVE: You can, but I shan't believe you. Why?

PSMITH: Because you were going to be here. That was enough for me.

EVE [*rather breathlessly*]: Oh!

PSMITH: And that reminds me of something else. I'm very glad that you've found out that my name is not McTodd. By the way, how did you find out?

EVE: Mrs McTodd rang me up last night from London.

PSMITH: Cynthia! Again I am very glad. Naturally you would like to know why I am very glad.

EVE: No, I would not.

PSMITH: Then I'll tell you. Because as McTodd I was a married man. As Psmith I am a bachelor. The joyous cry rings round the marriage market: 'Psmith is free! Psmith is eligible!' [*Going to her.*] Eve!

EVE [*backing away indignantly*]: Are you trying to make love to me?

PSMITH: We've got further than that, I hope. I am breaking it to you that no impediment now stands in the way of our marriage.

EVE: Don't add impertinence to everything else. You came to Blandings to steal those diamonds.

PSMITH: I came to Blandings to see you. The diamonds were a

joke. Anybody can have all the diamonds in the world so far as I'm concerned. I only want you.

EVE: Is that true?

PSMITH: Absolutely.

EVE: You are prepared to prove it?

PSMITH: On the spot.

EVE [*holding out her hand*]: Then give me back Lady Middlewick's necklace.

PSMITH: With the greatest pleasure. [*He goes to a stuffed pheasant on a bracket over the mantelpiece. He takes the bird down and produces the necklace from under its wing.*] There! [*Smiling at her.*]

EVE [*smiling too*]: The only place where we didn't look!

[*They both laugh.* PSMITH *hands her the necklace.*]

PSMITH: Now what have you got to say to me? [*She looks up at him.*] Would you care for the future to address me as Ronald Eustace?

[*The door opens suddenly, and* COOTES *and* MISS PEAVEY *appear.* COOTES *is holding a revolver.*]

COOTES [*fiercely*]: Hey – hands up! [EVE *whirls round with a cry, drops necklace and puts her hands up.*] I thought so! [*To* MISS PEAVEY:] More funny business! Trying to slip the stuff to a skirt! [PSMITH *backs quietly and tries to get his revolver off the mantelpiece.*] Ah, would you? Hands up! [*To* MISS PEAVEY, *proudly:*] He can't fool me!

MISS PEAVEY [*to* COOTES]: Eddie, don't talk so much – and take your finger off of that trigger! Do you want some person to get hurt around here?

PSMITH: Comrade Cootes, by rights you ought to be pressing my evening trousers. Miss Peavey, how is it that you're not laying foundation-stones?

MISS PEAVEY: Because I prefer to be picking them up. [*Picking up the necklace from the floor.*]

COOTES [*with great satisfaction*]: Well, that was pretty slick. [*To* PSMITH:] You poor hick! [*Turning to* MISS PEAVEY.] Now, is Momma pleased with her little Eddie?

MISS PEAVEY: Momma will be more pleased when we've gotten safe out of this health-resort.

COOTES: Well, let's tie these birds up and make our get-away. [*He advances towards* PSMITH. MISS PEAVEY *interposes.*]

MISS PEAVEY: Eddie, try to remember that what you've got balanced on your collar is a head, and not a billiard ball. Don't you see we've got the goods on them anyhow? They can't let out one little squawk about us without giving themselves away. [*Waving revolver away.*] And cover him, not me!

COOTES [*meekly*]: Yes, Lizzie. [*Lowering his gun.*]

MISS PEAVEY [*to* PSMITH *and* EVE]: I guess you can put your hands down now.

PSMITH: Thank you, Miss Peavey. Or should I say, Mrs Cootes?

MISS PEAVEY: Eh?

PSMITH: From your general attitude and manner of address towards Mr Cootes, I take it that you are married.

MISS PEAVEY: You're wrong.

PSMITH: I'm distressed to hear it.

MISS PEAVEY: Why the anguish?

PSMITH: Because I believe in marriage. I am shortly expecting to be married myself. If you and Mr Cootes settled down and got married, we might do a little mutual visiting. Do you play bridge at all, Mr Cootes?

MISS PEAVEY [*indignantly*]: Look what poker did for him! [*Pointing to* COOTS'S *thumb.*] But that's all over with now. [*She takes* COOTES' *arm.*] We're going to take your advice and get married and have a nice vacation together [*showing the necklace*] – on this. We shan't have to work the boats again for quite a while. Shall we, Ed?

COOTES: Oh, Honeybunch!

MISS PEAVEY: We'd better be getting out of this shack. Goodbye! [*She and* COOTES *go up to the door.*]

PSMITH: Good-bye, Miss Peavey. Goodbye, Cootes. [*Beginning to back towards the mantelpiece.*]

COOTES: Hey! Keep away from that fireplace. I nearly forgot my other gun. [*He takes the gun off the mantelpiece with a grin and returns to* MISS PEAVEY.] You ain't sore, brother? No hard feeling?

PSMITH: None whatever. There was no harm in trying, was there, guv'nor?

COOTES: None whatever. But you looked such a complete mug –
[*There is a sudden crash and shout from behind the staircase door. It is* FREDDIE *beating on the door.*]

FREDDIE [*shouting*]: Help! Help! Who's that? Help!

COOTES [*whirling round*]: Oh my, what's that?
[*His revolver goes off. A picture on the wall falls down with a crash. Next minute* PSMITH *has jumped on* COOTES'S *back and takes his two revolvers away. At the same time he gives* COOTES *a push with his knee and* COOTES *falls on his face.*]

PSMITH: Hands up, Cootes!
[COOTES *has risen. He puts his hands up and turns to* MISS PEAVEY.]

COOTES [*piteously*]: Liz!

MISS PEAVEY: You short, sharp pain in my neck! Don't ever you dare to speak to me again!

COOTES: Aw, Liz, have a heart! I couldn't help it! I was all nervous and wrought up –

MISS PEAVEY: You can switch off that record. I'm through with you. [*Going to the door.*] So long!

PSMITH: One minute. I'm afraid I must trouble you for that necklace, Miss Peavey.

MISS PEAVEY: You try to get it!

PSMITH: I'm a child in these matters, but I was under the impression that when you do *this* to anybody [*business with revolver*], their compliance with your wishes becomes – automatic!

MISS PEAVEY: I'll call your bluff. I'm going to walk right out of here and take this collection of ice with me. You won't do anything about it. Shoot a woman? Not you!

PSMITH: You're one up! I won't. [*He lays down the revolvers on the table, then takes one up again*] But I think I see a way out of the difficulty. I can't shoot you – but I *can* shoot Comrade Cootes!

COOTES [*frantically*]: Hey! Hey! Hey!

PSMITH: If you attempt to edge out of that door, Miss Peavey, I shall endeavour to plug your boy friend in the left leg.

COOTES: Say – listen!

MISS PEAVEY: Pull yourself together, Ed. He's only kidding.

PSMITH: I'm a poor shot, and I may hit him in some more vital spot; but at least he will know, before he breathes his last, that I did my best and meant well.

COOTES: Brother – !

MISS PEAVEY: Come on, Ed! He won't shoot!

PSMITH: I'm going to count three, Miss Peavey. One-two-

COOTES: Say – wait! [*Rushing to* MISS PEAVEY, *snatching the necklace from her, and throwing it on the floor.*] There!

PSMITH [*picking it up*]: Thank you, Cootes. [*Handing the pheasant to* COOTES.] The bird!

[COOTES *makes a despairing gesture to* MISS PEAVEY *as if asking for forgiveness.*]

MISS PEAVEY [*to* PSMITH]: I suppose you think you're smart?

PSMITH: Just a turn of Fortune's wheel, that's all. Would you care to take Mr Cootes away now?

MISS PEAVEY: I guess I'd better. [*To* COOTES:] Come on – you! It's back to the boats for us.

COOTES [*incredulously*]: Us?

MISS PEAVEY: Sure!

COOTES: Liz – you ain't through with me?

MISS PEAVEY: Through with you? I ain't got a hope!

COOTES: You're still going to marry me?

MISS PEAVEY: I've gotta marry you. What would become of you if I didn't – you poor oil-can? Pick up the Henry Fords! [*Taking* COOTES'S *arm and turning on* PSMITH.] You big bully – scaring my little ducksie wucksie! [*To* COOTES.] Oh, come on! C'mon!

[*They go out together. A moment later they appear walking past the window.* COOTES *stumbles along, half dazed:* MISS PEAVEY *glares defiance at* PSMITH *until they disappear.*

As they do so, PSMITH *quietly drops the necklace into* FREDDIE'S *hat, on the small table by the staircase. He now goes to* EVE, *who has been watching the whole scene from the fireplace.*]

PSMITH: Now, where were we when interrupted?

FREDDIE [*off*]: Help! Let me out!

[FREDDIE *begins to knock on the staircase door again, more cautiously this time.*]

PSMITH [*goes to the door and shouts*]: Shut up!

FREDDIE'S VOICE [*inside*]: Sorry!

PSMITH [*returning to* EVE]: Now, to resume.

[PHYLLIS *appears at the window and looks in. She has the receipt for £5,000 in her hand.*]

PHYLLIS: Hallo!

PSMITH [*with forced politeness*]: Oh-hallo!

PHYLLIS: Do you happen to know where Freddie is?

PSMITH [*to* EVE]: Let me see, do we happen to know where Freddie is?

EVE [*demurely*]: I think he's in there. [*Pointing to the staircase.*] Do you want him, Miss Jackson?

PHYLLIS: Yes. I've got a receipt for him for £5,000.

PSMITH: Come in!

[PHYLLIS *disappears.* PSMITH *goes up to the door and opens it.* PHYLLIS *enters.*]

Good morning, Miss Jackson! [*Going to staircase door.*] You will find your young hero in here. Will you please take him up to my bedroom and wash his face? [*Opening the staircase door wide.* FREDDIE *is seen sitting on the stairs, still with a black face.*] Topsy, here's Eva!

PHYLLIS: Freddie – darling! [*She runs upstairs to him.*]

[PSMITH *closes the door on her, then glances out of the window. There is a sound of rain.*]

PSMITH: Hallo – raining! Well, you and I aren't afraid of a shower of rain, are we? We were brought together by a shower of rain.

EVE [*looking up at him*]: By Mr Walderwick's umbrella!

PSMITH: Eve! Call me something!

EVE [*softly*]: Persmith!

PSMITH: Darling!

[BAXTER, LORD *and* LADY MIDDLEWICK, ETHELBERTA, WALDERWICK, AGATHA *and* MR *and* MRS MCTODD *suddenly appear walking in single file past the window, all with umbrellas up, and disappear on their way to the door.*]

[*Despairingly*]. Gurr! What is this? The United Empire Party! [*The door is opened by* BAXTER. *He stands aside while the others file in.*]

BAXTER: You see, Lord Middlewick. I was right. Here they are – together. We've caught them both!

PSMITH [*cheerfully*]: Good morning, Baxter. How's your cold? [BAXTER *glares at him.*] Lady Middlewick, let me find you a seat.

LADY MIDDLEWICK: Where's Freddie?

PSMITH: Having his face washed.

> [*He turns the settee right way up.* LADY MIDDLEWICK *sits down on it.* ETHELBERTA *sits beside her.* LORD MIDDLEWICK *stands behind the sofa.* WALDERWICK *and* AGATHA *go up to the window. The* MCTODDS *stand behind the table. There is a solemn silence.*]

LORD MIDDLEWICK: I perceive by your attitude that you would like to say a few words.

LADY MIDDLEWICK: He would. Say them, Eustace.

LORD MIDDLEWICK: Sir, Mr Baxter makes a very strange charge against you.

PSMITH: Whatever else I may be, I am not a woman in man's clothes, Baxter.

LORD MIDDLEWICK: A very strange charge, sir. He says that you are not Mr Ralston McTodd.

PSMITH: Well, after all, comparatively few people are.

LORD MIDDLEWICK: Please don't interrupt me. Mr Baxter goes so far as to assert that this gentleman [*indicating* MCTODD] –

BAXTER: Our material witness.

LORD MIDDLEWICK: Silence! – whom he has produced from somewhere, and who is an entire stranger to me –

MCTODD: Well, I'll be damned! Brussels sprouts to you!

CYNTHIA: Hush, darling!

LORD MIDDLEWICK: Step forward, sir. He asserts that this gentleman is Ralston McTodd.

BAXTER [*to* PSMITH]: And you know he is!

LORD MIDDLEWICK: Baxter, will you kindly refrain from putting in your oar?

BAXTER: But he is, sir! He returned to London yesterday, from Merthyr Tydvil –

LADY MIDDLEWICK: Why did he go to Merthyr Tydvil?

CYNTHIA: To have a brainstorm.

LORD MIDDLEWICK: This lady with him insists that she is his wife.

EVE: Of coürse she's his wife. [*Going to* CYNTHIA.]

CYNTHIA: Darling!
    [*They embrace.*]

LORD MIDDLEWICK: Please don't do that! It confuses me! [*To* PSMITH:] Now, sir, are you Ralston McTodd?

PSMITH: You want me to be perfectly frank with you, sir?

LADY MIDDLEWICK: Of course he does!

PSMITH: Very well. Lord Middlewick, I am not this gentleman.

LADY MIDDLEWICK: You admit it?

PSMITH: Proudly.

MCTODD [*annoyed*]: Say! Say! Lay off on the pride.

LORD MIDDLEWICK [*to* MCTODD]: But who shared my lunch with me? Was it you?

MCTODD: Well, I shared a table with you.

LORD MIDDLEWICK [*to* PSMITH]: Where did you come in?

PSMITH: In the lounge, *after* lunch. Mr McTodd had taken umbrage. [*To* MCTODD:] Hadn't you?

MCTODD: It was all there was to take.

LORD MIDDLEWICK: But why did you come to Blandings?

PSMITH: Because I had just learned that a determined attempt was to be made to rob Lady Middlewick of her diamonds.

LORD MIDDLEWICK: Who was your informant?
    [*Enter* FREDDIE, *now clean again, and* PHYLLIS, *from staircase.* FREDDIE *gives* PHYLLIS *his hand down the last step, then turns, to find the room full of people.*]

ALL: FREDDIE!

FREDDIE: What is this? Community singing?

PSMITH: Come in, Freddie! There is my informant, Lord Middlewick. [*Loudly.*] Just in time to corroborate everything I say.

FREDDIE: Hallo, Dad – laid it?

LORD MIDDLEWICK: Laid it? Frederick, am I a domestic fowl?

LADY MIDDLEWICK: Eustace, don't cackle! Freddie, did you tell this gentleman that somebody was going to steal my diamonds?

FREDDIE [*after a nod from* PSMITH *and a nudge from* PHYLLIS]: Yes, I believe I did.

LORD MIDDLEWICK [*to* PSMITH]: And *that* was why you came down here – to give Frederick any help that might be necessary?

PSMITH: Exactly.

LORD MIDDLEWICK: Well, I must say, Anastasia, I think we owe this young man an apology. You do, Baxter, anyhow.

BAXTER: May I ask a question? [*To* PSMITH:] Why didn't you explain who you were?

PSMITH: And put the criminal on her guard? Baxter, I'm surprised at you?

LORD MIDDLEWICK: Don't be a damn fool, Baxter.

LADY MIDDLEWICK [*rising*]: Do you say, on *her* guard?

PSMITH: I did.

LADY MIDDLEWICK: Was it a woman?

PSMITH: Alas, yes!

LADY MIDDLEWICK [*triumphantly*]: Ethelberta!

ETHELBERTA: Anastasia, how dare you?

   [*They face one another threateningly, and break into a furious altercation.*]

LORD MIDDLEWICK [*to* PSMITH]: Do something! Pull them off!

PSMITH: It was another lady.

LADY MIDDLEWICK [*turning round*]: Who?

PSMITH: Miss Peavey!

LADY MIDDLEWICK: Miss Peavey? That darling? But diamonds make her cry! She told me so herself. It's impossible!

PSMITH: Blinded by tears, she still managed to grab them.

LADY MIDDLEWICK: She stole them from me – in the dark?

PSMITH: She did.

LADY MIDDLEWICK: Oh!

ETHELBERTA [*sternly*]: Anastasia, you invited her here. I hold you responsible. The family holds you responsible.

LADY MIDDLEWICK [*thoroughly frightened now*]: But, Ethelberta dear, I'll make it up to you. I'm ordering some nice new ones.

ETHELBERTA: The original diamonds, Anastasia – or exposure and disgrace.

LADY MIDDLEWICK [*collapsing on settee*]: Oh!

FREDDIE: You shall not put her photograph in the 'News of the World.'

PSMITH [*calmly*]: As I was saying, when interrupted, Miss Peavey secured the diamonds. But at the last moment, when all seemed lost, they were recovered.

ALL: Recovered?

LADY MIDDLEWICK: By whom?

PSMITH: Whom would you expect? Who is the most intelligent person in this room? Who detected the original conspiracy? Baxter? Pooh! Myself? Pooh! Pooh!

ALL: Who?

PSMITH: The Honourable Frederick Bosham! Look in his face; his name is Red-hot Stuff. He will now give you back your diamonds, Lady Middlewick.

FREDDIE: *Me?* But – [PHYLLIS *gets her elbow into his ribs just in time*] – you flatter me!

PSMITH: Sherlock, do not play with us any longer. Show Lady Middlewick what is in your hat.

FREDDIE: My hat? [*Picking up his hat from the table beside him and staring into it.*] My hat! [*He gapes.*]

[PHYLLIS *glances into the hat, then quickly takes it from him, and hands it to* LADY MIDDLEWICK. LADY MIDDLEWICK *puts in her hand and takes out the diamonds.*]

LADY MIDDLEWICK: Oh! [*Exclamations from everybody.*] My dear child! My clever boy! Bless you both! [*She embraces* PHYLLIS *and* FREDDIE *in turn, then turns to* ETHELBERTA.] What a relief this will be to the family – and to you – darling!

PSMITH: Three cheers for Freddie!

FREDDIE: Hurray! Hurray! I'm sorry.

[ETHELBERTA *bursts into tears and walks out.*]

[LADY MIDDLEWICK *puts her arm round* PHYLLIS *and* FREDDIE. *They all go up to the window together, there* PHYLLIS *fastens on the necklace for her.* BAXTER *comes to* LORD MIDDLEWICK, *and sneezes suddenly into his ear.*]

BAXTER: Lord Middlewick, I resign.

LORD MIDDLEWICK: Thank the Lord for that! Any particular reason, this time?

BAXTER: I regard this gentleman's story as most unconvincing. We do not even know his name.

LORD MIDDLEWICK: What the devil does that matter? He helped Freddie to get the diamonds back, didn't he? [*To* PSMITH.] What is your name, sir?

[PSMITH *hands card to* BAXTER.]

LORD MIDDLEWICK [*to* BAXTER]: There you are, Baxter! He's got a name all right. I knew he would have.

BAXTER: But nobody knows anything about him.

WALDERWICK: Don't they? I do. He got my umbrella back for me when everybody else had given it up for lost.

BAXTER: Has he any written references, or testimonials?

LORD MIDDLEWICK: They don't mean a thing. Yours were wonderful, Baxter – and damn it, look at you!

BAXTER [*going up to the door and turning*]: All I can say is – [*Sneezes, and goes.*]

LORD MIDDLEWICK: Now, Mr Per Smith!

PSMITH: Psmith. The 'P' is silent, as in 'pshrimp'.

LORD MIDDLEWICK: Very well. I like you. Would you care to be my secretary?

PSMITH: May I bring my wife as assistant secretary?

LORD MIDDLEWICK: You're married?

PSMITH: I hope to be shortly; but I'm not absolutely sure. We'll ask Miss Halliday; she'll know for certain. Eve! [EVE *comes to him.*] Am I going to be married?

EVE: So far as I know – yes.

PSMITH [*putting his arm round her*]: And are you? [EVE *looks up at him, then buries her face on his shoulder.*] The 'U' is silent – as in 'unanimous' – and 'umbrella'!

[*He takes* WALDERWICK'S *umbrella from him, opens the umbrella and puts his arm round* EVE. *They walk up towards the door, under the umbrella.*]

CURTAIN

Come On, Jeeves

A farcical comedy in three acts by P. G. Wodehouse and
Guy Bolton

AUTHOR'S NOTE

Unless I have got my figures wrong, this – I allude to *Come On, Jeeves* – is Guy Bolton's eighty-ninth play. It is the twentieth he and I have written together, and a few words on the subject of our methods of collaboration may be of interest.

I don't know how Beaumont and Fletcher and Massinger and Ford did it, but with us what usually happens is that Guy comes to me and says he has a corking idea for a show. I say 'Ah, yes?' and we sit down and work out a plot. This done, Guy starts writing and goes on writing till the thing is finished. But do not think that I am idle while he is doing this. Twice or thrice a day – sometimes oftener – I look in and say 'How's it getting on?' and he says 'All right', and I say 'Good. Good.' And so, little by little and bit by bit, the work gets done.

I suppose all collaborations are more or less like this – Fletcher used to look in on Beaumont and say 'How goeth it, my heart of gold?' – but what is so remarkable about ours is not the excellence of the work it has produced, though this is considerable, but the fact that after forty years of churning out theatre-joy for a discriminating public we are not merely speaking to one another but are the closest of friends. If Guy saw me drowning, he would dive in to the rescue without a moment's hesitation, and if I saw Guy drowning, I would be the first to call for assistance. How different from most collaborators, who in similar circumstances would merely throw their partner an anvil.

For practically all theatrical collaborations blow up with a loud report on the morning after the first failure, Dramatist A. blaming Dramatist B. for being the sole cause of it and Dramatist B. coming right back at him. Shaftesbury Avenue and Broadway are congested with collaborators whom a single flop has turned from pals together to relentless foes. Indeed, whenever the body of a playwright is found with its head bashed in by a blunt instrument, the first thing the Big Four at Scotland Yard do, I believe, is to inquire into the movements of his former collaborators. 'Didn't deceased write a stinker with George Robinson a couple of years ago which came off after the second night?' asks the Assistant Commissioner. 'I thought so. Detain Robinson for questioning. If he hasn't a cast-iron alibi, he's for it.'

This has not been so with Guy and me. Forty years have passed since we first came together, but our mutual esteem still persists. Any time he has a good idea for a play, I am always willing to help him out. He knows that he can count on my moral support. It is not always convenient for me to go over to his house and say 'How are you getting on?' but I never fail him.

A footnote. All students of the best in English literature are familiar with the novel *Ring for Jeeves*, and many must have supposed that *Come on, Jeeves* is a dramatization of that book. This is not so. After I and Guy had written the play, I turned it into a novel, and if anyone has not read it, there is a genuine treat in store for him. ('This amusing trifle' – *Peebles Advertiser*, '8 by 10½, 255 pages' – *Times Literary Supplement*.)

P. G. WODEHOUSE

CHARACTERS

LORD CARMOYLE [RORY]
LADY CARMOYLE [MONICA], *his wife*
JILL WYVERN, *engaged to marry*
THE EARL OF TOWCESTER [BILL]
JEEVES, *Bill's butler*
ELLEN, *Bill's housemaid*
MRS SPOTTSWORTH, *a wealthy American widow*
CAPTAIN BIGGAR, *a 'White Hunter'*
COLONEL BLAGDEN, *Chief Constable*

SCENES

The action of the play takes place in the living-room at Towcester Abbey, Bill's home, near Towcester, England

ACT ONE

Late afternoon in June.

ACT TWO

The same evening, after dinner

ACT THREE

Afternoon, the following day

ACT ONE

Scene: The living-room at Towcester Abbey.
This is a big, comfortable, shabby room in a very old fabric. Up right,
some french windows opening into garden; up left, a door into an adjoining
library; down left a fireplace equipped with a club-fender in rear wall.
Centre: double doors opening into hall.

It is June, the day before the running of the Derby, and the french
windows are open, as are the doors to the hall, through which we see the
wide hallway and the foot of a staircase.

The furnishings are nondescript, but create a pleasant effect. There is a
telephone on table that stands behind a settee. There are two easy chairs
and an oak chest.

Time: Late afternoon.

The stage is empty. Then enter MONICA *from hall, followed by*
RORY. MONICA *is a pretty, lively woman in her thirties;* RORY, *more*
formally known as Lord Carmoyle, is a man in the forties, cheery and
blundering, the sort of man who, twenty years ago, was one of the Drones
Club Boys but has now, perforce, bowed to the inevitable. He is a
shopwalker at Harrods.

MONICA [*calls*]: Hi! [*Crossing to window.*] Anybody here?
   Coo-ee! [*Out of window. Turns and speaks over shoulder to her
   husband.*] I say, what *is* this, the Palace of Sleeping Beauty? [*Pulls
   bell.*]
RORY: It looks the part. I bet if you shook those curtains a couple of
   bats would fly out.
MONICA: Well, poor old Bill can't afford to keep up a castle on a
   cottage income. [*Opens library door and calls into it.*] View hallo!
   Tantivy! Tantivy!
RORY: Why doesn't Bill get a job like the rest of the poverty-ridden
   peerage? Nowadays the House of Lords is practically empty,
   except on evenings and bank holidays.

MONICA: Don't put on airs, darling, just because you're in trade. We Towcesters are lilies of the field. Grandpapa never so much as learned to tie his own bootlaces. [*She indicates a portrait of grandpapa.*]

[JILL *enters. She is a pretty girl in her early twenties.*]

JILL: Hello, was that you calling?

MONICA: Yes.

JILL: There should be a housemaid but the bells are not very dependable.

MONICA: I know.

JILL: Yes, of course you do, you're Lady Monica . . . I mean Lady Carmoyle, aren't you?

MONICA: Yes.

JILL [*with a little laugh*]: What a wonderful suntan!

MONICA: Oh, good. I was working on it for three months in Montego Bay. [*Sits sofa.*]

RORY: She says she's that colour all over. Might raise a question or two with an old-fashioned husband – but I s'pose it makes for variety.

MONICA: This is my husband, as you may gather.

JILL: Oh, I know Lord Carmoyle, but I see neither of you remember me. I [*offers cigarettes to* MONICA.] was at your wedding.

MONICA: Goodness, you don't look old enough.

JILL: I was fifteen. They gave me the job of keeping the dogs from jumping on the guests. It was pouring, you may remember, and they all had muddy paws.

MONICA: Ah, yes! I know you now. You're one of Lord Cowfold's girls.

JILL: The middle one, Jill.

MONICA: Of course. I suppose you don't happen to know where my brother is?

JILL [*crosses to* RORY *with cigarettes*]: He's off somewhere in the car.

MONICA: Oh, he manages to keep a car, does he?

JILL: He's taken the butler with him, but I'll see if I can't get the gardener to deal with your bags.

MONICA: Don't worry, dear. Rory is in the luggage department at

Harrods . . . But butler, gardener? Are you sure they're not brokers' men in disguise?

JILL: Oh, no, they're real, all right. Jeeves – that's the butler – is the most terrific find.

RORY: You don't mean *the* Jeeves – Bertie Wooster's man?

JILL: Yes. Bill has him on Lend Lease.

RORY: But what the devil does Bertie do without him?

JILL: I believe he's away somewhere.

MONICA: So this was the little girl who was at our wedding? I do apologize for not recognizing you at once.

JILL: Why should you? The last time you were staying here I was just coming out.

MONICA: The getting-ready-for-the-market stage? How well I remember it. Off with the glasses and the teeth-braces.

RORY: On with things that push you in or push you out – whichever you needed.

MONICA: What do you know about it?

RORY: Oh, I get around in our ladies' foundation department.

MONICA: And the agonized conferences with mama about those hockey-player's hands.

JILL [*laughs*]: I used to walk around for hours holding mine in the air. [*She illustrates.*]

MONICA: How did you make out? Has it paid off yet?

JILL: Paid off?

MONICA [*confidentially, woman to woman*]: A man, my dear? Did you catch anything worthwhile?

JILL: I think so. I'm going to marry your brother.

MONICA: *Really?*

RORY: Does he know about it?

JILL [*with a little laugh*]: We're engaged. Look! [*She holds out her hand, displaying ring.*]

MONICA: Oh, yes, family heirloom. You must take care of that, dear. You could pop it for quite a tidy sum.

JILL: I should hate to do that.

MONICA: Nonsense. Through three generations of Towcesters that ring has been in and out of Uncle's, God knows how many times.

RORY [*peering at it*]: Yes, seems like there's something a bit significant about the way those three round-cut diamonds are set.

MONICA: Mama used to hide it during the flat-racing season. Perhaps you'd better, too; gambling runs in the family.

[*The telephone, which stands on table behind settee, rings.*]

Good heavens, don't tell me the telephone bill's been paid.

[RORY *picks up phone.*]

RORY: Hullo . . . yes, this is Towcester Abbey . . . No, Lord Towcester isn't in at the moment. This is his brother-in-law speaking, Lord Carmoyle . . . No, I'm damned if I do. Hold on a minute . . . [*To* JILL.] Do you know the number of Bill's car, Jill?

JILL: No. Why are they asking?

RORY: No, we don't know. Why are you asking? [*Jiggles hook.*] He's rung off.

JILL: If it had been an accident they'd have told us.

RORY: Where did the old blighter go?

JILL [*sits*]: Somewhere on his job. Often he's away for a week at a time.

MONICA: *Job*? Bill's got a job?

RORY: What sort?

JILL: Something to do with the Farm Board. He never seems to want to talk about it, so I'm pretty vague.

MONICA [*incredulously*]: The *Farm* Board?

JILL: Inspection, I suppose . . . checking up on all those questionnaires. He's not very good at figures – that's why he takes Jeeves with him.

MONICA: That's wonderful. I used to be so worried about him dashing from race-course to race-course in a grey topper that he carried sandwiches in.

JILL: I don't suppose he makes much at it.

MONICA: I only hope he isn't having to sink it all in keeping up this ancient ruin.

JILL: The Abbey is quite a drain.

MONICA: If only I could sell if for him!

JILL: You can't, can you?

MONICA: I have strong hopes, that's why I've dashed over here the day of landing.

JILL: Bill offered it for a song as a Home for Reclaimed Delinquents, but they turned it down on the grounds that it was damp.

MONICA: So it is, dear. Towcester is famous for its rheumatism. The dear old Abbey is very warmly spoken of in Harley Street.

RORY [sits]: As I said to Bill, in summer there's a charming river at the bottom of your garden, and in winter there's a charming garden at the bottom of your river. [Laughing.]

MONICA: And being a prize at putting your foot in it, I fully expect to hear you repeating the laboured witticism to Mrs Spotts-worth.

JILL: Mrs. Spottsworth? Is she – ?

MONICA: The mug . . . pardon me, the *friend*, I have in mind. American – I met her on the boat and gave her the hell of a sales talk.

JILL: Rich, I suppose? [*Rises*.]

MONICA: *Rich*? The poor woman suffers agonies from coupon-clipper's thumb . . .

JILL: Is she coming to look at it?

MONICA: Arriving any moment. Stick around.

JILL: I'll be back, but I'm afraid I'll have to ask you to excuse me now. When I heard your call I was dealing with Bill's bitch.

MONICA: Oh, is that wretched cook giving trouble again?

JILL: This is a canine bitch I'm treating for mange. I'm the local vet.

RORY: You're a vet?

JILL: Fully licensed.

MONICA: And doesn't your father mind you running about the country ministering to our dumb chums?

JILL: Oh, no, we're all working at something – that is, all except my brother. He won a Vernon's pool, and he's gone frightfully upper-class. [*She goes out through french window*.]

MONICA: Nice girl.

RORY: Yes, damn pretty legs.

[MONICA *gives him a wifely 'look'. The phone rings again.* MONICA, *who is nearer this time, picks up receiver.*]

MONICA: Hullo? Yes? . . . What, the *police*?

RORY: What the devil?

MONICA: Nothing has happened to his Lordship, I hope? . . . Oh, I'm relieved to hear that . . . Chief Constable Blagdon? . . . I'll tell him, Chief Constable, as soon as he comes in. [*She hangs up.*]

RORY: What's going on here?

MONICA: Oh, it's nothing, I suppose. Bill may have forgotten to renew his car licence or his insurance.

RORY [*rises, spreading his hands*]: Speaking of cars, *I* could do with a wash.

MONICA [*crosses to hall door – RORY follows*]: Come one, we'll go and find ourselves a room. [*She opens hall door.*]

RORY [*staring at it*]: S'pose that radio works?

MONICA: Why?

RORY: I'd like to know what won today.

MONICA: Now don't you start talking about racing around Bill. He's sworn off. [*She turns and goes out.*]

RORY [*following her*]: That's a nice one – mustn't mention racing and tomorrow's Derby Day! [*He also goes out.*]

[*After a moment's pause the grinding of brakes is heard. An instant later BILL enters through french window. He is wearing a very loud check coat with voluminous, bulging pockets and a flamboyant tie. He wears a quite substantial, though not exaggerated, moustache. He also has a huge round badge pinned on his coat on which are the words: 'Honest Patch Perkins'. He speaks over his shoulder to someone he evidently imagines to be following him.*]

BILL [*enters, takes cigarette*]: Well, we got here, Jeeves. I suppose the whole thing turns now on whether the blighter got our car number.

[*As he speaks, he proceeds to the middle of the room, then, getting no answer, turns and sees he is alone.*]

Oh!

[*He moves back toward window, then suddenly sees his reflection in the mirror.*]

Good God!

[*He removes the badge and pockets it, then, bending and peering*

*closely in mirror, he pulls off the moustache, the operation being
clearly a somewhat painful one.*]

Oo-oo-oo.

[*As he finishes removing the moustache,* ELLEN, *a very refined
housemaid, enters from hall. She coughs.* BILL *quickly pockets
moustache.*]

ELLEN: Pardon me, my lord.

BILL: Yes, Ellen?

ELLEN: I just wanted to inform your lordship that Lord and Lady
Carmoyle are here.

BILL [*his mind on other things, scratches ear, finds cigarette*]: Are they
indeed? Well, well. [*To drinks table for matches.*]

ELLEN: I have put them in Nell Gwynne's room.

BILL: Won't that make them all rather crowded? [*Suddenly
realizing.*] Oh! Nell Gwynne's room . . . of course, of course.
My mind was wandering.

ELLEN: Lady Carmoyle inquired what time your lordship would
be having tea.

BILL: Oh, any time that suits them – any time they're ready.

ELLEN: Thank you, my lord. [*Exit, closing door.*]

[BILL *goes back to window and calls through it in a low,
conspiratorial voice.*]

BILL: Jeeves! [*He whistles.*]

[JEEVES *enters from hall. He carries over his arm a coat and, with it,
a tie of conservative pattern.* JEEVES *is a man in his middle forties of
impressive dignity.*]

JEEVES: You whistled, m'lord?

[BILL, *who is half way out of the french window, spins round.*]

BILL: How the devil did you get over there?

JEEVES: I ran the car into the garage, m'lord, and then made my
way to the servants' quarters. Your coat, m'lord.

BILL: Oh, thanks. I see *you've* changed.

JEEVES [*helping* BILL *on with coat*]: I deemed it advisable, m'lord.
The fellow was not far behind us and may appear unexpectedly.
Might I suggest that your lordship discard that somewhat
distinctive tie?

BILL: By Jove, yes. And put the coat away somewhere.

JEEVES: Very good, m'lord. I fancy this coffer will serve for the moment. [*He takes coat and tie and, opening oak chest, carefully folds and lays them inside it.*]

BILL: Rather humiliating, Jeeves, having to fly like that.

JEEVES: It was not an actual flight, m'lord – merely a 'strategic retreat'. Your lordship fully intends to pay the man.

BILL: Of course I do. But he'll jolly well have to wait until I can scrape together a little matter of three thousand pounds.

JEEVES: We were not equipped to incur so heavy a risk.

BILL: I know, I know. You begged me to lay the bet off.

JEEVES: I had misgivings. It is true, the probability of two such rank outsiders combining in a double seemed very remote.

BILL: I didn't think the fellow had an earthly. Lucy Glitters at a hundred to six, and Whistler's Mother at thirty-three to one . . . I thought it was the easiest five pounds I'd ever made.

JEEVES: When I saw Whistler's Mother pass us on her way to the starting post, I was conscious of a tremour of uneasiness. Those long legs, that powerful rump . . .

BILL: Tell me, Jeeves, if the worst came to the worst, couldn't I plead the Gaming Act?

JEEVES: I fear not, m'lord. You took the person's money. A cash transaction.

BILL: A prison offence?

JEEVES: The sentences are not severe.

BILL [*sits*]: But think of the papers! The Ninth Earl of Towcester, whose ancestor held the field at Agincourt, *fled* the field at Epsom.

JEEVES: Unquestionably the circumstance of your lordship having become a Silver Ring bookie would be given wide publicity.

BILL: Do you think if I met this johnny, the fellow who booked the double, d'ye think he'd recognize me?

JEEVES: I incline to think not, m'lord.

BILL: I had a patch over one eye and a *crêpe* moustache.

JEEVES: True. And two weeks ago at Newmarket you encountered several gentlemen of your acquaintance –

BILL: And none of them spotted me.

JEEVES: But, while he might not recognize your lordship in

persona proper, you dare not appear in the character of Patch Perkins.

BILL: True.

JEEVES: So the only course now is to try and raise the needed funds as quickly as possible.

BILL: It will take some doing.

JEEVES [*impressively*]: Three thousand and three pounds, six shillings and eight pence.

BILL [*torn*]: I would be grateful, Jeeves, if you wouldn't keep intoning those words. They are etched on my retina in glorious technicolour.

JEEVES: Very good, m'lord. [*He turns to go.*]

BILL [*rises*]: Hang on a moment. [JEEVES *turns.*] What do you think? Should I tell Miss Wyvern what's happened?

JEEVES: Is Miss Wyvern aware of your lordship's connection with the turf?

BILL: No. I had a feeling she would not be entirely sympathetic.

JEEVES: Then it would appear an ill-chosen moment to acquaint Miss Wyvern with the facts. Ladies are inclined to take a more broad-minded view in cases where the enterprise is paying dividends.

BILL: H'm, ah, yes. Maybe you're right.

[JILL *enters from garden.*]

JILL: So you're back?

BILL: Hello, my sweet. Come in and tell me how Adelina is doing.

[JEEVES *withdraws, closing door, as* JILL *replies.*]

JILL: Almost in the clear. That new American stuff is a miracle worker.

BILL [*to her*]: You're the real miracle worker. Ooh! When I'm dull and depressed, you come into the room and immediately the sun starts to shine.

JILL: Pretty speech.

BILL: Whenever I'm with you, I feel as if I had a flower in my buttonhole.

JILL: *Two* pretty speeches! Now I'm beginning to get suspicious. What have you been up to?

BILL: Me? Nothing. Just plodding the same daily round.

JILL: Your sister couldn't believe it when I told her about your job.

BILL: My sister?

JILL: Yes, she's here, she and Lord Carmoyle.

BILL: Good Lord! However did he manage to tear himself away from Harrods?

JILL: He seems to be awfully keen on his job.

BILL: Since they made him a floor-walker he's become a complete snob.

JILL: Your sister says she's dashed here from wherever it was she landed, to help you sell the Abbey.

BILL: Sell the Abbey? Don't be absurd. The only way to get rid of the Abbey would be to hire a couple of good arsonists and turn them loose with petrol and matches.

JILL: She says she's sure she can sell it – to a rich American.

BILL: An American buy this antiquated flea bag? Americans demand self-confident heating systems and proud plumbing. My ancestors were a rugged people who held the view that too many baths acted detrimentally on the natural body oils.

JILL: Heaven knows there's plenty of space to add bathrooms.

BILL [sits sofa]: If they'd content themselves with shower baths there are a good many places where the roof would oblige them.

JILL: You're a bit of a wet blanket, darling.

BILL: You'd feel out of place in Towcester Abbey if you were a *dry* one.

JILL: Seems you're not quite your old, lighthearted self this afternoon.

BILL: Had a rather patchy day.

JILL: Why? Aren't the crops rotating properly? Or are the pigs going in for birth-control?

BILL: My chief problem today was concerned with horses.

JILL [sits sofa]: Oh, those lovely farm horses with the big, shaggy hooves! People are always raving about spindle-legged race-horses, but for me – give me a good Shire.

BILL: I think you've got something there.

JILL: Let's buy a farm, darling. I'm sure we'd do well at it – me as a vet and you with all your expert farming knowledge . . .

BILL [vaguely]: H'm, yes – yes, of course.

JILL: If we could scrape enough money together we might start a prize herd . . . that really pays.

BILL: So I'm told.

JILL: Told? If you don't know, who does?

[*Enter* MONICA *from hall.*]

MONICA: Hiya, Bill

BILL: Hullo, Moke. [*Rises.*]

MONICA: I'm not breaking up any fond dalliance, I trust? Anyway you needn't mind sister Monica. My motto is 'love and let love' – with the one stipulation that people who love in glass houses should breathe on the windows.

[JILL *rises.* MONICA *goes to* BILL *and they embrace. As they do so* RORY *enters in his wife's wake.*]

RORY: What ho, Bill!

BILL: Hullo, Rory, how come you are straying so far away from the Brompton Road?

RORY: Holidays . . . Our new stagger system, two days a week for ten weeks. The Efficiency Director thinks that way one doesn't lose one's grip on things.

MONICA [*sits. To* BILL]: I hear that you've also become a horny-handed worker while I was away lotus-eating in Jamaica.

BILL: Yes . . . I've pitched in at last.

[JILL *sits sofa*]

RORY: Well, don't go it too hard at first. We ex-drones have got to learn how to use our latent energies. That's what I keep preaching to the chaps under me. Most of 'em listen, but there's one lad – younger son of a duke he is – in the ladies' shoe department . . . You've never seen such drive.

BILL: Really?

RORY: That boy's going to burn himself out before he's fifty.

BILL: I'll keep your warning in mind.

MONICA: Also hearty congrats on this rare specimen of girl that you've snaffled! I couldn't approve more.

RORY: Hear, hear!

JILL: Thank you.

RORY: How did you do it?

BILL: Oh, the usual way, just chased her until she caught me.

[RORY *sits.*]

MONICA: Has Jill told you about the reason for this uninvited visit – Mrs Spottsworth?

BILL: Mrs Spottsworth? No.

JILL: The rich American.

BILL: Oh, the pigeon – ? Is that her name, Sapworth?

MONICA: Not *Sap*-worth – Spottsworth. Tell me, what's your rock-bottom figure?

BILL [*promptly*]: Three thousand and three pounds, six and eightpence.

RORY: That's a damned funny sum.

JILL: Yes, surely it's worth a bit more than that.

BILL: I doubt it. Anyhow the way I'm situated I'd sell for almost anything. [*Sits sofa.*]

MONICA: You're hard up?

BILL: Stony.

RORY: But if you're so broke, old boy, whence all these retainers, butlers, housemaids, gardeners?

MONICA: Not to mention cars and paid-up telephone accounts.

BILL: I had a brief period of affluence.

MONICA [*rises*]: It sounds suspiciously as if you'd been gambling again. [*To* JILL.] It took him years to get it through his fat head that the punters haven't a hope against the bookmakers.

BILL: And now I *do* know it, I'm not so sure that it's true.

JILL [*patting* BILL'S *cheek maternally*]: Oh yes, you are, dear. [*To* MONICA:] Bill's always saying what idiots people are who think they can bring off fantastic doubles . . . win thousands of pounds with a single fiver.

RORY: It comes off once in a while and I must say I'm always tickled to death to see a punter give one of those damn bookies a kick in the pants.

MONICA: It wouldn't happen to Bill. He always chose the kind of horse that chases all the other horses home.

RORY: By the way, did you tell Bill about the police?

RORY: You had a call from the local gendarmerie. Chief Constable Somebody.

MONICA: He wants you to call him back. [*Cigarette out. Sits.*]

JILL: Surely that wasn't the police that called while I was here?

MONICA: No, that was another one.

RORY: Some mysterious bloke with a voice that sounded as if he ate spinach with sand in it. He was inquiring about the licence number of your car.

BILL: What!!!

MONICA: You haven't run into somebody's cow, have you? I understand that's a very serious offence nowadays.

BILL: Did this chap who phoned you give any name?

MONICA: No.

JILL: I would have been a bit worried if I hadn't remembered what a wonderful driver you are.

BILL [*crosses to hall door*]: I'll go and phone the Chief Constable.

MONICA: Why don't you use this phone?

BILL: I'll disturb you. Be back in two shakes.

JILL [*rises*]: *I* must be going, Bill. I have a couple of patients to call on.

RORY: Patients?

JILL: A battered tom cat and an expectant lady pig.

BILL: I'll see you to your motor cycle.

JILL [*to* MONICA *and* RORY]: Bye. See you later.

BILL: You're coming for dinner, remember.

[*He and* JILL *go out.*]

MONICA [*rises*]: Rory, there's something wrong here. Bill's got the wind up.

RORY: Oh, you imagine things . . . Naturally, we workers have our problems. We're not like your crowd of Jamaican sunbathers – those morons with less on.

MONICA [*looking to door*]: I tell you Bill's in some trouble. I know my brother a little better than you do. [*Picks up phone and listens.*] I'd love to hear what it is the Chief Constable has to say.

RORY: That's a bit hot, isn't it? Wire tapping. Just goes to show that women aren't gentlemen.

[*The hall door opens and* JEEVES *appears.* MONICA *has her back to him.*]

MONICA [*listening on phone*]: He's not on yet. [*Covers phone with hand.*] Perhaps he hasn't put in the call.

JEEVES: I am afraid that instrument is turned off, m'lady. There is a switch in my pantry.

MONICA [*putting back receiver*]: Oh yes, of course . . . And someone is using the phone, are they?

JEEVES: Yes, m'lady. His lordship.

MONICA [*crossing to chair, sits*]: Jeeves, there are strange things going on in this house.

JEEVES: Indeed, m'lady? I have noticed very few phenomena of late. Your ladyship's ancestress, the Lady Agatha, has not appeared for several months.

RORY: A lot of tosh.

JEEVES: I am not sure, m'lord. Mrs Piggott, the cook, a most reliable woman *and* a strict teetotaller, assures me that she saw Lady Agatha come down the Long Gallery and disappear into the bathroom.

RORY: I hope she doesn't make a habit of it. I don't want any Lady Agathas popping in while I'm taking a bath.

MONICA: These are not the kind of strange things I meant, Jeeves. I am not interested in the Towcester Abbey ghosts pro or con. It is the present Lord Towcester I am concerned about.

JEEVES: His lordship remarked to me only this morning that he had never felt so completely in the pink since the last time he rode to hounds.

MONICA [*rises*]: His health appears right enough, but what about this business with the police?

JEEVES: The police, m'lady?

MONICA: They rang up just now.

JEEVES: Ah, that would be with reference to their annual sports, one imagines. No doubt they wish his lordship to present the prizes.

MONICA [*eyeing him closely*]: I see. Someone also telephoned asking the number of Lord Towcester's car.

JEEVES [*without a flicker*]: We were obliged to replenish our petrol tank at a farm. They need the number for their books.

MONICA [*faintly ironical*]: Good, very neat.

JEEVES: Thank you, m'lady. I endeavour to give satisfaction.

MONICA: I understand Lord Towcester takes you with him on these daily journeys of his?

JEEVES: Yes, m'lady. There is a good deal of figure work involved, and I happen to have a head for figures.

MONICA [*sits*]: You must be invaluable to Lord Towcester in *many* ways. I can see that.

JEEVES: Your ladyship is too kind.

RORY [*rises*]: How the devil is Bertie Wooster managing without you?

JEEVES: Mr Wooster is attending a school, m'lord, which does not permit its student body to have personal servants.

MONICA: A school?

JEEVES: Designed to teach the aristocracy to fend for itself. Mr Wooster, while at present financially sound, feels that it is prudent to build for the future.

RORY: I see what you mean. Can't live on capital for ever.

JEEVES: Precisely, m'lord. The course Mr Wooster is taking includes shoe-cleaning, sock-darning, bed-making and primary grade cooking.

RORY: Well, I'm blowed. One doesn't realize how far the social revolution has gone.

MONICA: The man who holds a diploma from such a school will be the eligible party of the future.

JEEVES: Possibly, m'lady, but I must confess it is not without emotion that I picture Mr Wooster seated on a bed that he has made, in a room that he has swept and dusted, darning his own socks.

[*Enter* BILL *from hall.*]

BILL: Oh, Jeeves, we shall be five for dinner tonight. [*To* MONICA:] Or is your friend bringing anyone with her?

MONICA: Not that I'm aware of.

BILL: Between ourselves, Jeeves, there is some faint hope that we may be able to sell this house.

JEEVES: Indeed, m'lord? A consummation devoutly to be wished.

BILL: So I suggest you remove the two buckets that stand under the upper hall skylight.

JEEVES: Very good, m'lord. I will also put some more thumb tacks in the wallpaper.

MONICA: Mrs Spottsworth will be staying the night. Which room has the best climate for someone inclined to fibrositis?

JEEVES: The South Tower room, I should say, m'lady. I will put a wire screen in the flue, to discourage intrusion by the bats that nest there. Would there be anything further, m'lord?

BILL: No, that's all. Thank you, Jeeves.

JEEVES: Thank you, m'lord. [*Exit* JEEVES *to hall.*]

MONICA: That man is a treasure.

BILL: One of Nature's noblemen.

RORY [*sits sofa*]: Moke was trying to pump him, but she hadn't a hope. The Mona Lisa in butler's clothes.

BILL [*coldly*]: What was it you were trying to find out, Moke?

MONICA: Nothing, Rory's an ass.

BILL: Unquestionably . . . But it's also true, darling, that you're a bit of a Nosy Parker.

MONICA: There's gratitude for you. If I did make a few inquiries it was only because I can't bear to think that you're in trouble.

BILL [*taking cigarette from box on phone table*]: Who says I'm in trouble?

MONICA: You're as nervous as a rabbit's nose.

BILL: Rot. [*Starts to light cigarette.*]

RORY: . I always say when a chap's in a bit of a tizzy he ought to stop smoking cork-tip cigarettes.

[*He points a finger at the cigarette* BILL *is lighting, at the wrong end. As* BILL *throws it in ash-tray and takes another, door-bell rings.*]

MONICA: Is that the door-bell?

BILL [*listening tensely*]: Yes.

RORY: Perhaps it's the evening paper. I'd love to know what won today. [*Goes up to hall door.*]

BILL: Whistler's Mother, thirty-three to one.

RORY: Good Lord! [*He stands in the doorway looking off.*]

MONICA: How do *you* know?

BILL: I've a radio in the car . . . Look, old girl, why don't you pop up to the Tower Room, make sure it's properly aired, put some flowers around, etcetera?

MONICA: You want to get rid of me . . . Who are you expecting, the police?

BILL: The police *might* drop in. We're on very friendly terms.

RORY [*turning back into the room and speaking in low voice*]: Female of the species – looks like the Rock of Gibraltar in skirts.

MONICA: It's my American ... [*To* BILL:] She *is* a bit overpowering.

[*Turns to hall door as* JEEVES *appears.*]

JEEVES [*announcing*]: Mrs Spottsworth.

[*Enter* MRS SPOTTSWORTH. *She is in her early to mid-forties, large, handsome, and commanding. She is a devotee of the esoteric. She wears flowing draperies that, she feels, reflect her personality.*]

MRS SPOTTSWORTH: Greetings, greetings! Bienvenu!

[JEEVES *withdraws – closing door.*]

MONICA: Oh, come in, Mrs Spottsworth. So glad you found your way here all right. This is my borther, Lord Towcester.

BILL: How do you do?

MONICA: And my husband.

RORY: Haryar?

MRS SPOTTSWORTH: What a *wonderful* old place you have, Lord Towcester.

BILL: A bit shabby, I'm afraid.

MRS SPOTTSWORTH: The patina of Time. I adore it.

BILL: Oh, it's *old*, no mistake about that.

MRS SPOTTSWORTH [*rapidly with closed eyes and arms half-spread*]: The dead, twelve deep, clutch at you as you go by. [*Opens eyes, smiles.*] But I'm going to tell you something odd, something you will probably laugh at ... It struck me so strongly when I came in that door that I had to sit down for a moment ... Your butler thought I was ill ...

MONICA [*solicitously*]: You aren't, I hope?

MRS SPOTTSWORTH: No, not at all, I was simply – overcome. I realized that I've been here before.

BILL: We used to have shilling viewers Tuesdays and Fridays throughout the summer months.

MRS SPOTTSWORTH: Oh, I didn't mean that I had been here in my present corporal envelope. I meant in some previous incarnation. I'm a Rotationist, you know.

MONICA: Rotationist?

MRS SPOTTSWORTH: Yes. We Rotationists believe we are reborn as one of our ancestors every ninth generation.

MONICA: Ninth? [*Sits sofa. She begins to count on her fingers.*]

MRS SPOTTSWORTH: The mystic ninth house. Of course you've read your Zend Avesta?

BILL [*sits chest*]: I'm afraid not.

RORY: Is it good?

MRS SPOTTSWORTH: Good? I would say it's essential.

RORY: I'll put it on my library list.

MONICA [*completes her calculation*]: Ninth . . . That seems to make *me* Lady Barbara, the leading tart of Charles the Second's reign.

BILL: She had some stiff competition, for the title, what with pretty Nelly, etcetera.

MRS SPOTTSWORTH [*she gives a little laugh*]: I suppose I should be calling you Lady Barbara and asking you about your latest love affair.

MONICA: I only wish I could remember . . . You'd have quite an earful if I did.

RORY: Did Babsie get herself sunburned all over? Or was she more of an indoor girl?

MRS SPOTTSWORTH [*passing a hand slowly across her brow*]: There's a chapel here . . . I remember a chapel.

BILL: A ruined one.

MRS SPOTTSWORTH [*in the same medium-like manner*]: I knew it, I knew it! And there's a long gallery? [*She spreads her arms, illustrating.*]

BILL: There is indeed. A duel was fought in it over a gambling dispute in the eighteenth century.

MONICA: Yes, you can still see the bullet holes in the walls.

MRS SPOTTSWORTH: And dark stains on the floor, no doubt . . . The place must be full of ghosts.

BILL [*heartily*]: Oh, don't worry. Nothing like that in good old Towcester.

MRS SPOTTSWORTH [*tremulously, turns to Bill*]: But I *want* ghosts. Don't tell me there aren't *any*?

[*She stares from one to the other with woebegone eyes.* BILL *is obviously at a loss.* MONICA *comes to the rescue.*]

MONICA: There's a haunted bathroom. [*Rises.*]

MRS SPOTTSWORTH [*brightening*]: Really? Tell me what happens?

MONICA: Every now and then, when there's nobody near it, the loo will suddenly flush.

MRS SPOTTSWORTH: How extraordinary! Our Psychic Research Group would be very interested in that.

RORY: And at any time of family crisis it just keeps going and *going*.

MRS SPOTTSWORTH: Oh?

MONICA: What Rory means is that the phenomenon occurs at shorter intervals.

MRS SPOTTSWORTH: A form of poltergeist. But are there no bodily manifestations? [*To* BILL.] Ectoplasms?

BILL: I've never seen any.

MONICA: Plenty of other people *have*. Jeeves was telling us just now about seeing Lady Agatha come down the Long Gallery . . .

RORY: Bound for the bathroom.

MRS SPOTTSWORTH: Who was Lady Agatha?

MONICA: The wife of Sir Caradoc the Crusader. Described on his tomb as ye fairest knight of chivalry.

BILL [*to* MONICA]: He kept rescuing Saracen maidens from castles and taking them to *his* castle.

MRS SPOTTSWORTH: Fascinating, fascinating. And now let *me* take you to the Long Gallery. Don't tell me where it is. Let me see if I can't find it for myself.

[*She presses her fingertips to her temples, makes some little bobbing motions and then starts off. Hall door opens and* JEEVES *appears.* MRS SPOTTSWORTH *stops in front of him.*]

JEEVES: In reference to Mrs Spottsworth's dog, I would appreciate instructions as to meal hours and diet.

MRS SPOTTSWORTH: She usually dines at five but she's not at all fussy.

JEEVES: I took the liberty of giving her a bowl of water and sent her in charge of Ellen, for a turn in the garden.

MRS SPOTTSWORTH [*vaguely*]: In the garden?

JEEVES: I thought it expedient to save her the embarrassment of a possible *faux pas*.

MRS SPOTTSWORTH: Oh, yes, yes, of course . . . But now I must concentrate. [*She again applies fingertips to her temples.*] This is a test. [*She bobs about, as does a homing pigeon before it settles on its direction.*] Follow please, Lady Carmoyle – you too, Lord Towcester. I propose to take you *straight* to the Long Gallery. [*She goes out to hall,* MONICA *following.* BILL *brings up the rear of the procession. He makes a motion of revolving wheels beside his head which indicates* MRS SPOTTSWORTH *is a screwball. He goes out.*]

RORY: Definitely scrammy.

JEEVES: Mrs Spottsworth informed me on her arrival that she had week-ended here some time in the seventeenth century.

RORY: There seems to be a lot of crackpot ideas floating about in the States.

JEEVES: They give the American something to chat about when alone with his psycho-analyst.

RORY: Too rich – that's their trouble, Jeeves. Nothing like having to scratch for a living. I'm twice the man I was since I took up shopwalking.

JEEVES [*emptying ashtrays on phone table*]: 'Tis deeds must win the prize, to quote the bard.

RORY: Speaking of winning prizes, what about tomorrow?

JEEVES: Tomorrow, m'lord?

RORY: The Derby . . . any ideas?

JEEVES: I fear not, m'lord. It seems an exceptionally open race.

RORY: Voleur is favourite, I believe.

JEEVES: Fifteen to two at last night's call-over, but I fancy the price will shorten to sixes or even fives for the S.P.

RORY: I like the Boussac stable.

JEEVES: Quite so, m'lord, but the animal in question is rather small and lightly boned for so gruelling a contest. We have, to be sure, seen such a handicap overcome. I refer to Manna, the 1925 winner, and Hyperion, another smallish horse, which broke the course record previously held by Flying Fox; accomplishing the distance in two minutes, thirty-four seconds.

RORY: Zowie! You know your stuff, don't you?

JEEVES: It is part of my curriculum to be reasonably well informed on such matters.

RORY: Yes, jolly useful. [*Goes to door.*] You might tell his lordship that he'll find me in the billiards room.

JEEVES: Thank you, m'lord.

RORY: I'll have another little consultation with you tomorrow before I put my bet on. [*Exit to hall.*]

[*JEEVES flicks phone table, coffee table, etc., and empties ashtrays. A man appears in french window. This is CAPTAIN BIGGAR. He is a weather-beaten colonial, with a bronzed face, a clipped moustache and the air of being a tough customer.*]

CAPTAIN: Good evening.

[*The voice has a familiar ring to JEEVES, but he turns with great calm and continues to dust out ashtrays and polish them with a cloth he has taken from the drawer.*]

JEEVES: Yes, sir? May I suggest that the front door is round to the right, the tradesmen's entrance to the left?

CAPTAIN: I've just been having a dekko at your Austin.

JEEVES: Your allusion, I presume, is to the car of my employer, the Earl of Towcester?

CAPTAIN: The Earl of Towcester – ? That's true, then, is it? The police said . . . [*He comes into the room.*]

JEEVES [*interrupting*]: You are possibly unaware, sir, that your entry into this room constitutes a trespass?

CAPTAIN: That be damned. When you're chasing crooks –

JEEVES: Crooks?

CAPTAIN: People who take your money and don't pay what they owe are *crooks*. And we don't stand on ceremony with them in Kuala Lumpur.

JEEVES: You appear to be under some misapprehension. If you have any business with his lordship, will you kindly state it briefly and at once?

CAPTAIN: My old Wolseley would have caught up with that car if the police hadn't nabbed me for speeding. I told them I was chasing a welshing bookie and his clerk and gave them the car number – [*Points off in presumed direction of garage.*] – *that* car number.

JEEVES: Since the police presumably informed you that the car in question is the property of Lord Towcester, I find your presence here bordering on the incomprehensible.

CAPTAIN: Listen. You're coming it very grand, but let me tell you, my good man, that I'm used to dealing with Rajahs, Viziers and three-tailed Bashaws.

JEEVES: There is no question of being grand. I am, however, dressed in a little brief authority, and I shall exercise it by asking you to leave this room at once.

CAPTAIN: I've not finished saying my say . . .

JEEVES: I see I shall have to summon the police. [*He goes to telephone, picks up receiver.*]

CAPTAIN [*beginning to crack*]: Wait a minute. I've not come to make any trouble for Lord Towcester. Seems someone borrowed his car today . . . with or without his permission . . .

JEEVES: Nobody borrowed his lordship's car. Of that I can assure you. It is a clear case of mistaken identity. [*He replaces receiver, but stands with his hand on it.*]

CAPTAIN: Don't tell me! That car was used today by a bookie called 'Honest Patch Perkins' and his clerk.

JEEVES: In the kindliest spirit I suggest that your eyesight needs medical attention.

CAPTAIN: My eyesight? My eyesight? Do you know who you're talking to? I am Sahib Biggar.

JEEVES: I regret to say that the name is unknown to me. However, Sahib, I can only repeat . . .

CAPTAIN [*cutting in on 'Sahib'*]: In this country I use my title of Captain.

JEEVES: Sahib or Captain, I still say that you have made the pardonable mistake of misreading a licence number.

CAPTAIN: Look, perhaps you're not up on these things. I am a white hunter, the most famous white hunter in Malaya, Indonesia, Africa. I can stand *without fear* in the path of an oncoming rhino . . . and why? Because I know I can get him in that one vulnerable spot before he's within sixty paces.

JEEVES: I concede that you may have trained your eyes for that purpose, but, poorly informed as I am on the subject, I do

not believe that rhinoceri are equipped with number plates.
[BILL *appears in hall doorway. He stops dead as he sees the*
CAPTAIN. JEEVES *turns to him with reassuring calm.*]

Ah, your lordship. This gentleman is Sahib Biggar . . . he is
insisting that your car was used today by some race-course
characters against whom he appears to nurse a grievance.

BILL: Really? How do you do? [*Turning to* JEEVES.] What did you
say his name was?

CAPTAIN: Captain Biggar. I'm sorry to intrude like this, but I'm
after a blackguardly bookie –

BILL: Bookies! Stinkers, the whole lot of them. I'd like to have the
money they've taken from me.

CAPTAIN: I'll bet you never got the sleeve across the windpipe the
way I did today.

BILL: Had a bad day, did you?

CAPTAIN: Bad? It was the best day I ever had. I've done a lot of
race-going . . . Calcutta, Hong Kong, Singapore. I flatter
myself I've an eye for horses.

BILL: You pick them yourself, do you?

CAPTAIN: Always. I prefer a rangy animal with a strong rump.

BILL: Ah yes, like Whis – [*He checks himself, staring at* JEEVES,
appalled by his near slip.] – like my Aunt Augusta, I mean. Won
the hurdles at Girton in 'ninety-four.

CAPTAIN: A hundred-to-six and a thirty-three-to-one shot . . .
combined in a double . . . what do you think of that?

BILL: Good heavens, you mean that you . . . What was it, a quid
each way?

CAPTAIN: A *quid*? Five pounds on the nose.

BILL: Five pounds? . . . Are you listening to this, Jeeves? . . . You
must have won a small fortune . . .

CAPTAIN: Over three thousand quid . . . And then the bookie
does a bolt.

BILL: No!

CAPTAIN: I assure you.

BILL: I don't wonder you're incensed at this – this . . . what is it
Shakespeare calls such a man?

JEEVES: An arrant, rascally, beggarly, lousy knave, m'lord.

BILL: That's it.

JEEVES [*grateful at having been asked to quote Shakespeare*]: A whoreson, beetle-headed, flapeared knave; a rascal, an eater of broken meats; a beggarly, filthy, worsted-stocking . . .

BILL: Woa, Jeeves . . . Jeeves is a great Shakespeare student; he's read the old boy from cover to cover. [*As* JEEVES *opens hall door.*] Don't run away, Jeeves . . . Just give that fire a good stir.

JEEVES: It isn't lighted, m'lord.

BILL: Ah, no more it is! I'm all upset, hearing this appalling story. Won't you sit down, Captain? Cigars, Jeeves.

CAPTAIN [*sits. Holding up a hand*]: Thank you, not now. I'm after big game.

BILL: Big game?

JEEVES: The gentleman is a white hunter.

BILL: Is he, though? And now you're hunting bookies. [*He gives a mirthless laugh.*]

CAPTAIN: All I say is I wish I could meet that rat in Kuala Lumpur.

BILL: Kuala Lumpur? That's the place Maugham writes about. Rather a strange lot of birds out there, I gather.

CAPTAIN: Do you know what happens to a welsher in Kuala Lumpar?

BILL [*nervously*]: No, I don't believe I've ever heard. Hang on, Jeeves – Here's an ashtray you've missed. [*Hands* JEEVES *ashtray.*]

CAPTAIN [*impressively*]: We give the blighter three days to pay up. Then someone calls on him and leaves a loaded revolver.

BILL: You mean he's expected to . . .? Isn't that a bit drastic?

CAPTAIN [*rises*]: It's the code, sir. Code! That's a big word with the men who live on the frontiers of empire. Morale can crumble very easily, out there. The steps down are drink, women, unpaid gambling debts. [*He indicates the steps with his hand.*]

BILL: That one's the bottom, is it?

CAPTAIN: We've got to set an example, we bearers of the white man's burden. Can't let the Dyaks beat us on code. [*Sits.*]

BILL: Do they try?

CAPTAIN: A Dyak who defaults on a debt has his head cut off.

BILL: Does he really? Did you hear that, Jeeves?

CAPTAIN: The head is then given to his principal creditor.

BILL: Good Lord! You couldn't run a business that way over here. Imagine the arguments there would be. Eh, Jeeves?

JEEVES: Profoundly true, m'lord.

BILL: What about the weekend guests who slip away Monday forgetting the Saturday night bridge game? Still, I can see it would make everybody a damn sight more careful in their bidding. [*A pause.*] But, getting back to this business of my car, what makes you think – ? [*To* CAPTAIN.]

JEEVES: The gentleman is under the impression that an individual known as Patch Purvis borrowed your lordship's automobile.

CAPTAIN [*cutting in*]: Patch Perkins. 'Honest Patch Perkins', his sign says.

BILL: What an extraordinary idea. I never lend my car to anyone. And I keep the keys in my pocket. Show him the keys, Jeeves.

CAPTAIN [*he is beginning to realize that* BILL *is nervous*]: You don't know Honest Patch Perkins, Lord Towcester? Or *do* you? [*Rises.*]

BILL: Never laid eyes on him. But let me tell you something, Captain. I think this chap'll pay you.

CAPTAIN [*backing* BILL *round in front of sofa*]: I know damn well he'll pay me. I'm going to find him, and then he'll pay me . . . or *else* . . .

BILL: Or else – what?

CAPTAIN: Just as a start I'll have him barred for life from every racecourse in England.

BILL: But suppose he's only trying to gain a little time?

CAPTAIN: *I'll* give him time. I'll see that he gets plenty. Then, after he comes out, I shall attend to him personally. [BILL *sits sofa.*] I'll show him what it means, to try any nonsense with a white hunter.

BILL: Pretty tough chaps, I fancy.

CAPTAIN: We have to be. [*Sits sofa.*] Of course out East there's more leeway. If they know you for a straight shooter, and the other chap's a wrong 'un – well, there aren't many questions asked.

BILL [*nervously*]: Questions about what?

CAPTAIN: They're glad to be rid of him. The fewer there are of such vermin the better for Anglo-Saxon prestige.

BILL: I see.

CAPTAIN: There are a couple of notches on *my* gun that aren't for Brahmany bulls.

BILL: Really?

CAPTAIN: Cheaters of various sorts.

BILL: Cheetahs? Those are those leopard things that go as fast as racehorses.

JEEVES: Somewhat faster, my lord. A half-mile in forty-five seconds.

CAPTAIN [*rises*]: I am not talking about cheetah, the animal – though I have shot some of those, too.

BILL: *Too*? [*Rises*.]

CAPTAIN [*nodding his head significantly*]: *Too*.

BILL: Well, well, this is all very interesting. We must have another chat some time, eh, Jeeves?

CAPTAIN: I'll communicate with you again. I'm going back to the police station now. The Chief Constable may have found out something.

BILL: Let's hope . . . I'll get him on the phone after you've gone and tell him to call off that speeding charge. And take a cigar, won't you? Oh, no, I remember, you said you wouldn't.

[*Enter* MRS SPOTTSWOTH *from hall, followed by* MONICA.]

MRS SPOTTSWORTH: I found the Long Gallery. I'm sorry you didn't stay the course, Lord Towcester.

[JEEVES *goes out to hall.*]

BILL: I got a bit mixed up myself on that detour through the servants' wing.

MRS SPOTTSWORTH: I know, I know. I missed the Influence for a moment.

MONICA: But it wasn't bad after three hundred years.

BILL: Mrs Spottsworth, may I present Captain Biggar?

MRS SPOTTSWORTH: How do you do?

BILL: And my sister, Lady Agatha – I mean Lady Carmoyle.

MONICA: Good evening, Captain Biggar.

264

BILL: Captain Biggar is straight from Malaya, Burma and points East.

MRS SPOTTSWORTH: Ah, from the shadowlands of Mystery. How interesting! You must have seen many strange things!

CAPTAIN: I have indeed, ma'am. Barefooted believers treading the path of Ahura-Mazda over burning coals.

MRS SPOTTSWORTH: How marvellous!

CAPTAIN: I have practised Yoga myself and I know its power.

MRS SPOTTSWORTH: Really? Oh, Captain Biggar, we must have a talk.

BILL: Unfortunately, Captain Biggar can't stop.

MRS SPOTTSWORTH: Not for a little while?

BILL: No, I'm afraid I've wasted all too much of his precious time. He's on safari, you see.

MONICA: Safari? In *England*?

[*Hall door opens.* RORY *enters.*]

RORY: Oh, here you all are, back from your travels.

MONICA: Rory, this is Captain Biggar. My husband, Lord Carmoyle. [*Sits.*]

RORY: Haryar?

CAPTAIN: How d'ye do?

RORY: Bigger, eh? Captain Biggar – reminds me of that game we used to play when we were kids . . . The Bigger Family.

BILL: Ah, yes, I remember.

RORY: Do you? [CAPTAIN *to window.*] Which is bigger, then, Mr Bigger or Mrs Bigger?

MONICA: Rory, *really!*

RORY: Mr Bigger, because he is Father Bigger. Which is bigger, Mr Bigger or his old maid aunt?

MONICA: You're not a child now, you know.

RORY: The aunt, because, whatever happens, she is always Bigger.

[JEEVES *enters from the hall, carrying evening papers.*]

Perhaps Jeeves can answer. Jeeves knows everything.

JEEVES: What is the point, m'lord, on which you are seeking information?

RORY: Which is bigger, Jeeves, Mr Bigger or Master Bigger?

JEEVES: Master Bigger, because he's a little Bigger.

[*During this* MRS SPOTTSWORTH *has been inspecting the room and has come on the dower chest.*]

MRS SPOTTSWORTH: Oh, what a lovely dower chest!

MONICA: Yes, it used to be full of the most wonderful old costumes. They have been quite marvellously preserved in piles of lavender. [*Makes a move to raise the lid.*]

BILL [*sharply*]: They're not in there – I've had them all moved.

MONICA: Oh . . . I'm sure Mrs Spottsworth would enjoy seeing them.

MRS SPOTTSWORTH: I would indeed.

MONICA: There's a quite romantic story attached to that dower chest. The Earl Towcester of that period wouldn't let his daughter marry the man she loved – a famous discoverer . . .

RORY: The old boy was against discoverers. He was afraid they might discover America. [*Laughs.*] Oh, I beg your pardon.

MONICA: The lover sent this chest, filled with silks and rare embroideries he had brought back from the East.

RORY: Earl Towcester wouldn't let his daughter have them. He sent for the lover to take the chest away.

BILL [*butting in*]: The funny part of the story was the old blister following the chap down the drive saying: 'Get that damn thing out of here!'

MONICA: And inside it was his bride.

RORY: All ready for immediate use.

MRS SPOTTSWORTH: What a delicious story. [*To chest. She raises the lid of chest.*]

JEEVES [*trying to head off disaster*]: Be careful, madam –! The lid is very heavy.

[MRS SPOTTSWORTH *opens chest.* MONICA *dives at it, and pulls out* BILL'S *bookie coat.*]

MONICA: Golly, what's this?

BILL [*half under his breath*]: That's torn it.

MONICA: What a coat! Don't tell me you go around in a thing like this, Bill?

RORY [*fishing it out*]: And this tie! You'd better nip round and see my haberdashery clerk. We've got a sale on.

CAPTAIN: Let me look at that, may I? [*He takes coat, and putting his hand in pocket, pulls out a black patch.*]

JEEVES: Pardon me, m'lord, will Captain Biggar be remaining for dinner?

BILL: Can . . . can you manage that, Captain? M-might give us a chance for a bit of a chat.

[*Pause.*]

CAPTAIN [*eyeing BILL grimly*]: Yes, I'll stay. In fact, I'll spend the night.

JEEVES: Which room, m'lord?

BILL: The Bloody Mary room, Jeeves.

CURTAIN

ACT TWO

Same as Act One.
It is the same evening after dinner and the ladies have left the table.
JILL, MONICA, *and* MRS SPOTTSWORTH *are sitting drinking their coffee, and* MONICA *and* MRS SPOTTSWORTH *have liqueurs. A tray containing coffee apparatus, bottles, etc., is on a table, in front of* MONICA. *All three are in evening attire.*

MONICA [*helping herself to brandy*]: Sure you won't have some more coffee, Jill?

JILL: No, thanks.

MONICA: I don't know why I'm playing hostess. You're the future Lady Towcester.

JILL: I wonder? Many a slip, you know.

MRS SPOTTSWORTH: Yes, if I had the Interpreter here, he could tell you what the Ordaining Power has decided about you and Lord Towcester.

JILL [*coldly*]: Really?

MONICA: Who is the Interpreter?

MRS SPOTTSWORTH: The leader of our Rotationist Circle, Chundra Ram Bose.

MONICA: Qutie a cosy religion, us all being reincarnated together nine generations hence. Like Old Home Week. That is the idea, isn't it? We all foregather in 2253 or whenever it is?

MRS SPOTTSWORTH: Yes, people in the same Life Stream keep meeting and meeting. I was explaining that to Captain Biggar. He has been in contact with the Mystics of India and he says that out there you realize that the word impossible simply doesn't exist. Why, he's seen ropes tossed in the air and little boys shinning up them in swarms.

[*As she speaks,* RORY *enters from hall. He is smoking a cigar.*]

MONICA: He talked of nothing but tigers to me, and when it comes to hunting stories, I have a very low boiling point.

JILL: Not to say boring. And apparently he's still at it, sitting in a machan with his trusty Martini-Henry.

RORY: No, he's got off the subject at last. They're talking business. Bill asked me if I'd make his excuses to you ladies.

JILL: What business can Bill have with a man like the Captain?

RORY: Yes, seems pretty odd, I must say, sitting over the dinner table till nearly ten o'clock.

MRS SPOTTSWORTH: At what hour might one expect Lady Agatha to appear?

MONICA: I don't know that she keeps to any hours.

MRS SPOTTSWORTH: Did you ever see her, when you lived here as a child?

MONICA: No–o, but I've often heard the thump-thump-thump of that stick of hers.

RORY: Just a door banging in the wind.

MONICA [*ignorning him*]: She walks back and forth, back and forth.

MRS SPOTTSWORTH: Waiting for news of her husband from the Holy Land, poor faithful soul!

RORY: The old boy hadn't much faith in her, judging by those things they found in the attic.

MONICA: Shut up, Rory.

RORY: Those old Crusaders played it safe. The husband ordered his clothes from the blacksmith and his wife's from the locksmith.

MONICA: Really, Rory! Jill is an unmarried girl.

RORY [*unabashed*]: Dash it all, if anyone should know the facts of life it's a veterinary.

MRS SPOTTSWORTH [*her mind still on Lady Agatha*]: I do wish she would manifest herself while I am here. What a thrill I could give our Group when I get back to Pasadena. [*She rises.*] But now I must go and get Pomona and take her for a run in the garden. Such an angel, but you can't expect her to wait for ever. [*She goes out through the hall door.*]

JILL: What do you suppose is going on in there? [*She indicates direction of the dining-room.*]

MONICA: I can't imagine.

RORY: I'll tell you one thing: Bill is scared stiff of the feller.

MONICA: He seems to have some hold on him.

[JILL *closes door.*]

RORY: It's like those stories of the chap who comes back from the wilds to hunt down the partners who cheated him out of his share of the buried treasure . . . The Captain is just the type.

JILL: But Bill isn't.

MONICA: No.

RORY [*struck with a sudden idea*]: You don't suppose it's a baby?

JILL: Baby? Whose baby?

RORY: Bill's and this beggar Biggar's daughter. A poor, foolish little thing who loved not wisely, but too well.

MONICA [*protestingly*]: For heaven's sake, Rory!

RORY: I'm just advancing a theory . . . Girl back in England, no mother to guide her, meets a handsome young earl.

MONICA: You seem to take a delight in being tactless.

RORY: Oh, but, dash it all, there's nothing to worry about. Biggar can't make Bill marry her . . . Elephant-guns are barred at weddings in this country.

[*Raised voices are heard from dining-room.* RORY *cocks his head.*]

RORY: Hullo, that sounded like a lion's roar. Biggar must have changed continents.

JILL [*desperately*]: I'm going to go and listen. I must know what it's all about. [*She goes out, leaving door open.*]

RORY: Be careful you don't get the key poked in your eye. I had a door open suddenly once.

MONICA: You've upset the poor girl with your silly suggestions.

RORY: Well, there's something fishy going on here.

MONICA: I quite agree but –

RORY: Well, you're the girl with a nose for fish.

[*Enter* MRS SPOTTSWORTH *from hall carrying dog.*]

MRS SPOTTSWORTH: I just sent Pomona out on the lawn. Was that Miss Wyvern listening at the dining-room door?

MONICA: Yes, we heard raised voices.

MRS SPOTTSWORTH: Really? The Captain seems such a calm man. Yoga does that, of course. Wonderful training. He was telling me about the fakirs who sleep on beds of spikes . . . and, think of it, insomnia practically unknown. [*She goes out into garden.*]

MONICA: Whatever's happening I trust it won't upset her. I think she's quite sold on the Abbey.

[JILL *reappears in doorway.*]

JILL: The most extraordinary thing – Jeeves is joining in the conversation, leading it, in fact!

MONICA: Could you hear what he was saying?

JILL: Not really. It was something about someone's mother. I think the name was Whistler.

RORY: You girls will have to excuse me. The television set is in the library, isn't it?

JILL: Yes.

RORY: It's the Derby Dinner tonight. All the top owners are coming on the screen to say what they think of their chances tomorrow. [*He goes to door.*]

MONICA: I'll be with you in a minute.

RORY: I've got rather a liking for a beast called 'Oratory'. The Brompton Oratory is bang opposite Harrods – bit of an omen, what? [*Exit* RORY *into library.*]

MONICA: I've warned him not to talk about racing in front of Bill.

JILL: Pretty hard to keep the subject from popping up with Derby Day tomorrow.

MONICA [*as we hear voices, off*]: Here they are.

[CAPTAIN *enters from hall, followed by* BILL.]

MONICA: We thought you were never coming.

BILL: The Captain has been telling me about some of his adventures. You'd never believe how many times he's been within that of being killed. [*Holds two index fingers three inches apart*] . . . Sometimes even that. [*Holds fingers an inch apart.*] It was only by the worst . . . the damnedest luck, I mean, that he wasn't.

CAPTAIN [*regarding* BILL *dourly*]: Did your butler say there was a phone in the pantry?

BILL: Yes, but there's also one right here.

CAPTAIN: I prefer to talk privately.

MONICA: Oh, Captain! A girl friend?

CAPTAIN: My daughter, madam!

MONICA: What!

CAPTAIN: I must tell her I shall not be home tonight.

JILL: You have a daughter?

CAPTAIN: I have indeed, Miss Wyvern. That is the main reason I came back to the old country. Thought it wasn't fair to the girl to keep her penned up in Kuala Lumpur.

MONICA: You kept her shut up?

CAPTAIN: Not shut up. I said 'penned up'. I'm a widower, and when I was on safari the girl had to stay in her old missionary school.

[*Exit by hall door.*]

MONICA: Good Lord! Don't tell me Rory is becoming clairvoyant.

BILL: Clairvoyant? What are you talking about?

MONICA [*sits*]: Never mind.

JILL: Bill, what's wrong?

BILL: Wrong?

JILL: Has this Captain Biggar got you in his power?

BILL: Of course not.

MONICA: Then what is it? You look as worried as a hen that finds she's strayed into a fox farm.

BILL: It's nice of you girls to be so solicitous, but there isn't anything wrong. I'm happy. Why wouldn't I be? Look at the girl I've got. [*Puts his arm round* JILL'S *waist.*]

MONICA: What's bothering us is the Captain you've got.

[JEEVES *enters from hall, starts to gather coffee cups on tray.*]

BILL: Jolly old Biggar? He has his points.

MONICA: So has a porcupine.

[*Library door opens.* RORY'S *head appears.*]

RORY: Come in here, someone. I need help. Boussac's speaking in French.

BILL: What is it? The Derby Dinner?

JILL: Yes. But Monica says your gambling instincts mustn't be aroused.

BILL [*releasing her*]: Run along, then. [*To* RORY:] This girl can speak French with both hands.

RORY: Good, then 'op it quick, will you? Don't know why the devil Boussac's got to talk in French. Sounds so damned affected. [*Exit.*]

JILL [*as she and* MONICA *follow*]: I've told Monica you're not interested in racing any more. [*She says it back over her shoulder.*]

[MONICA *and* JILL *go out, leaving the door partly open.*]

BILL [*indicating it*]: Close that door, will you, Jeeves?

JEEVES: Certainly, m'lord.

BILL: The ladies seem to be suspicious.

JEEVES: They have noted that your lordship's gait is not as lightly tripping as usual.

BILL: It shows, does it?

JEEVES: I'm afraid it does, m'lord. I realize the situation is grave, but it is a time for the stiff upper lip, and the piece of steel down the spine.

BILL: You're right . . . We must try to make the best of it.

JEEVES: If I may remind your lordship Confucius observes that the man of philosophic spirit when treed by a lion may make use of the opportunity to admire the scenery.

BILL: But I'm not treed by a lion, I'm treed by a lion hunter.

JEEVES: I have been thinking, your lordship, the Captain threatens, if not paid by tomorrow morning, to go with his winning ticket to both the police and the Jockey Club.

BILL: I've told him I'll pay him within thirty days, but that's not good enough.

JEEVES: I know – I heard him – the deadline is tomorrow morning.

BILL: And there isn't an earthly . . . [*Sits*]

JEEVES: Oh, but there is, your lordship . . . if we could possess ourselves of Captain Biggar's ticket your position would be notably stabilized.

BILL: Get the ticket away from him? Good – but how?

JEEVES: By what I might describe as direct action.

BILL: Set on him, you mean? Scrag him? [*Rises.*]

JEEVES: That is my suggestion.

BILL: But, Jeeves, have you seen him? That bulging chest, those rippling muscles.

273

JEEVES: I agree that Captain Biggar is well-nourished, but we would have the advantage of the element of surprise. The Captain is now talking on the telephone in my pantry. [*He picks up receiver and puts it to his ear.*] When he stops speaking he will return to this room. The switch for these lights and those in the hall are together beside that door. You follow my thought-processes, m'lord?

BILL: Yes, yes, I get the idea. We grab him in the dark.

JEEVES: Precisely, m'lord. He has displayed the ticket on several occasions. We know that he carries it in his inside breast pocket. If your lordship is prepared for a little rough work . . .

BILL: I am, indeed, but it won't be any Maypole dance. We shall have to take some means of stifling his roar until I have reasoned with him. [*He picks up sofa pillow.*] I think this should – [JEEVES *holds up his hand.*]What's the matter?

JEEVES [*in a low voice, his hand over mouthpiece*]: He is talking with some race-course acquaintances. [*Listens again.*] There is a big job on . . . The Irish horse, Ballymore . . . It has had two trial gallops on the Epsom course and broken the record both times. [*Listens again.*] The individuals with whom Captain Biggar is in communication appear to be the same persons who gave him his two winners today.

BILL: So that's why he insists on being paid tomorrow? [*He starts to make feints with the pillow.*]

JEEVES [*still listening*]: The 'wise' money is to go on at the last moment, distributed among a dozen different turf accountants.

BILL: Well, there's nothing else for it, Jeeves. We've got to get that ticket. [*He presses pillow against* JEEVES' *face.*] He'll cut up pretty rough, I expect.

[BILL *removes pillow,* JEEVES *speaks as if nothing had happened.*]

JEEVES: Not if your lordship makes speedy repayment dependent on seemly behaviour. Once we have deprived him of his evidence, your lordship is in a position to dictate.

BILL: Exactly. I'll treat him fairly, of course. Monthly instalments. And if Mrs Spottsworth buys the house –

JEEVES [*cutting in*]: He has hung up. [*He hangs up.*] The moment approaches, m'lord. Stiffen the sinews, summon up the blood.

BILL: I'll shove the pillow over his face, you go for the ticket.
[*They take stations on either side of the door.*]

JEEVES [*stage whisper*]: I will switch off the lights as he starts to open the door.

BILL [*stage whisper*]: Glad now I did that Commando training.
[*Listens.*] He's coming.

JEEVES: Yes, m'lord.
[*They are either side of the door.*]

BILL: Now!
[*Lights go out, plunging the stage in darkness.*]

BILL: I've got him!

JEEVES: So have I.

BILL [*strangled utterance*]: He's choking me.

JEEVES: Punch him in the stomach, m'lord.

BILL: Right. [*He speaks in a muffled voice, and an 'ouch!' is heard.*] Trip him up. Get him on his back. [*There is a yelp of pain.*] Are you getting the ticket?

JEEVES [*strangled voice*]: Almost.

BILL: Ah, I've got the pillow over his face now. Tell me when you've got it, Jeeves . . . Jeeves, why don't you answer?
[*There is a crash as if a chair had been knocked over.*]
He almost tripped me, but I've still got the pillow over his face. Jeeves, are you still here?

JEEVES [*muffled voice*]: Got it.

BILL: Good work. Now listen, Captain Biggar, you're going to be paid . . . paid in full . . . if you behave yourself.
[*Lights are suddenly switched on by* CAPTAIN, *who enters, stopping inside the doorway, surveying the two figures on the floor.* JEEVES *is on his back and* BILL *sits astride him with a pillow pressed over his face.*)

CAPTAIN: And what is going on here?

BILL [*surprised*]: Why – why, Captain Biggar! [*He takes the pillow off* JEEVES' *face.*]

CAPTAIN: Fighting with your butler, eh? I'm learning something about life in high society.

BILL [*rising*]: We're not fighting. Poor Jeeves had a seizure, one of his spells.

CAPTAIN: You're subject to fits?

BILL: Not fits exactly, but one has to help him get hold of himself. Have you got hold of yourself now, Jeeves?

JEEVES: Yes, thank you, m'lord. My breathing is almost back to normal.

[*They rise, dusting themselves, adjusting ties, etc.*]

BILL: I think you ought to see a psychiatrist, Jeeves.

CAPTAIN: Psychiatrists – a lot of American rubbish! A man who is fool enough to go to a psychiatrist ought to have his head examined.

JEEVES: It dates from my batman days. Our dugout was blown up while I was passing the summer pudding.

BILL: And the mess was a mess, ha-ha!

[CAPTAIN *regards him stonily.*]

CAPTAIN: You seem to be in a light-hearted mood, Patch Perkins.

BILL [*with a glance at library door*]: I wish you wouldn't call me that.

CAPTAIN: It's your professional name, isn't it? And let me tell you, Perkins, there's to be no more beating about the bush. I have just had a word with some big insiders, and they want me to come in on a bet tomorrow that'll put me on easy street for the rest of my life. So – ! [*He holds out his hand, palm upward.*]

BILL: As I've told you a hundred times, I haven't got the damned money!

CAPTAIN: Borrow it.

BILL: Who from?

CAPTAIN: You must know plenty of the nobility.

BILL: I do. But it has evidently escaped the notice of Kuala Lumpur that the British peerage is on its uppers.

CAPTAIN: You also know Americans.

BILL: Have we any Americans among our *clientèle*, Jeeves?

JEEVES: Not that I'm aware of, m'lord.

CAPTAIN: What about the one that's here tonight?

BILL: You mean Mrs Spottsworth? I am hoping she is going to buy this house. If she *does* . . .

CAPTAIN: I can't wait for any 'ifs'. I've got to have that money by noon tomorrow. As Shakespeare says: I have an enterprise of great importance.

JEEVES [*pained*]: 'Enterprises of great pith and moment' is the exact quotation, sir.

CAPTAIN: You'd better speed up this house deal, Perkins. Get a down payment tonight.

BILL: If I rush it, it may kill the sale. [*Sits.*]

CAPTAIN: You'll have to take your chance on that. I'm damn sure you can get the money, if you want to. And if you don't some very unpleasant things are going to happen. [*Goes to window.*] What sort of going will they have at Epsom tomorrow? The air smells fresh, but perhaps it's just the contrast to these musty old rooms. [*He takes a long breath, thumping his chest.*] Don't see any stars. [*Exit* CAPTAIN *through french window.*]

BILL: I like that man the more I see him – less.

JEEVES: His suspicions were aroused when he saw us struggling on the floor but I think your lordship's happy invention –

BILL: Ah, your seizure – yes, he fell for it, I think. By the way, I'm sorry about that swat in the stomach.

JEEVES: It was my own suggestion, m'lord.

BILL: What's that thing you're holding?

JEEVES: It appears to be Miss Wyvern's photograph. I extracted it from your lordship's pocket under the impression that it was the Captain's ticket.

BILL [*taking proffered photograph*]: What are we going to do now, Jeeves?

JEEVES: I suggest, m'lord, that we have a second go.

BILL: Another surprise attack?

JEEVES [*to window*]: Precisely, m'lord. [BILL *rises.*] If I draw the curtains – over this window – it will be necessary for the Captain to enter through them. We will see him fumbling, and in that moment a good tug from either side will bring the curtains down on top of him. [*He goes to curtains and draws them. They cover window completely.*]

BILL: Enmeshing him, as it were.

JEEVES: The technique of the Roman, Retiarius.

BILL: Oh, was that the bird who fought with net and trident?

JEEVES: Precisely, m'lord.

BILL: This time we can quell his outcries with the heavy velour.

JEEVES: Yes, your lordship will not need your sofa-pillow.

BILL [*pulling back his sleeves and taking stand by the window*]: It's in the bag, Jeeves.

JEEVES: An appropriate image, I trust, m'lord.
   [*Sound of singing off.*]

BILL: What's that filthy noise?

JEEVES: The Captain, m'lord, warbling his native wood-notes wild.

CAPTAIN [*singing off*]:

The regiment's in 'ollow square, they're hanging' him today,
They've taken of his buttons off an' cut his stripes away,
And they're hangin' Danny Deever in the morn—ing!

BILL [*whispering*]: Charge, Chester, charge! On, Stanley, on!
   [*They are either side of the window. The voice draws nearer. A form is seen pushing against the curtains.*]

JEEVES: Now!
   [BILL *and* JEEVES *give them a tug. The curtains come down, bringing the pole with them.* BILL *grabs the enmeshed figure, and they topple to the floor. There is a cry. The library door opens.* JILL *appears, followed by* RORY *and* MONICA. *Just off stage Pomona starts to bark furiously.*]

JILL: What on earth is happening?
   [*Bill is still kneeling beside the shrouded figure.* CAPTAIN BIGGAR *appears in the window. He has Pomona in his arms.* BILL *looks up at him with an astonished expression.*]

JEEVES [*addressing the group*]: The fault, I fear, is mine. Lord Towcester instructed me to have the curtain bracket seen to some days ago.
   [BILL *pulls the curtains away, revealing* MRS SPOTTSWORTH *in a dishevelled condition. He helps her up.*]

MRS SPOTTSWORTH [*feeling the top of her head*]: I felt a blow on the head. What was it? A poltergeist?

RORY: No, a curtain-pole-tergeist.

MRS SPOTTSWORTH [*dazedly*]: I distinctly felt a hand fumbling with the neck of my dress.

BILL: As long as you're not hurt.

[JEEVES *starts to gather up curtains, detaching them from pole.*]

RORY: Practically everything in the bally place is falling to pieces.

MONICA [*between her teeth*]: Shut up!

RORY [*as usual, remembers too late*]: I forgot. Sorry.

MONICA [*going to* MRS SPOTTSWORTH]: Come with me. I must bathe your head with eau de cologne.

MRS SPOTTSWORTH: Thank you, my head's all right. I was going to take Pomona to the kitchen. She hasn't had her supper.

[JEEVES, *folding the curtains, rises to offer his services, but* JILL *comes forward.*]

JILL: I'll look after that. I'm the registered dog's nurse. [*She takes Pomona from* CAPTAIN.]

BILL: Better let me.

JILL [*coldly*]: I fancy you have more serious matters to attend to. [*She goes out with Pomona.* MONICA *leads the still dazed* MRS SPOTTSWORTH *to door.*]

BILL [*following them*]: I'm frightfully sorry about this, Mrs Spottsworth.

MRS SPOTTSWORTH: It's nothing, really. I just want to repair my make-up. [*She stops abruptly in the doorway.*] Listen! Is that the thump-thump of Lady Agatha's stick?

MONICA: I don't hear anything.

MRS SPOTTSWORTH [*as they go out*]: I suppose I am a trifle dazed. [*Exeunt* MRS SPOTTSWORTH *and* MONICA. BILL *goes to double doors and shuts them.*]

RORY [*with a heavy wink*]: Funny that business about a spirit hand fumblin' with the lady's dress. Damn silly place to choose for that sort of thing. [*Exit* RORY *into library, closing door.*]

[JEEVES *is still kneeling down, folding the curtains.* BILL *and the* CAPTAIN *face one another.*]

CAPTAIN: Look . . . let me tell you two beauties something . . . I'm a champion at kushti, the jiu-jitsu of India. So if you want an arm or a leg broken, just try and take that ticket away from me.

BILL: What on earth are you talking about?

CAPTAIN: For a minute, I thought it was the lady's pendant you were after.

BILL [*indignantly*]: Pendant? Do you really think – ?

CAPTAIN: And that gives me an idea. Why not the pendant?

BILL: Are you, a bulwark of the Empire, a man who goes about setting an example to Dyaks, seriously proposing to rob one of my guests?

CAPTAIN: Not me. You.

BILL: What? You think that I would steal – ?

CAPTAIN: Not steal. I suggest that you borrow that pendant till tomorrow afternoon.

BILL: Do you hear this, Jeeves?

JEEVES: Yes, m'lord. If I understand Captain Biggar rightly, his proposal is that the object in question shall be abstracted and pawned, and the proceeds used to back the horse Ballymore in tomorrow's Derby, the odds on which are quoted at fifty-to-one.

CAPTAIN [*startled*]: How do you know all that?

JEEVES: At the conclusion of the race the pendant would be redeemed and discovered, probably by myself, in some corner of the Abbey, where Mrs Spottsworth might have dropped it.

BILL: I still call it stealing.

CAPTAIN: Even if it were, it would only be a piece of rough justice. That emerald is stolen property.

BILL: What?

CAPTAIN: I recognized it at a glance. It's a case of the green eye of the little yellow god. Two chaps were well and properly hanged for pinching it from the Temple of Vishnu in Bhomo with a little spot of murder thrown in.

BILL: So it is what the Americans call a bit of hot ice? That puts a different complexion on things, eh, Jeeves?

JEEVES: Distinctly m'lord.

BILL: The biter bit, as it were.

JEEVES: 'An eye for an eye' would seem to be the *mot juste*, m'lord.

BILL: Yes, it's one up on the moral end, but there are several 'buts', eh, Jeeves?

JEEVES: Precisely, m'lord . . . Can one be certain beyond the peradventure of a doubt that Ballymore will win?

CAPTAIN: No doubt at all. The course record is held by Mahmoud, two minutes thirty-three and a half seconds.

Ballymore, in a secret gallop, covered the course in two seconds over two minutes.

BILL [*impressed*]: Golly! That's official, is it?

CAPTAIN: Straight from the feed-box . . . Look, I'm a poor man, but I'm proposing to put my all on Ballymore's nose.

JEEVES: May I be permitted to ask a question?

BILL: Go ahead.

JEEVES [*turning to* CAPTAIN]: Who would undertake the pawning, sir? Would you?

CAPTAIN: All I want is my three thousand quid.

JEEVES: In other words you wish to keep your skirts clear?

CAPTAIN: I happen to have a rather high standard of honour.

JEEVES: So, if I may so, has his lordship.

CAPTAIN: Come off it! His lordship did a dust-off after the race today with a fiver of mine in his pocket.

BILL: I've told you I have every intention –

CAPTAIN [*cutting in*]: All right, Lord Towcester, I'll give you the final proof of how sure I am that Ballymore will win the Derby . . . I will involve myself. You get it, I'll pawn it.

BILL: Plus two record trial gallops, plus the Sahib's willingness to risk his all, that adds up to as near a sure thing as I ever heard of.

JEEVES: Quite, m'lord. Nevertheless . . .

BILL: To hell with nevertheless! Captain Biggar, it's a deal.
  [*He puts out his hand,* CAPTAIN BIGGAR *takes it.*]

CAPTAIN: Right . . . Is there any whisky going?

JEEVES: I was about to bring in the tray, sir. [*Makes move towards hall door.*]

CAPTAIN: Where do you keep it? You had better stay here and give counsel.

JEEVES: You will find the decanter in my pantry, beside the telephone.

CAPTAIN: Good. That gives me a chance to kill two elephants with one shot. I'll call my friends again and make arrangements to get that money on. [*Exit* CAPTAIN *by hall door.*]

BILL: Seems pretty confident, doesn't he?

JEEVES: Your lordship is, of course, aware that the task to which you have somewhat lightly committed yourself involves considerable danger?

BILL: Of exposure and humiliation?

JEEVES: Precisely, m'lord.

BILL: Let me remind you that exposure and humiliation are already threatened by the Captain if his money is not forthcoming tomorrow.

JEEVES: True, m'lord.

BILL: I have an impression that a peer of the realm cuts a better figure caught in the act of borrowing a valuable jewel than legging it away from the races with a punter's fiver in his pocket.

JEEVES: Your lordship feels that in larceny, as in other matters, it is more dignified to be grand than petty?

BILL: Precisely. But these niceties need not concern you. Understand, Jeeves, this is an adventure in which you are to play no part.

JEEVES: That is extremely considerate of you, m'lord, but in the relationship of thane and vassal –

BILL: I applaud your feudal spirit, Jeeves, but I must insist that this is a case of single jeopardy.

[*Enter* CAPTAIN *from hall, carrying a tray containing decanter, syphon and glasses.* JEEVES *takes tray to drinks table.*]

CAPTAIN: I thought you might be needing a bracer yourself.

BILL: Very matey of you, Sahib, I do.

CAPTAIN: I've made the financial arrangements, and my friends will have in readiness a pawnbroker not given to asking questions.

BILL: You have useful acquaintances.

CAPTAIN: I shall now go and do my exercises. [*He goes to window.*]

BILL: Daily jerks at this time of night?

CAPTAIN: Breathing exercises . . . Yoga. Yoga came to my rescue when I was caught without my Snider by a Bengal man-eater. It was a clear case of him or me.

BILL: Well, I have no doubt he made a better looking rug than you would.

CAPTAIN: It can calm the nerves and steady the hand as nothing else.

[*He goes out into garden.*]

BILL: Yoga, make a note of that, Jeeves. But for the moment, I shall have to depend on a glass of the old reliable. Pour me one – will you? – while I concentrate on the *modus operandi*.

JEEVES: Yes, my lord. I have a thought in regard to your problem . . .

BILL: No, no, Jeeves, keep aloof.

[*As he speaks* MRS SPOTTSWORTH *enters from hall with* MONICA. *She seems quite freshened up.*]

MRS SPOTTSWORTH: Well, here I am, as good as new. [*Looks round.*] Where's Pomona?

BILL: Still busy with her dinner, I fancy.

MONICA: If you'll excuse me, I'll pop in and have a word with Rory. [*She goes towards library.*]

MRS SPOTTSWORTH: It's the Derby, is it, that you're all so interested in?

MONICA: Just our silly little annual flutter.

MRS SPOTTSWORTH [*sits sofa*]: If you find something promising I might have a tiny little gamble . . . not more than a grand across the board.

MONICA: A thousand dollars!

BILL: We'd call that putting our shirt on it.

MONICA: That would be not only my shirt but my stockings and pantie-girdle as well. [MONICA *goes into library, closing door.*]

MRS SPOTTSWORTH: Your sister gave me a brandy, and – do you know? – I feel like having another.

BILL: Oh, do, [*Looking at tray.*] Jeeves, we seem to be caught short on brandy.

JEEVES: I will see to it at once, m'lord. [*He goes out into hall.*]

MRS SPOTTSWORTH: This wonderful old house! It makes me feel so romantic.

BILL [*sits sofa*]: Monica was saying that you might be interested in buying it.

MRS SPOTTSWORTH: I would indeed. There is only one thing that makes me hesitate.

BILL: Oh?

MRS SPOTTSWORTH: Your English climate! Damp is death to me.

Fibrositis, you know, and sciatica. [*She pats her hip joint by way of illustration.*]

BILL [*disappointed*]: I see.

MRS SPOTTSWORTH: But I am thinking it over, thinking it over very seriously. [*Drops handkerchief.*]

BILL [*picking it up*]: Well, I can't pretend that the place isn't damp . . . not all of it, of course, but some of the older quarters . . .

MRS SPOTTSWORTH: So honest . . . that's what I like about the English. The most honest people on earth.

BILL [*uncomfortably*]: Yes-es.

MRS SPOTTSWORTH: So different in America. Gangsters. Look at this thing I've got around my neck tonight. I practically never dare to wear it in America.

BILL: No?

MRS SPOTTSWORTH: It's unique . . . a flawless emerald of perfect colour. Indian, of course . . . It's said to be stolen; I feel rather guilty when I stop to think about it.

[*Enter* JEEVES *from hall with a small tray containing brandy and a glass.*]

BILL [*rises*]: Ah, there you are. You've been the dickens of a while bringing it. A Saint Bernard dog would have been there and back in half the time.

JEEVES: Sorry, m'lord. I slipped at the top of the cellar stairs.

BILL: Well, that shouldn't have taken you long. Brandy and soda, Mrs Spottsworth?

MRS SPOTTSWORTH: No, straight. About three fingers. [*As he pours.*] Where's that White Hunter man got to?

[*Breathing noise from off.*]

BILL: Captain Biggar? He's in the garden doing his Yoga callisthenics. [*To her with brandy.*]

MRS SPOTTSWORTH [*taking the brandy*]: Really? Such a fruitful visit I am having! Towcester Abbey with its familiar spirits, and then this delicious Captain, a fellow believer, a Zoroastrian. [*Rises, moves off to inspect a grimy portrait.*]

JEEVES: May I freshen that for your lordship?

BILL: No, must keep my wits about me.

JEEVES: Quite so, m'lord.

BILL [*speaking in monotone*]: I'm going to unfasten it. Stand by to pick it up.

[BILL *goes over to* MRS SPOTTSWORTH *and stands immediately behind her.*]

MRS SPOTTSWORTH [*studying the portrait*]: Is that Sir Caradoc?

BILL: No, that's his father, Sir Oughtred. He gave the famous banquet where King John ate the four helpings of stewed eels . . . Tell me, are you afraid of spiders?

MRS SPOTTSWORTH: What do you mean?

BILL: There's rather an outsize specimen crawling on the back of your hair.

MRS SPOTTSWORTH: Knock it off.

BILL: Strange. I can't see it now. Protective coloration, I suppose.

MRS SPOTTSWORTH: I must have got it off those curtains.

BILL: Yes, that's it.

JEEVES: If I could be of assistance, m'lord?

MRS SPOTTSWORTH [*sharply*]: I can feel it on my neck.

[BILL *undoes clasp of pendant.*]

BILL: There it goes.

[*The pendant is unfastened at back, slides down the bosom of* MRS SPOTTSWORTH'S *gown.*]

MRS SPOTTSWORTH: Is it off?

BILL: Yes, it's off.

[MRS SPOTTSWORTH *searches about the floor.*]

MRS SPOTTSWORTH: Where is it now?

BILL [*also searching on floor*]: That's what I'm wondering.

MRS SPOTTSWORTH: I don't see it.

BILL [*on hands and knees*]: Nor do I. Can you see it, Jeeves?

JEEVES [*looking about*]: No, m'lord.

BILL [*speaking sotto voce to* JEEVES]: It slipped into the Midland Bank.

MRS SPOTTSWORTH: You wouldn't think it could disappear completely.

BILL: No, there's not much cover. Must have caught on something.

MRS SPOTTSWORTH: Anyway, I'm glad you didn't kill it. That's bad luck.

BILL: It's terrible luck.

MRS SPOTTSWORTH: Oh, well, never mind.

BILL: Yes, let's forget it. Turn on the gramophone, Jeeves. I feel like a dance.

[JEEVES *goes to gramophone, raises lid and turns it on.*]

MRS SPOTTSWORTH: You want to dance?

BILL: Yes, with you. American women are such beautiful dancers.

MRS SPOTTSWORTH [*as they dance*]: I love dancing. The one unpunished rapture left on earth.

BILL: The old Charleston . . . do you remember it?

MRS SPOTTSWORTH: You bet I do. [*They start to dance the Charleston.*]

BILL: Shake that shimmy, shake, sister.

[*He shakes her in an effort to dislodge the pendant.* MONICA *and* RORY *enter from library.*]

MONICA: Good God!

RORY: The old boy cuts quite a rug, doesn't he?

MRS SPOTTSWORTH: One drifts like a piece of thistledown. I hardly know I've got feet.

MONICA: If you danced with Rory, you'd now you've got feet.

[JILL *enters from hall, carrying Pomona. She stands watching in amazement as* BILL *does a lift, bringing* MRS SPOTTSWORTH *back on her feet with a bump.*]

JILL [*icily*]: Here is your dog, Mrs Spottsworth.

MRS SPOTTSWORTH [*stopping dancing*]: Oh, thank you. [*She goes to* JILL.] Has mother's little angel-rabbit had a nice din-dins?

[BILL *and* JEEVES *are both looking anxiously about the floor.* MRS SPOTTSWORTH, *about to take* POMONA, *utters a cry and puts a hand to her hip joint.*]

MONICA: What's the matter?

MRS SPOTTSWORTH [*hobbling to a chair*]: I've twisted something. [*Sits.*]

[RORY *makes a dive at something on the floor.*]

RORY [*picking it up*]: I say, I say, what's this? [BILL *reacts with an involuntary wince of agony.*] This bauble is yours, isn't it, Mrs Spottsworth? [*He carries it over to her.*]

JILL [*giving* BILL *a cold look*]: It's hardly surprising you lost it. The way Bill was dancing.

MRS SPOTTSWORTH [*to* RORY, *taking pendant*]: Oh, thank you . . . Yes, we were being rather silly and nostalgic. Those dear Twenties! . . . Oh gee, I hope this is just a twist and not sciatica. [*She rises rather gingerly.*]

   [MONICA *and* RORY *assist her.*]

RORY: Upsy-daisy.

MONICA: I think you had better get straight into bed with a nice hot-water bottle.

RORY: Wish I had one of our new electric pads to offer you. We have three speeds – Autumn Glow, Spring Warmth and May West.

   [*They move towards the hall.*]

JILL: Here.

   [JILL *hands Pomona to* BILL. RORY, MRS SPOTTSWORTH *and* MONICA *go out.*]

BILL: Righto-ho.

JEEVES [*offering to take dog*]: Shall I, m'lord?

BILL: No, thanks, Must make sure she's all right. She may want a doctor. [*He goes out, carrying Pomona.*]

JILL: Jeeves, will you do something for me?

JEEVES: Certainly, miss.

JILL [*taking off her ring*]: Will you say good night to Lord Towcester and give him this ring?

JEEVES [*displaying ring*]: Am I to infer, miss, that there is a symbolical significance attached to the gesture?

JILL: Yes, I am putting his lordship back into circulation.

JEEVES: If I might be permitted a word of counsel –

JILL: It won't do any good, Jeeves.

JEEVES: His lordship will wish to know the cause of your annoyance.

JILL: My annoyance, as you call it, has nothing to do with Lord Towcester's infatuation for this wealthy American trollop . . . Let us have that quite clear.

JEEVES: Yes, miss.

JILL: The trouble is that I object to not being trusted. There are, quite clearly, things that Lord Towcester is keeping from me.

JEEVES: Possibly from a desire to spare you anxiety.

JILL: I want to share the bad as well as the good. I don't care if we have as many ups and downs as a man in an aisle seat.

JEEVES: A very apt simile – nevertheless . . .

JILL: I'm in no mood for arguments. That is why I want to go before Lord Towcester returns. Good night, Jeeves.

JEEVES: Good night, miss.

> [*Exit* JILL *through hall door.* JEEVES *looks at ring, shakes his head and sighs. He puts it in his pocket. Once again there comes from the garden the sound of the* CAPTAIN *singing. This time he is in romantic mood.* JEEVES *shuts the window.*]

CAPTAIN [*off*]: Pale hands I loved, beside the Shalimar,

Where are you now? I sink beneath your spell . . .

La, la, la . . . la, la, la, la, la.

Where are you now? Where are you now?

> [BILL *re-enters briskly.*]

BILL [*cheerily, but low-voiced*]: Well, I managed to spot the whole set-up. She put it in a jewel case, unlocked and left lying on top of the dressing table. [BILL *looks round.*] Where's Miss Wyvern?

JEEVES: I fear I have something of a blow for you, m'lord.

BILL: What is it? Explode your bomb and bury my fragments.

JEEVES: Miss Wyvern has taken her departure. She desired me to give you this. [*He hands* BILL *the ring.*]

BILL: Oh . . . Ah . . . I see. The brusheroo, eh?

JEEVES: I believe that is the term.

BILL: What seems to be the trouble, Jeeves? [*Sits sofa.*]

JEEVES: Miss Wyvern explained with the utmost emphasis that it has nothing to do with her finding you romping with Mrs Spottsworth, nor with that lady's unfortunate allusion to a hand fumbling with the neck of her dress.

BILL: Good.

JEEVES: So, knowing the way of the gentler sex in these matters, I should say that that is unquestionably what it is.

BILL: I see . . . Well, as a matter of fact, the thing has its fortunate side. If I got caught tonight, my *fiancée* would be in an embarrassing position.

JEEVES: May I ask if it is your lordship's present purpose to enter Mrs Spottsworth's room after she had fallen asleep?

BILL: It is.

JEEVES: She may be a light sleeper.

BILL: True.

JEEVES: A silk handkerchief concealing the lower part of the face is, I believe, the ruse generally favoured by the underworld on these occasions.

BILL: I had thought of wearing the old moustache and my black patch.

JEEVES: I would not advocate it, m'lord. A lady, discovering such an apparition in her room, might quite conceivably utter a piercing scream.

BILL: Something in that. [*Rises.*]

JEEVES: But may I point out that there is one figure which, terrifying to most ladies, would not alarm Mrs Spottsworth in the least?

BILL: Who's that?

JEEVES: The Lady Agatha.

BILL: The Lady Agatha? [*Turns.*] H'm . . . Yes . . . Food for thought there, Jeeves!

JEEVES: I think your lordship might find it the safest approach.

BILL: If we can only escape from this predicament, Jeeves!

JEEVES: Yes, m'lord, the future would look fair indeed.

BILL: Who knows? – next year we might even find ourselves at the Derby on the right side of the course.

JEEVES [*raptly*]: Tattersall's!

BILL: The ring at Tattersall's! No harm in day-dreaming, is there, Jeeves? [*He goes out to hall.*]

> [JEEVES *places the brandy decanter on the larger tray and puts the used glasses on the smaller tray. Then he goes out to hall on his way to pantry. There is a second's pause . . . and then the* CAPTAIN *enters from the garden.*]

CAPTAIN [*calling in a conspiratorial way, as he enters.*]: She's coming down. [*He looks around, sees no one is there, goes to hall, calls.*] Lord Towcester. [*No one answering, he hurries to library and calls inside.*] Quick! Lord Towcester. This is your moment –

[*There is no one there, and again he turns to hall door. As he does so,* MRS SPOTTSWORTH *appears in front of him. She wears a seductive négligé of a silvery blue shade. She limps slightly.*]

MRS SPOTTSWOTH: Well, mighty Orion, here I am!

CAPTAIN: You looked so charming standing up there on your balcony.

MRS SPOTTSWORTH: Don't I look charming now that I've come down?

CAPTAIN: You do indeed, ma'am.

MRS SPOTTSWORTH: You mustn't call me ma'am. This is most un-Romeo-like. My name is Rosalinda.

CAPTAIN: Pretty. A pretty name for a pretty lady.

MRS SPOTTSWORTH [*sits sofa*]: Oh, you are gallant, aren't you? What is your name, by the way, [*Patting sofa.*] your little name?

CAPTAIN: Cuthbert. [*Sitting sofa.*]

MRS SPOTTSWORTH: Cuthbert, the White Hunter . . . no, not the White Hunter, the White Knight.

CAPTAIN: I'm just a very plain ordinary sort of man, I'm afraid.

MRS SPOTTSWORTH: You're not. I won't have that. You're not ordinary at all. I called you Knight, and that's what you are – the nearest thing to one that modern life affords.

CAPTAIN [*wriggling*]: You're making me feel very uncomfortable, Rosalinda.

MRS SPOTTSWORTH: Why? You know you're braver than other men. You know you are stronger, more honourable. Your code is higher.

CAPTAIN [*rises*]: I wish you hadn't said that, Rosalinda. I feel pretty small. As we say out East, 'I could wear a topee and walk under a duck'.

MRS SPOTTSWORTH: Why do you say that?

CAPTAIN: Suppose I'd asked you to leave your room and come down here not for a good reason, but for a bad one?

MRS SPOTTSWORTH: A *naughty* reason, you mean?

CAPTAIN: Call it naughty, if you like.

MRS SPOTTSWORTH [*rises*]: I understand. You said my *négligé* looked like a moonbeam. What you were thinking was – I'd love to have her dance for me out here on the grass, clad only in moonbeams.

CAPTAIN [*horror-stricken*]: Oh, no Rosalinda, ma'am, you mustn't think things like that about me. I'm a clean-minded man.

MRS SPOTTSWORTH: Silly boy, I don't mind.

CAPTAIN: What I meant was . . . no, I can't tell you.

MRS SPOTTSWORTH [*with a little laugh*]: You Englishmen! But I even like your clumsiness. You ring true. As I said to Lord Towcester, you Englishmen are so honest.

CAPTAIN [*with a groan, leaning over chair*]: Oh, God! I can't take it . . . this thing you're doin' to me . . . making me feel like . . . like . . .

MRS SPOTTSWORTH: Like an embarrassed schoolboy. It's all right. You'll get over that.

CAPTAIN [*desperately*]: Rosalinda, listen. [*Sitting on chair.*] Rosalinda . . .

MRS SPOTTSWORTH: Yes, a little rose, that's what I am. Pluck me before my petals fall. [*She nestles against him.*]

CAPTAIN [*with a groan*]: If the boys in Pago-Pago could see me now!

MRS SPOTTSWORTH: Kiss me, Cuthbert.

[*She puts her arms round his neck and gives him a passionate kiss. BILL enters from hall.*]

BILL: Well, I'll be damned!

[*They break.*]

MRS SPOTTSWORTH: Oh, Lord Towcester, you caught us. This romantic old house quite got the better of us.

BILL: That's all right.

MRS SPOTTSWORTH: Just as well, perhaps, that you came when you did. Cuthbert was stumbling into a proposal . . . whether or not of marriage, I don't know. Probably it's a little soon for that . . . Good night, Cuthbert. Good night, dear Lord Towcester. I'm off to beddy-bye.

[*She goes to hall door which BILL opens for her. With shaking hands the CAPTAIN slops some whisky into a glass.*]

BILL: How's the old hip joint?

MRS SPOTTSWORTH: I beg your pardon?

BILL: That muscle you strained?

MRS SPOTTSWORTH: Oh, I hardly feel it. Romance is such a wonderful medicine. Bye! [*Exit.*]

[*The* CAPTAIN *drinks whisky and pours another.* BILL *closes the hall door.*]

BILL: What the devil was all that about?

CAPTAIN [*brokenly, dropping into a chair*]: She came out on her balcony when I was in the garden doing my Yoga breathing. I asked her to come down. I thought it would make it easy for you to nip into her room and snaffle that damned pendant.

BILL: Why on earth didn't you say so?

CAPTAIN: I tried to, I rushed in here, expecting to find you . . . and then . . . she started saying things that made me feel like a dingo-dog. She called me a knight . . . She said I had such a high code of honour . . .

BILL: She's taken a fancy to you.

CAPTAIN: Oh, God! [*Buries face in hands.*]

BILL: It's your fault for being so fascinating.

[*During these speeches* BILL *has gone to chest and opened it. He takes out some garments. He produces a woman's mediaeval head-dress and puts it on his head. The* CAPTAIN *turns and sees him.*]

CAPTAIN: What the hell? Have you gone mad?

BILL: I'm going up there to get you that pendant. [*He takes a stick, and starts to stump about with it, practising. The woman's dress he has taken from the chest is thrown over a chair.*]

CAPTAIN: Mad as a hatter.

BILL [*suddenly*]: Sh! Listen . . . LISTEN!

[*They listen. From above comes a clump-clump-clump of a stick. It seems to be descending the stairs.*]

BILL [*staccato*]: My God, do you hear that? It's the real one! It's Lady Agatha!

CAPTAIN [*awed whisper*]: Then that story is true?

BILL: Perhaps the old girl is sore that I was going to pretend –

[*The* CAPTAIN *grips* BILL'S *arm, stopping him.*]

CAPTAIN: It's getting nearer.

BILL: Yes, she's coming down the stairs.

[*The door opens and Lady Agatha stands there. The lights in the hall are out. She is framed in darkness. She wears the tall, conical hat and the drooping wimple. Her face and arms are the colour of chalk.* BILL *recoils.*]

CAPTAIN [*uttering a yell of fear*]: YOW!

[*The figure raises its hand and holds it out to* BILL.]

THE FIGURE: The pendant, m'lord!

BILL: Jeeves!

JEEVES: And now – the ticket, please, Captain Biggar.

[*As the* CAPTAIN *mechanically takes ticket from his pocket . . . and hands it to* JEEVES, *the pendant is handed to him by* BILL.]

CURTAIN

ACT THREE

The Scene is the same.
It is early in the afternoon the following day.
MONICA *and* RORY *are seated a little distance apart. Each has a circle of newspapers on the floor, dropped as they are read.*

RORY: I tell you there's nothing in sight to beat Taj Mahal. The Aga has the mares, that's what counts. The sires don't begin to count compared with the mares.

MONICA: I'm glad to hear you pay that belated tribute to my sex.

RORY: I think for my two quid it's Taj Mahal on the nose.

MONICA [*striking out name with her pencil*]: That settles Taj Mahal for me. Whenever you bet on them, they start running backwards. Look at that dog race.

RORY: I admit my doggy let the side down on that occasion. But when a real rabbit gets loose on a dog track, it's bound to cause a bit of confusion.

MONICA: I thought your money was going to Oratory?

RORY: Oratory is my 'outsider' bet, ten bob each way.

MONICA: Well, here's another hunch for you – Escalator.

RORY [*struck*]: Escalator!

MONICA: Wasn't Harrods the first store to have escalators?

RORY: Yes, by jove.

MONICA [*buried in paper*]: Lester Piggott is riding it.

RORY [*rising and spilling papers on floor*]: Lester Piggott? Well, that's a clincher. L. Piggott is the name of our Ladies Underwear shopwalker, as fine a chap as ever punched a time-clock. That's a good enough omen for me. [*Looks at his watch.*] Two-twenty. I'm going to send my wire. [*He takes up phone.*]

MONICA: You can't send it on that telephone.

RORY: Why not?

MONICA: Bill. He's hovering about.

RORY: Don't worry. I'll pay the old agriculturist.

MONICA: That isn't the point. Bill's being very good . . . doesn't show the slightest interest in *what* wins the Derby . . . but I keep on telling you I don't want the devil in him roused . . . *can't* you understand that?

RORY: All right. No need to get ratty.

MONICA: And don't leave that *Racing News* lying about. Put it in your pocket.

RORY [*picking up paper and taking out cigarette case*]: Okay. But if you ask me, I'd say that a good healthy interest in sport wouldn't do old Bill any harm.

MONICA: What do you mean by that crack?

RORY: Mark you, I am perfectly aware that a lot of fine, manly chaps collect queer sorts of things . . . old costumes, for instance . . . *but* . . .

MONICA: But what . . .?

RORY: But, damn it all, they don't *wear* them.

MONICA: What on earth are you talking about?

RORY: I didn't mean to tell you . . . thought it wasn't quite cricket . . . but I came in here last night and found Bill and Jeeves dressed up in farthingales and wimples.

MONICA: I don't believe you.

RORY: It's true, old girl. I'd come down looking for a drink and . . .

MONICA: You mean to tell me that Jeeves . . . *Jeeves* was dressed up like some urchin playing Guy Fawkes?

RORY: Not *Guy* Fawkes – *Gladys* Fawkes.

MONICA [*rises*]: Wait. I've just remembered. Mrs Spottsworth says that she came downstairs to find a book, and that when she went back to her room, she saw Lady Agatha hanging about in the hall.

RORY: Waiting for a chance to get into the bathroom, I suppose.

MONICA: She was longing to see Lady Agatha, and Bill knew it.

RORY: Ah! I'm getting it. Yes, it's dawning.

MONICA: Clever old Bill, he knows she'd be twice as likely to buy the house if she were convinced it's got a real authentic ghost.

RORY: I see the idea. Salting the mine, as it were.

MONICA: Yes, that's the explanation, I'll bet you.

[*Enter* JEEVES *from hall.*]

JEEVES: Pardon me, m'lady. His lordship desired me to find Mrs Spottsworth.

MONICA: She's taken her dog for a walk. [*Sits sofa.*]

JEEVES: Thank you, m'lady. [*He gathers up some of the papers strewn on the floor*]

MONICA [*raising her voice a little*]: Mrs Spottsworth tells me she saw Lady Agatha last night.

JEEVES: Indeed, m'lady?

MONICA: Do you believe in ghosts, Jeeves?

JEEVES: I am open to conviction, m'lady. As Hamlet observed to his friend, Horatio –

[BILL *appears, coming in from the hall. His hair is disarranged, as if he had been running his hands through it.*]

BILL: Well, have you found her?

JEEVES: Mrs Spottsworth is walking her dog, m'lord.

MONICA: She won't be long. She hates exercise.

BILL: I've got to find her and settle this house business.

MONICA: Yesterday you didn't seem to care whether you sold it or not.

RORY: We'll see if we can find the lady for you. Moke and I are just popping down to the post office.

BILL [*loud and aggressive.*] Ha! Putting a bit on, eh? I thought that was what you were up to. [*Pulls paper from* RORY'S *pocket.*] *Racing News.* What do *they* say? Who's going to win it? What's the majority opinion? [*He spreads the paper open on table and starts to study it closely.*]

MONICA [*shaking her head at* RORY]: You see.

BILL: Guineas form . . . You can't go by the Guineas . . . Too many unknowns. Boussac . . . that's the chap I'm afraid of.

MONICA: Oh, Bill! Don't tell me you've fallen again?

BILL: No, no, nothing like that.

MONICA: Then why are you afraid of Boussac's entries?

BILL [*crushing 'Racing News' in crumpled ball*]: Patriotism. Naturally I want an English horse to win . . . er . . . er . . .

JEEVES: England's premier classic race, m'lord.

BILL: Thank you, Jeeves. Or an Irish horse. I love Irish horses. Had an Irish hunter once named Donegal. Remember, Moke? I never knew such a sure-footed animal. Kicked me three times in exactly the same place. For months after that, whenever I lay down on something soft, I'd leave a hoof-mark, ha, ha, ha! [*He laughs a forced laugh, his face changing to a lugubrious expression, as if he were about to cry.*]

[*JEEVES is putting their pages in proper order, a fairly lengthy task.*]

MONICA: What's the matter, Bill?

BILL: Nothing, nothing at all. Here, take this paper, Jeeves. Take the lot of them, burn them.

MONICA: There *is* something wrong, isn't there, Bill?

BILL: Of course there is. My girl's given me the heave ho.

MONICA: You mean the engagement . . .?

BILL: Definitely down the drain.

MONICA: Poor old boy! I am sorry.

BILL: Thanks and all that but don't hang around here making sympathetic noises. Go and find the Spottsworth. I want to sell this bloodsome house, and shake its dust from my feet for ever.

MONICA: Is there anything I can do –

BILL: There isn't.

RORY: Don't let it get you down, laddie. Jill's a nice enough kid, but remember what Shakespeare says: 'A woman is only a woman, but a good cigar is a smoke.'

JEEVES: Pardon . . . *Kipling*, m'lord.

RORY: And another profound truth: 'All cats are grey in the dark'.

MONICA [*her lips compressed*]: Splendid! Go on!

RORY [*laying a sympathetic hand on* BILL'S *shoulder*]: When it comes to love, there's a lot to be said for the 'à la carte' against the '*table d'hôte*'.

MONICA: What was the name of the lady who drove a spike into her husband's head while he was sleeping?

JEEVES: The name was Jael, m'lady. But the gentleman in the case was not the husband, merely a good friend.

BILL [*who has been listening*]: I shall go and shoot big game in Africa. [*Sits.*] I shall take the White Hunter with me. It is possible you may read of an accident. [*He breaks off.*]

RORY: Where *is* the Sahib? I haven't seen him since yestreen.

[BILL *does not answer. He once more drops his head between his hands and stares at the floor.*]

JEEVES: Captain Biggar went up to London, sir. He is returning –

[*He pauses and, taking a step to the table, taps on it for luck.*] – on the five-ten train, arriving here just before dressing time.

BILL [*rises*]: Look, will you please biff off and find me Mrs Spottsworth? She's pretty well sold – she told me so this morning.

MONICA [*rising and picking up her handbag*]: Yes, her increased interest is to be attributed to the fact that she saw Lady Agatha last night. [*Smiles at* JEEVES.] Ingenious, very ingenious. [*She goes to hall door and turns.*] Come on, à la carte. [*She goes out.*]

[RORY *follows, realizing belatedly that he has put his foot in it.*]

RORY [*as he follows her*]: I was only saying those things about marriage to cheer up old Bill. [*Exit.*]

BILL [*rises*]: What was all that heavy innuendo about Lady Agatha?

JEEVES: Lord Carmoyle, m'lord. It seems he caught a glimpse of us last night when we were in costume.

BILL: If anything comes out about there being a robbery, this business of playing ghost might look suspicious.

JEEVES: It might indeed, m'lord.

BILL [*with nervous irritation*]: And why *hasn't* it come out? Does she think it ill-bred to raise a rumpus over a mere ten-thousand-quid pendant?

JEEVES: It is, I agree, surprising there has been no explosion.

BILL: The suspense is awful. Nothing from Mrs Spottsworth and nothing from that offspring of unmarried parents, Sahib Biggar. *He* was sopposed to phone and tell us how much he got for the thing. [*Sits sofa.*]

JEEVES: Yes, he was to inform your lordship if the sum was sufficiently adequate to allow for an independent wager.

BILL: The hell with that. If I had anything more at stake on this blasted race, I should start sticking straws in my hair.

JEEVES: It is certainly a Derby to be remembered.

BILL: If the brute doesn't win, I suppose the only way to save face is to throw myself from the Abbey battlements.

JEEVES: The Captain's confidence in the animal appears to be complete.

BILL: Yes, but what of *our* confidence in the Captain?

JEEVES: I urged your lordship to let me accompany him.

BILL: I couldn't allow you to involve yourself any further. I realize what a scarifice you made for me last night, placing your good name in jeopardy . . .

JEEVES: Since the deed had to be done I felt better the vassal than the lord.

BILL: A gesture of loyalty I shall not lightly forget.

JEEVES: A privilege, m'lord.

BILL: You haven't an aspirin about you, I suppose?

JEEVES: Certainly, m'lord. As a matter of face, I have just been taking one myself. [*He takes a small tin box of aspirin from his pocket, and holds it out to* BILL.]

BILL: Thanks, Jeeves, and please . . . don't slam the lid.

JEEVES: May I suggest, m'lord, that you go and relax on the library settee? I will call your lordship as soon as Mrs Spottsworth appears.

BILL: Not a bad suggestion. I must husband my strength for this house-selling business. Then, even if Ballymore should lose, God forbid, I would still be in a position to redeem the pendant. [*He goes towards library.*]

JEEVES: Your lordship might be well advised to skim through the for sale advertisements in *Country Life*. The language is extremely persuasive.

BILL: Yes, I know the sort of thing: 'This lordly demesne, with its rondelays of historic oaks, its tumbling stream alive with trout and tench' – I'll go and mug up something.

[*He goes into library.* JEEVES *resumes his task of emptying ashtrays.* JILL *appears in french window. She is wearing jodhpurs.*]

JILL: Good afternoon, Jeeves.

JEEVES: Oh, good afternoon, miss. His lordship is in the library.

JILL: I haven't the slightest wish to speak to his lordship, thank you. I'm here in my professional capacity, to see how Adelina's mange is getting on.

JEEVES: Yes, miss.

JILL: Did you give Lord Towcester the ring?

JEEVES [*crosses to her*]: Immediately after you had left, miss. You had barely closed the door.

JILL: Really? It evidently didn't occur to him to come running after me with cries of protest.

JEEVES: His lordship seemed to feel that it might be all for the best.

JILL [*indignantly*]: For the best? He did, did he? I suppose I was cramping his style with this multi-millionairess?

JEEVES: Oh, no, miss, you interpret his lordship's attitude incorrectly. His lordship is, at the moment, in a sea of trouble, and he felt that it was better that you should not be involved.

JILL: Trouble? What sort of trouble? Money?

JEEVES: Yes, miss.

JILL: But he knows that I don't care a hang about money. If I did, would I have got engaged to him? There are two rich men I could have married.

JEEVES: Two miss?

JILL: Well, either one. Why didn't the silly man tell me he was in difficulties? That's the whole idea of marriage – having no secrets from one another.

JEEVES: A questionable theory, if you will allow me to say so, miss. If a young gentleman and a young lady know everything there is to know about each other, a certain *ennui* seems to be inevitable.

JILL: But, damn it all, Jeeves, when someone you love is in the soup, you want to help him, and you can't do that if you've no idea what it's all about.

JEEVES: May I be so personal as to inquire if you still love his lordship?

JILL: I suppose it will take me a little time to get over it. You can't turn love on and off as if it were the bathroom tap.

JEEVES: Then I will assume the responsibility of putting you *au courant* with the facts. You see, his lordship is a Silver Ring bookie.

JILL: A bookie?

JEEVES: Yes, miss. He had come to the conclusion, based on personal experience, that the bookie always comes out a winner.

JILL: Hold on a minute! Then the Farm Board – ?

JEEVES: A slight misrepresentation, I fear, miss.

JILL: A thundering lie, I'd call it.

JEEVES: On becoming betrothed to you, his lordship decided he must do something about earning a living.

JILL: So you're saddling me with the responsibility of this bookie business?

JEEVES: I would hardly express it in those terms, miss, but it is surely apparent that love played a large part in the matter.

JILL: But wasn't there anything else – ?

JEEVES: In selecting an occupation his lordship, on my advice, sought the help of the Classified Trades Directory.

JILL: But you got no further than 'bookie'?

JEEVES: 'Turf Accountant' is a considerable distance through that volume.

JILL: I would like to ask one question: did it pay?

JILL: In three days at Doncaster we cleared four hundred and twenty pounds.

JILL: Quite a pretty penny. But you said 'money troubles'. Has the tide turned?

JEEVES: What smote his lordship was not so much the tide as a tidal wave: Captain Biggar.

JILL: The Captain copped a winner?

JEEVES: A double, miss. Five pounds on Lucy Glitters at a hundred-to-six, all to come on Whistler's Mother, S.P.

JILL: What *was* the S.P.?

JEEVES: I regret to say, miss, thirty-three to one.

JILL: Suffering saints! [*Sits sofa.*]

JEEVES: Yes, miss.

JILL: That must be a ghastly amount.

JEEVES: In excess of three thousand pounds.

JILL: He can't pay it?

JEEVES: No, miss. Hence his lordship's urgency to sell the Abbey.

JILL: And hence his making up to Mrs Spottsworth?

JEEVES: Precisely, miss.

JILL: H'm, that clears up that . . . Thank you, Jeeves.

JEEVES: Not at all, miss.

JILL: In the library, you said? [*Crosses to library door, calls.*] Hey, Bill! [*Turning back to* JEEVES.] Anybody with him?

JEEVES: No, miss. His lordship is studying the advertisements in *Country Life.*

[BILL *appears in the library doorway. He has a copy of* Country Life *in his hand.*]

BILL [*taken aback*]: Why – why, Jill! Did you – ?

JILL: Yes, I called you. Jeeves has just told me everything.

BILL: Good Lord! When you say 'everything' do you mean – everything?

JEEVES: I acquainted Miss Wyvern with the fact that you are a turf accountant.

BILL: Ah, and now you know that – ?

JILL: As you know, I disapprove of your gambling – that is if you lose.

BILL: We haven't been doing too badly – Jeeves as my clerk, wonderful head for figures . . .

JILL: You mean you *hadn't* been doing too badly – until this Biggar business?

BILL: Oh, you know about that, too?

JILL: Didn't I just say, Jeeves told me everything?

BILL: And – ?

JILL: I'm not a girl to give her man the chuck because he's struck a bit of rough going.

BILL: That's my poppet! [*With an impulsive gesture he takes her in his arms.*] And did Jeeves tell you – ? [*He breaks off as, looking over* JILL'S *shoulder, he sees* JEEVES *wigwagging to him in race-course style.*]

JILL [*pushing herself free*]: Tell me what? Is there anything more?

BILL: I – I mean about my selling the house? It's urgent, you see.

JILL: Oh, that? Yes, of course it's urgent. You've got to pay blasted Biggar.

BILL: But frankly I don't know how Mrs S. can resist the place with its wealth of old oak, its yew-lined vistas, its tumbled profusion of rose and jasmine.

JEEVES: I think the matter will turn on the question of dampness. If your lordship could conclude the business before there is any rain.

BILL: Yes, if the pails have to appear the jig's up.

JEEVES: In case the worst should happen, I will see that each pail is provided with a cloth so that drops will fall inaudibly. [*He starts off.*]

BILL: You forget nothing, do you, Jeeves?

JEEVES: Thank you, my lord. One does one's best. [*Exit to hall.*]

JILL: Where's my ring?

BILL: Right here. [*He takes it from his pocket.*]

JILL: Did you hate losing me?

BILL: I couldn't sleep a wink.

JILL: Good. *I* slept like a top.

BILL: What!

JILL: But then, you see, I knew I was coming back – *you* didn't. [*She laughs.*]

BILL: You're a little swine, but at the same time you do my sleepless eyes good.

[*As he speaks,* MONICA *enters by hall door, accompanied by* MRS SPOTTSWORTH. MRS SPOTTSWORTH *is in attractive sports attire.*]

BILL: Ah, Mrs Spottsworth.

JILL: Good afternoon, Mrs Spottsworth.

MRS SPOTTSWORTH: Good afternoon, Miss . . . Miss . . .

JILL: The name is Wyvern.

MRS SPOTTSWORTH: Forgive me, I'm in rather a state.

BILL [*trying to sound casual*]: Oh, has anything happened?

MRS SPOTTSWORTH: Indeed something has happened. I just rushed off to the village to make my report.

BILL: You reported it, did you? And are the police coming up here?

MRS SPOTTSWORTH: The police? What have the police got to do with it?

BILL: You just said you made a report.

MRS SPOTTSWORTH: To the Psychical Research Society.

BILL [*relieved*]: Ah, the good old ghost-chasers?

MRS SPOTTSWORTH: I suppose you are aware of what happened here last night?

BILL: Yes . . . quite a night, wasn't it?

MRS SPOTTSWORTH: Have you told Miss Wyvern about it?

BILL: Jill knows everything.

MRS SPOTTSWORTH [*to* JILL]: Lady Agatha made a complete manifestation. She came right into my room.

JILL: You actually saw her?

MRS SPOTTSWORTH: As distinctly as I see you. The lights were turned off but there was a beam from the full moon, that filtered through a chink in the curtains. The apparition went straight to the dressing-table and peered about as if looking for something.

BILL: Some old trinket, no doubt, lost in the long ago.

MRS SPOTTSWORTH: It's extraordinary that none of the rest of you saw her.

MONICA: I distinctly heard the thump, thump of her stick.

MRS SPOTTSWORTH: I could point out the exact spot where she came through the wall.

JILL: If I'd been there I'd have gone through the opposite one.

MRS SPOTTSWORTH: Nonsense! I was delighted to see the good lady. I trust, if I should come to live in this house, we will establish oral communication.

JILL: That reminds me – you are thinking of selling, aren't you, Bill?

BILL: I've toyed with the idea . . . Of course, I shall miss those bowered walks, the charming prospect of park and pasture.

JILL: What I was going to say was that Mrs Burrage is looking for larger premises for her school, and I was wondering if the Abbey . . .

MRS SPOTTSWORTH [*breaking in*]: Oh, no, no, no! A lot of inky-fingered schoolgirls racing up and down Lady Agatha's gallery – it would be desecration.

BILL: If I decide to sell Lady Agatha will have to take her chances. She can't expect me to keep the place just for her to stump about in.

MRS SPOTTSWORTH: How much do you want for the Abbey, Lord Towcester?

BILL [*swallowing*]: Three thousand and three pounds, six –

MRS SPOTTSWORTH [*flabbergasted*]: What's that? Three thousand?

MONICA: Mrs Spottsworth isn't asking how much you want as a deposit. What's the total price? You said something about giving it away for forty thousand.

MRS SPOTTSWORTH: Forty? That seems cheap enough.

BILL: It needs a spot of paint here and there. It hasn't had a good doing up since James the First came for a week-end in sixteen-twenty.

MRS SPOTTSWORTH: James the First? Did he really?

BILL: I understand he commented favourably on the warmth of the place. It had relieved him of a 'misery of the royal knee'.

MRS SPOTTSWORTH: Rheumatism!

JILL: If you want it still warmer, I suppose there's plenty of room for a heating plant down below?

BILL: In the dungeons? Oh, rather – they're on the large side – as dungeons go.

MRS SPOTTSWORTH: Suppose I make out a cheque now, as a binder?

BILL: You're rushing me a bit but that's the way you Americans are . . . [*He picks up a small table, as he speaks, puts it in front of her and whips out a fountain-pen.*]

    [MRS SPOTTSWORTH *starts to look in her bag for cheque book.* RORY *enters from hall, leaving doors open.*]

RORY: Well, it's started to rain. That'll alter the going at Epsom.

BILL: Rain!

MRS SPOTTSWORTH: Will that alter the chances of my horse?

BILL: You have a horse?

MRS SPOTTSWORTH: I saw there was an animal in the race called Poltergeist. I thought that was rather an omen.

RORY: Hasn't a prayer.

MRS SPOTTSWORTH: Really? Well, I only put on five hundred.

RORY: At thirty-three to one.

JILL [*turning to* BILL]: Aren't those the same odds – ?

BILL [*with finality*]: Yes.

MONICA: The rain seems to be getting worse.

    [*As she speaks* JEEVES *goes by at back carrying two pails.*]

RORY: I hope you've put up the top of your car, Bill. That garage roof is practically non-existant.

[MONICA *makes a gesture of irritated despair.* MRS SPOTTS-WORTH, *having found her cheque book, pauses and looks round alertly.*]

MRS SPOTTSWORTH: The garage roof, you say?

BILL: One of the old barns. Nothing to do with the Abbey itself.

MRS SPOTTSWORTH: Oh, I see.

BILL: Since you're such pals I'll throw in the portrait of Lady Agatha.

MRS SPOTTSWORTH: Thank you.

[*As she bends over to write the cheque,* ELLEN, BILL'S *housemaid, appears in doorway.*]

ELLEN [*to* MONICA]: Excuse me, my lady. Could I have a word with Mrs Spottsworth?

BILL: Not now.

MRS SPOTTSWORTH [*turning her head*]: What is it, Ellen?

ELLEN: I was just laying out your evening things and I noticed that big emerald piece you were wearing last evening is missing.

MRS SPOTTSWORTH [*rising*]: You mean to say it's not in its case?

ELLEN: No, ma'am, not anywhere else. I had a good look.

MRS SPOTTSWORTH: Don't say that, it's my good luck charm. I wouldn't lose it for the world!

[*She hurries to door. As she passes out of sight there is a terrific metallic clatter.*]

BILL: My God, what's that?

MONICA [*following her, turns in doorway*]: Only Mrs Spottsworth falling over a pail. [*Exit.*]

JILL: That's torn it.

[ELLEN *also goes off after them.*]

BILL [*to* RORY]: Big Mouth.

RORY: Did I drop a brick?

BILL: If one followed you about for a month, one would have enough bricks to build a house.

RORY: The garage roof? Yes, I get it now – you were about to close the deal.

BILL: That moment of hesitation did it – and now that damned pail
— well, that's that!

RORY: About this lost pendant, if you'd like, I'll nip off in the car
and fetch the local constabulary.

BILL: Thanks a lot, but no. You'd better get into the library and
warm up the set. The Derby is in half-an-hour.

RORY [*looking at watch*]: By jove, so it is! Think of that silly woman
putting all that money on a thirty-three to one shot. [*Exit to
library*.]

JILL: What about this pendant, do you think it's been pinched?

BILL: We-ll . . .

JILL: That stuff about her going to the village with a report . . .
You thought she'd been to the police then.

[BILL *opens his mouth to speak but says nothing*.]

Now, now Towcester – come clean!

BILL: All right then – yes, it has been pinched . . . At least, not
actually pinched, just borrowed.

JILL: You took it to pay Biggar?

BILL: The Captain has a cast-iron tip on the Derby – the Irish horse
Ballymore. And, after the race, he's redeeming the pendant, and
bringing it back.

JILL: That is if Ballymore wins.

BILL: And now you really do know everything.

JILL: You're sure?

BILL: And if you want to break the engagement again I don't blame
you.

JILL: It's rather an odd sensation after falling in love with a peer of
the realm to find yourself engaged to a member of the criminal
class. It gives me rather a heady feeling . . .

BILL: When you say 'criminal' . . .

JILL: I mean criminal. But I'm sticking with you in spite of even
this.

BILL [*huskily*]: You mean it?

JILL: When you come through the gate, with your prison pallor
and close-cropped head I'll be standing there – waiting.

BILL: Gosh!

JILL: And at the trial just remember I'm on *your* side.

BILL: Yes, but you won't be on the jury.

JILL: Cheer up, old thing. Don't let's take it so tragically . . . Look, I'll send you one of those prison cakes. Only I'm such a rotten cook I won't know which ingredient to put in first – the file or the cold-saw. [*As* BILL *looks at her lugubriously.*] Well, aren't you going to laugh? Here I am making jokes to cheer you up.

BILL [*mirthlessly*]: Ha, ha!

[JEEVES *enters from hall.*]

JEEVES: Oh, excuse me, m'lord, I have been told by the girl, Ellen, that we have suffered a robbery.

BILL: It's all right, Jeeves, you can speak freely. Miss Wyvern knows everything.

JEEVES: Indeed, m'lord?

JILL: Oh, does Jeeves . . . ?

BILL: Yes, Jeeves knows everything, too.

JEEVES: His lordship did me the honour of seeking my assistance.

JILL: I feel rather like a gangster's moll. It's quite thrilling. You know, the Abbey would be a wonderful setting for the last stand of Scarface. Up with the drawbridge, down with the portcullis, fill up the cauldrons with boiling oil . . .

BILL: A thought has just occurred, Jeeves. That case the thing was in . . . How about fingerprints.

JILL: I thought for the modern burglar it was bad form to go without gloves?

JEEVES: I fear, m'lord that gloves were a detail of costume that was forgotten.

BILL: A serious oversight.

JEEVES: I fear so, m'lord.

BILL: Understandable in the heat of the moment.

JEEVES: The moment was certainly one of some warmth.

BILL: Any attempt to get at the case now would rouse suspicion?

JEEVES: Unquestionably, m'lord.

[*There is a sound of voices in the hall, followed by a metallic crash.*]

BILL: Good Lord, she's fallen over that pail a second time.

[JEEVES *hurries out.*]

JILL: I told you you ought to put a light in that hall.

[*Enter* MONICA *and* MRS SPOTTSWORTH. *The latter is limping.*]

MRS SPOTTSWORTH: Who is responsible for these booby-traps? [JEEVES *re-enters.*]

BILL: I'm frightfully sorry.

JEEVES: I'm afraid the man who was washing the hall floor left his pail.

MRS SPOTTSWORTH: My feet are soaking. I shall be crippled with rheumatism tomorrow.

JILL: Can't one of us get you some dry things?

MRS SPOTTSWORTH: No, thank you. After losing my good luck charm minor disasters are of little moment. [*To* MONICA.] How long did the police say they would be?

BILL: The police?

MONICA: Fifteen minutes – and it's half of that since I called them. [*Turning to* BILL.] Mrs Spottsworth hesitated about making the matter public.

BILL: But you insisted? [*To* JILL.] While others think, Monica acts.

MRS SPOTTSWORTH: I'm sorry to be making this unattractive scene.

BILL: Don't mention it.

MONICA: All Bill wants is to see the criminal caught, and put behind bars. [*As* BILL *does not now answer.*] Isn't it, Bill?

BILL: Of course.

MONICA: I've a pretty shrewd idea who the guilty party is.

JILL: Who?

MONICA: Someone who was in a terrible state of nerves this morning.

BILL: You – you don't mean – ? [*He swallows nervously.*]

MONICA: Do you want me to name names?

BILL: Yes, go ahead.

MONICA: The Sahib; didn't you notice the way his cup and saucer were rattling? He was as nervous as a tree full of elephants.

MRS SPOTTSWORTH: The Captain? Oh, no, no! That I won't believe!

MONICA: I'll lay odds that that's *one* White Hunter you'll never see again!

BILL: You've no right to – Moke.

MONICA [*overlapping*]: He'll vanish into the jungle with his sex-starved daughter and his ill-gotten gains . . . just like Doctor Livingstone.

MRS SPOTTSWORTH: If Captain Biggar were guilty, I should lose my faith in human nature. Suspect *him!* I would as soon suspect Lord Towcester. [*Laughs.*]

BILL: Those are strong words.

MONICA: What about the case the pendant was in? It may well show some fingerprints.

MRS SPOTTSWORTH: I'll go and get it.

JEEVES: Permit *me*, madam.

BILL: Yes, *you* go, Jeeves. But be sure and hold it by the edges.

JEEVES: I will exercise the greatest care, m'lord. [*Exit to hall.*]

[*As he does so, the front doorbell rings.*]

JILL: There they are. [*Rises.*]

BILL: Quick work. But then our police are like that, always darting after some wretched rabbit like a lot of pink-nosed ferrets.

[CHIEF CONSTABLE'S *voice heard off.*]

CHIEF CONSTABLE: [*off*]. I understand there's some trouble here, what?

[JEEVES *appears in doorway.*]

JEEVES [*announces*]: Chief Constable Blagden.

[CHIEF CONSTABLE *enters, a strongly-built, deep-voiced man of middle-age.* JEEVES *goes out, closing doors.*]

CHIEF CONSTABLE: Afternoon, Lord Towcester. Afternoon, Lady Carmoyle. Afternoon, Miss Wyvern. [*He looks inquiringly at* MRS SPOTTSWORTH.]

MONICA: This is my friend, Mrs Spottsworth, Colonel.

CHIEF CONSTABLE [*bowing*]: How de do, Mrs Spottsworth? Sorry to hear about this. Nasty business, a robbery. Makes everyone feel uncomfortable.

BILL: True, Colonel, true.

CHIEF CONSTABLE [*taking out note-book and pencil*]: You said on the phone that it looks like an inside job?

MONICA: That's what we think.

CHIEF CONSTABLE: Then I'll have a list of everybody in the house.

[*There is a knock at the door, sounding as if it had been gently kicked.* MONICA *turns and opens it, revealing* JEEVES. *He is carrying the pendant's case. He has a folded handkerchief at either edge and presses with his hands in an elaborate precaution not to touch the case.*]

JEEVES: Thank you, m'lady.

[*He advances to table and puts case on it, carefully.*]

MRS SPOTTSWORTH: Here is the case.

CHIEF CONSTABLE: Good. Glad to see you were careful about handling it.

JEEVES: Yes, sir. We fancied there might be some fingerprints.

CHIEF CONSTABLE: Now for the names.

BILL [*with an attempt at being jocular*]: Heading the list of suspects . . .

[*The library door bursts open and* RORY *enters.*]

RORY: I say, the most ghastly thing has happened.

BILL: Something more?

RORY: It caps everything.

CHIEF CONSTABLE: Who is this?

MONICA: My husband, Lord Carmoyle. Rory, this is Colonel Blagden, the chief constable.

RORY [*to* CHIEF CONSTABLE]: Do you know anything about television?

CHIEF CONSTABLE: No.

RORY: The ruddy thing has gone on the blink and it's almost time for the race to start.

JEEVES: The wireless will report the event, m'lord. [*He indicates the radio cabinet.*]

RORY: And it is in working order?

JEEVES: I think so, m'lord.

RORY: Come on, let's make sure.

CHIEF CONSTABLE: I was called here, Lord Carmoyle, to investigate a robbery.

RORY: Robbery? What robbery? Anyway, the devil with that. We want to hear the Derby.

CHIEF CONSTABLE: The first thing I want is a list.

RORY: Here you are. *Sporting Life*. You'll find the list of runners on page two.

CHIEF CONSTABLE: A list of the people in this house.

WIRELESS [*suddenly blares forth*]: They're all up there now circling about. I can see Sweet William, Garniture, Voleur – that's the French hope, and with Ray Johnstone up I wouldn't be surprised – ah, there's a horse giving trouble, rearing about and trying to throw his jockey. It's that Irish outsider, Ballymore.

CHIEF CONSTABLE: Lord Towcester, what servants have you here?

WIRELESS: They really are a splendid lot; Weymouth . . .

BILL: Jeeves.

WIRELESS: Simple Simon . . .

BILL: Jem Jones.

CHIEF CONSTABLE [*who is trying to jot them down*]: Not so fast.

WIRELESS: Dr Crippen.

CHIEF CONSTABLE: Dr Crippen?

RORY: He'll never stay.

BILL: He's the gardener.

CHIEF CONSTABLE: Crippen.

BILL: No, Jones.

CHIEF CONSTABLE: What's Crippen?

RORY: By King's Bench out of Pond Lily.

WIRELESS: Ah, there goes the flag. They're under starter's orders.

RORY: Quiet, everybody.

BILL [*in stage whisper*]: There's a cook, Mary Jane Piggott.

RORY: Piggott? Who said Piggott? If that boy wins I shall invite you all to kick me.

CHIEF CONSTABLE: I don't want to lose my temper, Lord Carmyole –

WIRELESS: They're off! Simple Simon is in the lead.

CHIEF CONSTABLE [*staring at his note-book*]: Is Simple Simon a horse?

RORY: The Derby is a horse race so naturally –

CHIEF CONSTABLE: I demand that you all give me your attention.

JEEVES: The record for the course is – I suggest that you wait . . .

WIRELESS: It's still Simple Simon, with Vaurien, the Boussac pacemaker, in second place. I see Escalator is trying to break through . . . I see Oratory.

CHIEF CONSTABLE: Perhaps if I talk to you, Lord Towcester . . .

WIRELESS: There's a horse coming up on the outside, coming very fast . . . It looks like the Irish outsider, Ballymore.

[BILL *deserts him on this, going to wireless together with* JILL.]

JILL: Come on, Ballymore!

BILL [*turns to wireless*]: Ballymore! Come on, Ballymore!

CHIEF CONSTABLE [*turning to* MRS SPOTTSWORTH]: Tell me, Mrs Spottsworth, when did you first miss – ?

WIRELESS [*overlapping*]: It looks like Ballymore is going to win it. Vaurien is falling back. Simple Simon is finished.

MRS SPOTTSWORTH: What was your question, Colonel? With this dreadful racket –

CHIEF CONSTABLE: I demand you turn that thing off.

WIRELESS: Wait! A horse has come through on the rails – it's Poltergeist.

[MRS SPOTTSWORTH *leaps up and, pushing the* CHIEF CONSTABLE *violently aside, makes for the wireless.*]

MRS SPOTTSWORTH [*shrilly*]: Poltergeist! Poltergeist!

JILL: Come on, Ballymore!

WIRELESS: It's Ballymore – no, it's Poltergeist – no, it's Ballymore!

RORY: Make up your mind.

WIRELESS: I tell you it's Ballymore.

[*The wild roaring of the crowd can now be heard.*]

JILL: Come on, Ballymore!

MRS SPOTTSWORTH: Poltergeist! Poltergeist!

CHIEF CONSTABLE [*catching the infection*]: Come on, Gordon!

RORY: Gordon isn't riding.

WIRELESS: Photo finish! First time in the history of the Derby – a photo finish! Vaurien in third place.

MRS SPOTTSWORTH: What will I win if it's Poltergeist?

BILL: Enough to buy yourself a couple of pendants.

CHIEF CONSTABLE: If you can stop talking horses for a minute I would like to inspect the scene of the robbery.

MRS SPOTTSWORTH: Certainly. One of you will stay and get the decision?

BILL: I will.

MONICA [*eyeing him sternly*]: You have no interest in the result. You never bet!

RORY: Then why was he yelling, 'Come on, Ballymore!'?

JILL: He knew *I* was on it.

RORY: I think you might have told us.

CHIEF CONSTABLE [*at hall door*]: Please, Mrs Spottsworth.

MRS SPOTTSWORTH: Yes, of course. Come with me, won't you, Lady Carmoyle?

[*She and* MONICA *go out,* CHIEF CONSTABLE *following.*]

RORY: What is all this about a robbery?

BILL: If you trot along with them you'll get all the facts.

RORY: Right, and I'll tell this policeman feller to see a list of those present doesn't get in the papers. I'm not concerned about my own name but I must think of Harrods. [*Exit.*]

BILL: What about a drink, Jeeves?

JEEVES [*turning to side-table*]: Certainly, m'lord.

JILL: One for me, too, Jeeves. A stiff glass of sherry.

BILL: They're taking the devil of a time with that photo.

JEEVES: The suspense is extremely trying.

JILL: It's agony.

BILL: And the sale of the old Abbey –

JILL: Oh, that's right down the drain.

BILL: It therefore rests with the photograph of the horses' noses whether I'm a respected peer of the realm or a felon.

JILL: Hsh! Don't say that out loud!

BILL: Let's hope Ballymore had sense enough to stick out his tongue.

WIRELESS: Here's the result at last. Hundreds of thousands hang in the balance. People stand with glasses focused as the number goes up.

JILL [*impatiently*]: For heaven's sake tell us – !

WIRELESS: It's Poltergeist!

BILL: Hell!

JILL: Oh, gosh. I think I'm going to cry.

JEEVES [*handing them the drinks*]: Your sherry, miss.

JILL [*in a choked voice*]: I don't want it. [*She turns, hurries through hall door.*]

BILL: Poor kid. I'm sorry I got her into this.

JEEVES: There is nothing that so unites two loving hearts, m'lord, as a shared sorrow.

BILL: I must go to her. [*He tosses down his drink at one gulp and goes out.*]

> [JEEVES *returns tray and glass to side-table. Bell rings off. He goes out to hall.*]

WIRELESS: Ballymore's defeat saves the bookies from a tremendous loss. A huge sum was bet on the Irish horse just before starting time.

> [*As these words are spoken,* CAPTAIN BIGGAR *enters through french windows. He goes to the radio, turns it off. Door opens and* MRS SPOTTSWORTH *enters from the hall. She stops dead as she sees* CAPTAIN. *They stare at one another. Mechanically she pushes the door to behind her.*]

CAPTAIN [*in an electric whisper*]: Rosalinda.

MRS SPOTTSWORTH: Cuthbert. I knew you'd come. They said you wouldn't, but *I* knew.

CAPTAIN: I couldn't do it, Rosalinda. I got to thinking of you and of the chaps at the club.

MRS SPOTTSWORTH: What club, Cuthbert?

CAPTAIN: The old Anglo-Malay in Kuala Lumpur, where men are white and honesty goes for granted. Yes, I thought of the boys. I thought of old Tubby Frobisher. Would I ever be able to look him in that one good eye of his? And then I thought of what you said . . . of how you trusted me because . . . because I was an Englishman. And I said to myself, it isn't only the old Anglo-Malay and Tubby and the Subadah and Doc and Squiffy . . . you're letting down the side, the whole blessed British Empire!

MRS SPOTTSWORTH [*in whisper*]: Did – did you take it?

CAPTAIN: I took it and I brought it back. It was only borrowed for the day, security for a gamble. But I couldn't do it. It might have meant a fortune, but I couldn't do it.

[*He takes pendant from his pocket and holds it out to her.*]

MRS SPOTTSWORTH: Put it round my neck, Cuthbert.

CAPTAIN: You want me to? You don't mind if I touch you?

MRS SPOTTSWORTH: No, my White Knight. I don't mind if you kiss me. In fact, I shall mind if you don't.

CAPTAIN [*brokenly*]: Rosalinda.

[*They embrace.*]

MRS SPOTTSWORTH: Now, this evening we'll make some plans. I'm going to take you back to California.

CAPTAIN: What would I do in California? I'm a White Hunter.

MRS SPOTTSWORTH: You can go white hunting on the films. You shall do a series. You'll live in the hearts of·twenty million children. You'll be the new Hopalong Cassidy.

[*As she speaks he clasps the pendant round her neck.*]

CAPTAIN: I-I can't take it in all at once. I only know that Tubby was right when he said honesty pays . . . That reminds me, I've got a taxi outside. [*He goes to french window.*] I came in to get some change – now I'll give him a quid. [*Exit through french windows.*]

MRS SPOTTSWORTH [*looking down at pendant*]: Thank you, dear lucky charm.

[JEEVES *re-enters from hall.*]

JEEVES: Excuse me, madam, the Chief Constable would like you – [*Breaks off as he sees pendant.*] But I see it isn't necessary, the pendant has been found.

MRS SPOTTSWORTH: Yes, I'd evidently dropped it in the chair there and it had slipped down between the cushions.

JEEVES: Most fortunate, madam. I am sure everyone will be much relieved.

MRS SPOTTSWORTH: I am sorry to have upset everybody in this charming house.

JEEVES: Might I inquire, madam, are you buying the Abbey?

MRS SPOTTSWORTH: No, Jeeves, I wish that I could but alas, the climate!

JEEVES: I admit our English summers are somewhat severe. May I make a suggestion, madam? Why not buy the Abbey and ship it to Pasadena?

MRS SPOTTSWORTH: Take it down stone by stone, you mean?

JEEVES: The feat has been accomplished by several of your millionaires.

MRS SPOTTSWORTH: It's a brilliant idea. I'll do it! Oh, but what about the haunt?

JEEVES: After six hundred years I fancy the Lady Agatha might enjoy a change of scene.

[*She goes to table, opens bag and takes out cheque book.* BILL *and* JILL *re-enter from hall.*]

BILL: The Chief Constable insists on our all going down – [*He, too, breaks off and gawks at the pendant.*]

JEEVES: Mrs Spottsworth found her pendant in that chair, m'lord.

BILL: I do believe in fairies, I do, I do.

JEEVES: And that isn't all.

JILL: What more can there be?

MRS SPOTTSWORTH: I am going to buy the Abbey. Here, Lord Towcester, your deposit. [*Hands him cheque.*] And now I'll go and make my apologies to that nice Chief Constable. [*She sweeps to the door.*] I'm shipping the Abbey to California. [*Exit to hall.*]

JILL: Shipping it?

BILL: Your idea, I fancy, Jeeves?

JEEVES: I did venture the suggestion.

JILL: Oh, Bill! Isn't it wonderful? [*Grabs and kisses him.*] But why am I kissing you? It ought to be Jeeves.

BILL: Jeeves, you must promise never to leave us.

JEEVES: I'm sorry, m'lord, but I fear Mr Wooster needs me. I have just received a summons to come to him.

BILL: But I thought the school rules wouldn't allow – ?

JEEVES: I regret to say Mr Wooster has been expelled.

BILL: Expelled?

JEEVES: Yes, m'lord. Mr Wooster was awarded the prize for darning socks. It was then discovered that he had used a crib . . . an old woman whom he smuggled into his study at night . . .

BILL: Poor old Bertie!

JEEVES: In his letter he says that, should the revolution come, he will have no course but to emigrate.

[CAPTAIN BIGGAR *enters through french windows.*]

CAPTAIN: Hullo, folks.

BILL: Why, Captain!

JILL: So you did come back?

CAPTAIN: Come back? Of course I came back.

[MRS SPOTTSWORTH *re-enters from hall.* MONICA *and* RORY *follow her.*]

MRS SPOTTSWORTH: Have you told them the news, Cuthbert?

JILL: *More* news?

MRS SPOTTSWORTH [*going to* CAPTAIN *and taking his hand*]: About us, I mean?

BILL: You and the Captain? Congratulations.

RORY: So you'll be Mrs Biggar? That reminds me – which is bigger, Captain Bigger, or Mrs Bigger?

[MRS SPOTTSWORTH, *as if to give point to the question, stands beside the* CAPTAIN.]

I bet you don't know the answer to that one, Jeeves.

JEEVES [*gravely*]: Mrs Bigger, because she became Bigger.

CURTAIN